Christians under the Crescent and Muslims under the Cross c.630–1923

This book examines the status that rulers of one faith conferred onto their subjects belonging to a different one, how the rulers handled relationships with them, and the interactions between subjects of the Muslim and Christian religions.

The chronological arc of this volume spans from the first conquests by the Arabs in the Near East in the 630s to the exchange between Turkey and Greece, in 1923, of the Orthodox Christians and Muslims residing in their territories. Through organized topics, Berto analyzes both similarities and differences in Christian and Muslim lands and emphasizes how coexistences and conflicts took directions that were not always inevitable. Primary sources are used to examine the mentality of those who composed them and of their audiences. In doing so, the book considers the nuances and all the features of the multifaceted experiences of Christian subjects under Muslim rule and of Muslim subjects under Christian rule.

Christians under the Crescent and Muslims under the Cross is the ideal resource for upper-level undergraduates, postgraduates, and scholars interested in the relationships between Christians and Muslims, religious minorities, and the Near East and the Mediterranean from the Middle Ages to the early twentieth century.

Luigi Andrea Berto is professor of History at Western Michigan University (USA). His research focuses on Medieval Italy and the Mediterranean, with a special interest in the use of the past in the medieval and modern periods, and the relationships between Christians and Muslims.

Christians under the Crescent and Muslims under the Cross c.630–1923

Luigi Andrea Berto

Routledge
Taylor & Francis Group

LONDON AND NEW YORK

First published 2021
by Routledge
2 Park Square, Milton Park, Abingdon, Oxon OX14 4RN

and by Routledge
52 Vanderbilt Avenue, New York, NY 10017

Routledge is an imprint of the Taylor & Francis Group, an informa business

British Library Cataloguing-in-Publication Data
A catalogue record for this book is available from the British Library

Library of Congress Cataloging-in-Publication Data
A catalog record has been requested for this book

ISBN: 978-0-367-60855-2 (hbk)
ISBN: 978-1-003-10074-4 (ebk)

Typeset in Bembo
by codeMantra

Contents

Maps

Acknowledgments

I wish to thank Laura Pilsworth for accepting this volume for publication, the staff at Routledge, Chiara Frison, Delphine, Stefano Trovato, my brother Massimo, Roberto Pesce, Massimiliano Vitiello, Joe Brandao, Jason Glatz, Tony Shugaar, and Matthew Trojacek for their help.

Introduction

At the beginning of the eighteenth century, in response to an ill-omened event (the appearance of a dog on Jerusalem's Esplanade of Mosques, an animal greatly despised by Muslims), the Ottoman authorities decided to eliminate all dogs. They, therefore, required all Christians to bring one, kill it in their presence, and pay a sum of cash; the Jews were assigned the task of burying the carcasses of those slain animals.

Harking back to relations with the faithful of Islam prior to the Balkan Wars in 1912, an Orthodox Christian woman of Anatolia declared: 'Before the war, we lived in peace with the Turks. We got along like brothers. They came to our homes, and we went to theirs. The Turks attended our religious celebrations, our weddings, and our funerals.'

Between 1184 and 1185, a Muslim traveled through Sicily, then under Christian rule for roughly a century at the time, and described how, during an earthquake, the servants of the royal palace had invoked the names of Allah and Muhammad and were greatly embarrassed when they saw the king, but they were reassured when the ruler said to them: 'Let each of you call upon the name of the God he worships and believes in.'

At the beginning of the sixteenth century, all of Spain's Muslim subjects, in contrast, were obliged to make a choice between converting to Christianity and abandoning their native land. Even the ones who converted were nevertheless expelled some hundred years later.

These are just a few examples of the considerable diversity of experiences encountered by Christian and Muslim subjects in territories under the government of rulers belonging to a faith different from their own. This situation developed in the aftermath of the victories and conquests of the believers in Islam between the seventh and ninth centuries, in areas between the Near East and the north of the

Iberian Peninsula inhabited by the faithful of Christ. Between the second half of the eleventh century and the beginning of the early modern era, the Seljuq Turks and, later, the Ottoman Turks occupied Anatolia, much of the Balkan peninsula, and certain areas in Eastern Europe. Between the end of the eleventh century and the fifteenth century, the Christians took back possession of certain of those territories, whose population had in the meantime largely become Muslim (the Iberian Peninsula, Sicily, and, for a little over a century, the region corresponding roughly to present-day Israel and Lebanon). With the exception of this latter area and a number of regions in the Balkans and Eastern Europe, the conquered peoples of both faiths evolved from a situation in which they had constituted a substantial majority of the inhabitants into one where they had shrunk to minority.

The aim of this book is to examine the status that was assigned to them, how the rulers managed relations with them, what relationships existed between the subjects of the two religions, and what methods were employed to eliminate or remove the corresponding minority in cases where its presence was considered deleterious. Taking into account the broad chronological sweep, the considerable regional differences, and the fact that the Muslims experienced that condition in the Middle Ages while the Christians underwent a similar experience until the end of the Ottoman Empire, the book is organized by themes, analyzing to the greatest extent possible both the similarities and differences of that multiplicity of experiences. I want to point out immediately that this approach does not spring from any wish to prove that everybody behaves in the same way in good and evil, but rather from a desire to point out how coexistence and conflict were conditioned by particular factors and circumstances, both of long-standing and general nature and others more recent and specific, and how they followed a given direction that was by no means, however, inevitable.

Since certain themes addressed in the book are rather controversial, I wish to emphasize that partisan sources will not be used to reconstruct the actual and factual nature of events, but rather to examine the mindset of those who produced them and of their intended recipients. As far as the chapter devoted to violence is concerned, I will consider only those cases in which the subjects were not involved in revolts and wars of independence and the suppression thereof. Those episodes, however, will be utilized to have a better understanding of the climate thereby created and to determine what repercussions they had on their co-religionists who were not involved in those conflicts.

This book is addressed to a nonspecialist audience, and therefore, issues related to sources, hypotheses, and historiographical debates will not be discussed here, and there will be no notes, explanations of terminology, or historical overviews in order not to weigh down the text. Those wishing to have a greater understanding and to delve deeper into certain topics can refer to the back matter for further bibliographic references, a glossary of technical terms, and a timeline of the main events covered in this book. In order to avoid too many repetitions of the terms *Christians* and *Muslims*, I will use the words 'faithful' and 'believers,' to which will be appended as necessary 'of Christ' and 'of Christianity' as well as 'of Allah' and 'of Islam,' respectively.

1

Prohibitions, laws, and justice

Treatment after the conquest

If the inhabitants of a city refused to surrender immediately but instead put up a fierce defense, then the Old Testament recommends killing all the men and selling the women and children into slavery. Both Muslims and Christians followed this line of conduct, and there was no shortage of episodes in which the civilian population was massacred after a city had been taken by storm. In the case of the faithful of Christ, such events occurred especially when the city or the territory was considered sacred. The most famous case occurred after the conquest of Jerusalem in July 1099. Even the Christian chroniclers provide accounts with extremely macabre details of the slaughters carried out on that occasion against the Muslims and the Jews of that city. The indiscriminate killing of Muslim civilians was hardly limited to the western Christians. According to the daughter of the Byzantine emperor Alexius Comnenus, her compatriots showed great cruelty against the Turks, going so far as to throw newborn Turkish babies into pots of boiling water. Though they are not comparable to those accounts, descriptions of the executions of Christian prisoners carried out after the conquest of a city or in the wake of a victory on the field of battle are not completely unknown in Muslim writings. This happened, for instance, a number of times during the conquest of Sicily in the ninth century, whose inhabitants, unlike the peoples of the Middle East and the Iberian Peninsula, had put up a very firm resistance against their attackers. Once Constantinople was taken in 1453, the Turkish Sultan Muhammad II gave free rein to his troops for the next several days.

If, instead, cities surrendered after putting up a fight for a certain period of time, the inhabitants were customarily asked to swear fealty, pay a tribute, and accept the presence of a garrison and a governor. If the conquered populace showed a ready willingness to collaborate and not many troops were available, the command was left to a local leader. The Normans of southern Italy adopted this strategy on many occasions over the course of their campaigns in Sicily and Tunisia. The Muslims did much the same at the beginning of their occupation of the Iberian Peninsula. In exchange, they guaranteed the protection of persons and property, administrative and judicial autonomy, and freedom of worship and movement. In 1085, the king of Castile and León showed himself to be generous toward the faithful of Allah in Toledo, bestowing upon them a large sum of money to be used to purchase foodstuffs and seeds and allowing them continue to use the main mosque of the city, which had previously been the cathedral of Toledo. In the centuries that followed, in many cases, Andalusian Muslims were required to reside outside the city walls for a year. In Seville, in 1248, the Moors had their lives spared, although they had put up a lengthy and stubborn defense before finally surrendering, but they were required to leave the city and choose some other place nearby to settle or to move to the Maghreb.

Given their symbolic importance, religious buildings were also subjected to treatment that depended on the nature of the conquest. The Muslims immediately transformed the most important churches of the cities that had refused to surrender into mosques. This fate befell the cathedral of Palermo, as well as Hagia Sophia in Constantinople, one of the most significant symbols of the grandeur of the Byzantine Empire. In order to legitimize the conversion of the church into a mosque, Ottoman authors later invented the story that Al-Khidr, the mysterious character who, in the Koran, imparts knowledge of God to Moses, had actually inspired the construction of the famous dome of Hagia Sophia. In the seventeenth century, the long war to capture Crete and the island's capital so inflamed the Ottomans' rage that they destroyed many of the religious buildings there and transformed the rest into either mosques or government edifices. Worried about the fact that many Christians had abandoned Crete, the governor of the island later ordered that they be allowed to have a church of lesser importance. Because the territories the faithful of Christ took from the Muslims had once belonged to them, that act symbolized the re-appropriation of the lost sacred space and the definitive victory over the infidels who had taken possession of Christian land. After the conquest of Palermo in 1071, the Normans immediately re-consecrated the main mosque of Palermo, while in Jerusalem, at the end of the eleventh century, they transformed all the Islamic buildings into churches, including those that had not been churches.

In places that had been occupied without much difficulty and that were characterized by a high number of inhabitants of the other faith, the speed with which the process of converting the most important buildings of worship belonging to the others unfolded was dependent on the dynamics playing out between the subjugated and their conquerors. Even though Thessaloniki had only been taken by the Ottomans after a lengthy and challenging siege in 1430, the transformation of the most important churches into mosques proceeded at a proportional rate to the slow increase of the Islamic population, and therefore it really began to take root only in the middle of the sixteenth century. Some fifty or so years after the occupation of Damascus, the Arabs demolished the church of St. John in order to enlarge the main mosque. In spite of the promise of the king of Castile and León made to the Muslim population of the city in 1085, when he left Toledo, the city's zealous archbishop retransformed the most important Islamic religious building in Toledo back into a cathedral, with the queen's approval. In contrast, the incredible beauty of the mosque of Cordoba preserved it from destruction when the Christians conquered that city.

Once they had consolidated their conquests, the Muslims followed the precept of the Koran, which called for attributing the status of dhimmis to their Christian and Jewish subjects, dhimmi means literally the 'people of the pact,' thus guaranteeing them freedom of worship and protection of their persons and their property. As a sign of their subjugation, male dhimmis aged approximately ten and up were required to pay a tax known as the jizyah, the amount of which varied depending on the income (three categories were created); usually ecclesiastics were exempted from it. In their turn, the Christian rulers imposed a similar tax on their Muslim subjects, and although they did consider them to be second-class citizens, they nevertheless deemed them to be legitimate subjects. On various occasions, they declared that even though those subjects did not follow a good religion, it was still wrong to rob Muslims or deprive them of their property by force. Anyone who dared to do such a thing was required to pay twice the value of what they had stolen. Believers in Islam were considered property of the sovereign and classed as *servi regis*, an ambiguous definition that placed them in a condition between servitude and slavery. They were therefore under the special protection of the king, and there were clearly established penalties for those who attacked them. What is more, they were not subject to the justice of the lords of the lands in which they lived, and they could not therefore be arrested, tortured, and sentenced to death without the sovereign's consent.

Prohibitions

With the increase in the number of Muslims in conquered territories between the eighth and the ninth centuries, there progressively began to emerge a determination to impose upon the dhimmis an ever lengthening list of limitations and prohibitions, which, along with the requirement that they pay the jizyah, clearly underscored the inferiority of Christian subjects and the desire to keep the members of the two communities separated, both physically and culturally. The insistence on the particular detail that the dhimmis must always be easily identified, especially in public places, can be explained by the fear that they might contaminate Muslim spaces and rituals. For that same reason, the sale and consumption of pork and alcoholic beverages, prohibited by the Koran, were also forbidden, as was the public display of anything that referred to the Christian religion (for instance, praying, ringing bells, and displaying crosses). Linked to that set of prohibitions was the law against teaching the Koran to their children, because it was feared that the faithful of Christ might distort and corrupt the words of Allah. There was also a strong determination to limit the number of Christian subjects, and it was therefore forbidden to proselytize, to erect new religious buildings, or to repair the ones that had fallen into disrepair. Aside from pointing out the inferiority of Christians, the prohibitions against owning weapons and using horses were also signs of the fear that the numerous Christian communities might organize dangerous revolts and make alliances with the enemies of the believers in Allah.

It is worthy of note that, in order to give that legislation greater legitimacy, it was backdated and presented as the well-established project of one of the earliest successors to Muhammad, the caliph Umar (634–44). There exist a variety of versions of those prohibitions. The most significant ones are as follows:

We shall not build, in our cities or in their neighborhood, new monasteries, churches, convents, or monks' cells, nor shall we repair, by day or by night, such of them as fall in ruins or are situated in the quarters of the Muslims.

We shall keep our gates wide open for passersby and travelers. We shall give board and lodging to all Muslims who pass our way for three days.

We shall not give shelter in our churches or in our dwellings to any spy, nor hide him from the Muslims.

We shall not teach the Koran to our children.

We shall not manifest our religion publicly nor convert anyone to it. We shall not prevent any of our kin from entering Islam if they wish it.

We shall show respect toward the Muslims, and we shall rise from our seats when they wish to sit.

We shall not seek to resemble the Muslims by imitating any of their garments, the qalansuwa, the turban, footwear, or the parting of the hair. We shall not speak as they do, nor shall we adopt their kunyas.

We shall not mount on saddles, nor shall we gird swords nor bear any kind of arms nor carry them on our persons.

We shall not engrave Arabic inscriptions on our seals.

We shall not sell fermented drinks.

We shall clip the fronts of our heads.

We shall always dress in the same way wherever we may be, and we shall bind the zunar round our waists

We shall not display our crosses or our books in the roads or markets of the Muslims. We shall use only clappers in our churches very softly. We shall not raise our voices when following our dead. We shall not show lights on any of the roads of the Muslims or in their markets. We shall not bury our dead near the Muslims.

We shall not take slaves who have been allotted to Muslims.

We shall not build houses overtopping the houses of the Muslims.

Some jurists added other rules and specified certain points. Around the year 800, one of them wrote to the caliph reminding him that, 'The Christians were allowed to live in the cities and conduct their trade there, but they were required to abstain from all actions that might insult the faithful of Islam, that is to say, selling pork and wine.' Alongside the prohibition against ever displaying the cross, he added that if ever such a display were to occur, then the cross in question must be destroyed. As for the prohibition against using horses, he specified that only humble donkeys could be ridden, and that they must be mounted sidesaddle, with both legs on one side (in other words, riding like women). The humbler jobs, such as cleaning latrines and collecting garbage, moreover, could only be done by those subjects. The jurist urged the ruler to apply these measures to the very letter and also to ensure that no one in his court should take advantage of his kindness and violate these rules.

The dhimmis, another jurist emphasizes, must neither attack nor twist the words of the Koran nor state that Muhammad had uttered falsehoods or attempt to separate Muslims from their faith. Nor were they allowed to approach a Muslim woman with intentions of having sexual intercourse or marrying her. Moreover, he recommended that Christians abstain from drinking wine in public. In order to avoid possible contaminations (some Muslims considered any object that had been touched by a Christian as impure), he went so far as to suggest not buying any type of meat from dhimmi butchers, advocated expelling them from the markets of the faithful of Allah and urged his people not to eat food prepared by Christians for their religious festivities and not to accept gifts from them on those occasions. In order to strengthen these prohibitions, it was pointed out that on Judgment Day, everyone would be judged similarly to the people they resembled. Prohibitions also concerned public baths, very popular in the Mediterranean basin with the faithful of all religions. According to a collection of Islamic laws, non-Muslims were required to wear a ring around their necks when they entered those baths. Caliph Al-Ḥākim (d. 1021), in contrast, at first ordered them to wear a cross and later ordered the faithful of each religion to frequent only baths used by their own coreligionists and also that the baths of dhimmis should be marked with a clearly visible symbol. Once Andalusia was subjugated toward the end of the eleventh century, the Almoravids presented themselves as the true messengers of Allah and imposed upon their non-Muslim subjects a series of prohibitions much harsher than those previously in effect.

Those discriminations also involved the purely economic sphere. Some legal experts, in fact, stated that dhimmi merchants had to pay a tax on their merchandise double that paid by the faithful of Islam. Some discriminatory rules were also created in the Ottoman era. Not wanting to have Christian neighbors, in the eighteenth century, an inhabitant of Aleppo obtained a verdict from the local Muslim religious leader concerning the fact that the faithful of Allah could force a Christian to sell his house to a Muslim if the Christian practiced his religious rituals in a Muslim quarter. In Sofia, in the early modern era, for instance, this very thing happened to a number of Christians who owned a home in a Muslim district because they had prayed aloud.

Not even in Christian realms was it immediately felt necessary to impose upon their Muslim subjects the obligation of making their diversity and inferiority immediately visible and keeping them separate from the faithful of Christ. That need was initially expressed by the churchmen though they never produced legislation comparable to that of the pact of Umar. The earliest instance of this kind of prohibitions can be found in the proceedings of a council held in 1120 in the kingdom of Jerusalem. On that occasion, the Muslims were ordered not to wear Frankish garb, which was a reference to European Christians, evidently in order to make those Muslims immediately recognizable and thus prevent any intimacy between members of the two faiths.

In 1215, Pope Innocent III, a legal expert and a pontiff forcefully engaged in the struggle to defend Christianity from enemies foreign and domestic, made sure to include a number of articles concerning the Jews and the Muslims residing in Christian lands in the final proceedings of the meeting held in Rome among all the principal ecclesiastical leaders. Driven by a desire to protect the physical and spiritual safety of the faithful of Christ as well as to provide a clear line of conduct for non-Christians, the pontiff expanded and fine-tuned the decisions issued the previous century in the Holy Land concerning the importance of ensuring that they were made immediately recognizable, in order to forestall eventual illicit relations between the faithful of different religions. Moreover, he established a barrier between Christians and non-Christians during the Holy Week, the most important period of the year for Christians, with the excuse that non-Christians mocked it (implicitly emphasizing that, by so doing, they contaminated those festivities).

> In some provinces, Jews and Saracens distinguished themselves from Christians by the different ways they dressed; but in other areas such unbridled confusion had emerged that there were no visible distinctions. It therefore sometimes happened that, by pure mishap, male Christians might have congress with Jewish or Saracen women, or that Jewish or Saracen men could dally with Christian women. To keep such deplorable unions from relying upon the excuse of innocent error, due to their clothing, we hereby decree that these people, of either sex, in all Christian provinces and for all time, must distinguish themselves in public by their style of dress from the rest of the population, as was ordered, for that matter, by Moses.
>
> In the days of lamentations and on Passion Sunday they must not dare to appear in public, given the fact that some of them on these days feel no shame in walking around dressed up more elaborately than usual and mock the Christians, who in commemoration of the holy passion of their Lord display all the signs of their mourning. We therefore forbid most severely that they dare to dance in joy making mockery of the Redeemer.

Some sixty years later, a council added that the Muslims were not to be allowed to engage in the public call to prayer, while in 1280, the bishop of Lleida (Catalonia) specified that anyone who visited the public baths with Muslims would be excommunicated.

In spite of the threats of the ecclesiastics, those laws were not put into effect by Christian sovereigns, especially those who ruled over substantial numbers of Muslim subjects; in certain zones under their dominion, they sometimes represented the majority of their inhabitants. The rulers of those areas had no desire whatsoever to give any cause for discontentment to subjects who were productive and had only recently been incorporated into their reign. In this connection, it is worth pointing out that we see the first requirements that the Muslim subjects wear distinctive markers around 1255 in the legislation of Castile, but no such requirement in the body of laws of Aragon, which included the recently conquered region of Valencia, characterized for many years by a considerable presence of Muslims. In conjunction with a progressive decline in the number of Muslim subjects, prohibitions began to appear in secular legislation. Not only were orders issued requiring Moors to make themselves immediately identifiable, they were also forbidden to show off their wealth. In Seville in 1252, the faithful of Allah were forbidden to wear garments colored white, red, and green or to wear white or golden shoes. A few years later, it was added that they had to wear long beards as demanded by their religion. Again, with a view to keeping Muslims from trying to pass for Christians, we start to see prohibitions in city legislation against Moors having Christian names.

Other prohibitions were aimed at separating the faithful of the two religions, in particular during Christian festivities. Muslims who practiced noisy professions, such as blacksmiths, were not allowed to work on Sunday and any other Christian holy days. In cities characterized by small Islamic communities, they were prohibited to have workshops outside of their quarter, but instead they were permitted to do so in towns with high numbers of Mudéjars. Their importance to the economy was so great that in some cases the need was felt to put that right to work in written form.

The fear of having excessively intimate relations even extended to wet nurses suspected of contaminating children. In the House of Islam, dhimmi wet nurses were strongly disapproved by legal experts, while in 1268 in a collection of the laws of a Spanish city under the Christian rule, we find a prohibition against using Muslim wet nurses; the punishment for violators of that law was to be sold into slavery. Their use during the Ottoman era, in contrast, created no problems for the Muslims but instead for Christian subjects. According to the most intransigent, those wet nurses were sinners. In a sixteenth-century fresco in a Bulgarian church, we see a depiction of a woman showing her breasts, which are being bitten by two snakes. According to an inscription set beneath that painting, this was the penalty for serving as a wet nurse for Turkish children.

In the late Middle Ages in the Christian kingdoms of the Iberian Peninsula, secular laws also began to regulate the use of public baths, but the rules were not the same everywhere. In general, in Portugal and in northern Castile, non-Christians were prohibited to enter the public baths of the faithful of Christ. In central and northern Spain, they were allowed to go there on certain days, while no prohibitions were issued in the rest of the Peninsula and in southern Catalonia. It is worth mentioning that in the laws of Tortosa, it is specifically stated that public baths were open to all and that the proceeds were to be devoted to the maintenance of the city walls. We should keep in mind that, in places where it was forbidden, a complaint had to be filed in order for violators to be punished, and furthermore the presence of numerous witnesses was necessary. And what is more, the fines were not very heavy.

Sharply discriminatory laws only started to spread through various zones of the Iberian Peninsula in the middle of the fifteenth century. For instance, in Castile, the faithful of Islam were allowed to live only in their own quarters and exclusively allowed to sell 'living flesh' to Christians, which is, to say, animals that had not yet been slaughtered. What is more, they were not permitted to practice the medical profession, severe penalties were established for those who dressed like Christians, and they were ordered not to show themselves in public during the course of celebrations of the most important Christian holy days. In one Catalan city, thirty lashes or heavy fines were set as the penalty for those who failed to kneel during the passage of the Corpus Domini procession or who sold meat to Christians or worked during the principal Christian festivities. In Burgos, Muslim stonemasons were punished with seventy lashes for having used Christian assistants. Well aware that commercial activities tended to flourish in the absence of injustice, even then the authorities chose not to pass laws that disadvantaged Muslim businessmen.

Putting prohibitions into practice

It is not possible to determine whether those prohibitions were completely or partially implemented in Muslim and Christian dominions. The reiteration of the majority of those laws suggests that they were not always applied and that they had been passed at moments of great tension between the faithful of the two religions or else between neighboring states, and by rulers who were zealots when it came to religious matters. In Egypt, for instance, during the persecutions against Christian subjects, the caliph Al-Ḥākim decreed that they would always have to wear a cross, visible around their neck, as well as wearing a sash. In that land, the same measures reemerged during the Mamluk period. That European pilgrims, who went to the Holy Land and to Egypt in the fourteenth and fifteenth centuries, describe certain Christian faithful of those regions as 'Christians of the Belt' indicates that those rules were followed especially in urban zones inhabited by members of both religions. The Ottomans seem to have implemented a prohibition against dhimmis wearing white turbans (the turbans worn by Christians were to be blue, and the ones worn by Jews, yellow). According to some western travelers of the nineteenth century, in the countryside in the

Syro-Palestinian area, the peasants of the various faiths were indistinguishable from each other, while the Christian peasants in Egypt could be identified by the cross tattooed on their wrists, in all likelihood, done by themselves.

Not everyone was willing to respect these requirements, and most likely the rules were not enforced with ironbound severity, but if discovered, transgressors were punished with considerable harshness. One episode that occurred in Cairo in the thirteenth century offers a clear illustration of what happened in practical terms. Requiring two witnesses for the signature of a document, a Muslim met in the marketplace two men of aristocratic appearance who accepted to perform that duty for him; it was later learned that the two men were Christians. Their act was considered to be a form of mockery, and the ruler ordered that they be caned and obliged to wear a belt and the distinctive marker of non-Muslims in order to ensure 'that they comply with the inferior position assigned to them by Allah.' In the seventeenth century in Istanbul, no dhimmi dared to wear a white turban, because the penalty was either to convert or else to face execution. These norms were not always applied in the following century, but it was not uncommon for members of the lower classes to abuse and molest dhimmis who failed to wear such markers of distinction.

With reference to the distinguishing marks in Spain, it is worth noting that as late as 1486, King Ferdinand mentioned the fact that many believers in Islam failed to wear them. Aside from stating that Muslim men thus enjoyed opportunities to have sexual relations with Christian women, he emphasized that the failure to implement that prohibition had allowed Granada's Muslims to infiltrate his kingdom so as to kill or rob Christians.

Likewise, prohibitions against publicly exhibiting the signs of the Christian faith and against erecting new religious buildings or repairing those in ruins were subject to the will of the Muslim rulers concerning the application of those rules and were largely influenced by relations between the faithful of the two religions. In Andalusia, the previously mentioned intransigence of the Almoravids resulted in the sound of bells being completely banished, as they claimed that such sounds should only be heard in the 'lands of the infidels.' In various areas of the Ottoman Empire, attempts were made to enforce that law, but in areas with a heavy presence of Christian subjects, such as the Balkans, that prohibition was roundly opposed, and in various places, the bells continued to be heard, causing disputes with the local Muslims.

When Egypt became part of the dominions of Saladin (d. 1193), who was battling fiercely against the kingdom of Jerusalem, tension toward Christian subjects increased considerably, and bells and crosses displayed outside religious buildings were removed. One particularly significant case concerned the large cross on the church of the Orthodox Christian patriarch of Istanbul, which was removed in the middle of the sixteenth century because it was displayed in a position that stood higher than the mosques. In that century in the Balkan Peninsula, the Ottomans forbade putting crosses along the roads leading to sanctuaries, but in the seventeenth century, it was possible to see them in remote areas between Serbia and Bulgaria.

The importance of maintaining good relations with the sizable Christian community in Egypt kept the Fatimid rulers from hindering the construction of new religious buildings, and they sometimes contributed funds for that purpose. Having been forced to destroy a monastery in the process of constructing a palace, the first caliph of that dynasty ordered a new one built in a different location. The second caliph, instead, permitted the restoration of a number of churches, one of which had been transformed into a warehouse. Al-Ḥākim's successors allowed Christians to reconstruct the religious buildings destroyed during the rule of that caliph and contributed to defray the costs of their reconstruction. When it was discovered that the Christians had taken advantage of the opportunity to erect new churches and had even displayed an inscription honoring the Holy Trinity, considered offensive to Muslims, they were, however, forced to remove the inscription, demolish the new churches, keep the others locked tight for a year, and pay a heavy fine (the patriarch of Cairo and many bishops were imprisoned until the entire sum had been delivered). Under the Ottomans, the repair and construction of houses of worship were allowed. In both cases, especially for the construction, though, permission had to be obtained from the local authorities, who were not always inclined to approve, prompting numerous complaints. It was not uncommon for the Christian communities to forward their objections to Istanbul. In a manual dating from the second half of the sixteenth century, drawn up in the Balkans, the author recommends destroying the entire building if so much as a single brick is added.

Even though the sale of alcohol to Muslims was not allowed and was punished with the destruction of the shop or the house involved, that trade remained rather widespread in various regions of the House of Islam, in particular in Andalusia, where judges frequently turned a blind eye. Measures were taken, however, in cases of flagrant flaunting of laws and during periods of tension with Christians. In 1343, for instance, Mamluk soldiers carried out a raid on the Armenian quarter of Cairo where pork and wine had been openly offered for sale, alongside a booming market in both male and female prostitution. An emblematic instance of how, under the far-from-strict rule of the Ottomans, prohibitions were generally subject to negotiations and the whims of the authorities and of judges can be found in the following occurrence that took place in Aleppo in 1658. A delegation of Muslims from a quarter of that city denounced several Christians residing in there for the sale of alcohol and public drunkenness. The faithful of Christ declared that they had been given permission by the Sublime Porte to conduct that sort of trade. The magistrate, however, replied that the license in question did not allow them to become drunk in public and therefore forbade them from selling alcohol in future.

When the Christian sovereigns of the Iberian Peninsula began to forbid the 'abominable name of Muhammad' from being mentioned aloud and publicly, they did not do so systematically and they showed that they were capable of changing their minds in cases where they needed to ensure the support of their Muslim subjects. Among the privileges bestowed upon the Mudéjar community during the course of a civil war in the fourteenth century in hopes of ensuring their loyalty, the king included the right to the call to prayer. That permission was granted frequently. In rural areas, many Christian lords pretended not to know that this was happening in their lands in order to ensure that they had happy and therefore productive, Muslim farmers. It was not until 1477 that the archbishop of Zaragoza managed to secure the demolition of the minarets in the Huesca district.

Finally, it is worth noting the immense challenges that the authorities encountered in Spain in preventing Muslims from owning weapons. This problem still arose in 1480 when King Ferdinand, worried about the military activities of the Turks in the Mediterranean, issued orders to disarm the Mudéjars in his kingdom. In the cities, some Muslims were fined for violating that decree, but in general, the royal officers decided that there was no danger and that it was sufficient to keep an eye on them. In the countryside, the lords and landowners absolutely refused to implement that prohibition and the Mudéjars continued to be armed 'to the teeth.'

Laws and justice

Both Muslim and Christian sovereigns allowed their subjects of a different religion to appeal for judgment in controversies involving civil law between their coreligionists from courts presided over by magistrates of their own faith, and in accordance with their own laws, provided that these verdicts did not go against the secular and religious legislation of the dominators. They were thus allowed a certain degree of autonomy, meaning that the rulers avoided acting against the religious precepts of their subjects. In the House of Islam, the Muslims by and large assigned this duty to the Christians' ecclesiastic leaders, who were thus given the duty of deciding what was allowed and what forbidden according to their holy books. In the eighth century, for instance, the patriarch of Damascus was given the duty of settling lawsuits between his faithful in cases of inheritances and marriages. The ecclesiastical hierarchies and the secular leaders of the dominated populace chose the judges, whose appointment was usually confirmed by the dominators. The magistrates, in turn, were permitted to delegate their powers to persons who were authorized to hand down verdicts in their absence. In the kingdom of Aragon, which could claim the distinction of having the highest number of Muslim subjects in the Iberian Peninsula, there was also a royal Muslim superintendent whose job was to oversee the activities of the Islamic courts of justice. Those courts offered a place to appeal for those who were unsatisfied with a verdict handed down by a local court of law.

If the various parties to the lawsuit belonged to different faiths, in the territories governed by the believers in Islam, it was their magistrates who administered justice. The same thing was true in the kingdom of Jerusalem. The situation varied, instead, in the Iberian Peninsula where, at the beginning of the conquest of Muslim territories, the Christians who had settled in those places often found themselves immersed in a sea of Muslims where, as a result, those cases were necessarily managed by Mudéjar judges and according to Islamic law. In general, this did not mean that the faithful of Allah received special treatment in those areas, but these legal procedures nonetheless spread discontent among the faithful of Christ. When the percentage of Christians rose in those areas, those procedures were increasingly administered by Christian magistrates. Until the fourteenth century, nonetheless, there were various regions where those changes did not take place.

As far as criminal trials among coreligionists were concerned, in the House of Islam a Muslim magistrate had to be present in order to ensure the correct application of the law. The religious leaders who served as judges were not, moreover, allowed to inflict penalties involving corporal punishment. In the Ottoman Empire, the Orthodox Christian patriarch of Istanbul was often required to ask the Muslim authorities to implement expulsion orders that he had handed down against Christians who were found guilty of having created problems in the capital through their behavior.

During the first period of the Christian conquest of Andalusia, crimes with significant legal penalties among the Moors wound up in the Islamic courts under the supervision of a royal functionary, in order to ensure that the guilty party was captured and the sentence carried out appropriately. Muslims, in fact, were not allowed to carry out corporal punishments and capital sentences, and what is more, they preferred not to prosecute crimes committed by groups of wrongdoers. In the fifteenth century, the Mudéjars of the Valencia region were quite happy to leave to Christian officials the task of arresting and trying fifteen Moors who, having forced entry into the home of a Muslim widow, then proceeded to rape her, along with her daughter. The penalties for crimes were very harsh, but the king's representatives often commuted them into fines or else the sale into slavery; thieves could thus avoid the amputation of a hand, for instance. The king's representatives were also expected to maintain public order and ensure that, in murder cases, the victim's family accepted compensation from the killer, rather than resorting to a vendetta. That a portion of that sum went to the Crown constituted an incentive for the application of this procedure. In the late Middle Ages, this kind of crime was increasingly tried and punished by Christian courts.

In practical terms, the way in which justice was handled in the Christian kingdoms of the Iberian Peninsula depended on the power relationships between and among the sovereigns, the aristocracy, and the Mudéjar communities. In periods when the royal authority was weak, noblemen and city authorities tried to take control at all levels. For instance, during the difficult years of the war between the Christian kingdoms of Aragon and Castile (1355–1366), roughly 90% of the lawsuits between the Muslim subjects of Aragon were heard by Christian magistrates. On other occasions, the Mudéjar communities arranged to take jurisdiction over those disputes, especially concerning crimes such as premarital sexual relations, adultery, insults concerning an alleged lack of chastity, theft, consumption of alcohol, and armed robbery. In some cases, they also managed to obtain the right to have laws applied under the supervision of a royal official in suits involving civil law, between the faithful of the two religions. At the end of the thirteenth century, in a village near Tortosa, the lord of the region gave the local Muslim chief the right to administer justice among the faithful of Islam and to hold trials of Christians accused of witchcraft and similar crimes in that village. Desirous of keeping the peace in his kingdom, in the second half of the fifteenth century, King Ferdinand of Aragon responded to the complaints of his Muslim subjects in Valencia concerning the interferences of Christians in that sector by decreeing that 'all disagreements, whether civil or criminal, involving a Moor against another Moor, must be resolved in accordance with sharia.' Anyone who violated that decree was to be levied the heavy fine of a thousand gold pieces.

Testifying against the other

In the House of Islam, Christians could bring lawsuits against Muslims in Islamic courts, but testimony from their coreligionists was not considered valid. This rule progressed in parallel with the Islamization of the occupied regions. Worthy of mention, in this connection, is the statement of a Syrian Christian who complained, in the 730s, that the testimony of the faithful of Christ was no longer accepted against a Muslim. According to the most extremist Islamic jurists, if the accused was a faithful of Allah, the dhimmis could not even provide evidence against him. They took for granted that an infidel was an immoral person, and this nullified any ability they might have to act legally in court. Some went so far as to emphasize that a dishonest Muslim was still better than an honest Christian. Dhimmis were allowed to testify or provide evidence only when there was no other evidence or testimony available. In places where there were good relations between the faithful of the two religions, such as in Candia (Crete) during the eighteenth century, the testimony of Christians of good repute was, however, accepted. Even there, in criminal trials, however, it was essential to have witnesses belonging to the faith of the dominators, and that, moreover, these witnesses be important and well respected. If the suspected murderer was a Muslim, dhimmis were absolutely forbidden to testify against him. In the eighteenth century, in Aleppo, a Muslim who had murdered a Christian who had refused to give him a job was not taken to court, because only Christians had witnessed the killing. In disputes among Islam's faithful, the testimony of Christians was completely out of the question. There was, however, an exceedingly rare exception to that rule in Bulgaria in 1618. Given that the case concerned the repair of a mosque, on that occasion, the Christian had probably provided an appraisal of the work carried out.

In Christian lands, the validity of the testimony of the dominated in the courts of the dominators was the object of fluctuations that reflected the dynamics in the demographic relations between the two groups and the standing of Muslim subjects in the administration and in the society. In the first few decades following the conquest of a certain area, they were accepted without question.

In Spain, in some collections of laws from those periods, it was specified that a Muslim was recognized to be guilty only when there was a coreligionist testifying against him. At the beginning of the thirteenth century in the kingdom of Jerusalem, it was noted that trials were considered admissible only when the witnesses offering testimony belonged to the same religion as the accused, Muslims included. In that period, the same rule was applied in numerous regions of Spain under Christian rule. In the Iberian Peninsula, the increase of the Christian population in those territories progressed in parallel with the progressive elimination of that legal corpus, and at the beginning of the fourteenth century, the testimony of Muslims was no longer considered valid in cases brought against the Christians. According to a 1301 edict from the king of Aragon, the testimony of two Christians of good repute was sufficient in a trial against a Mudéjar. In cases where testimony from Muslims was allowed, that testimony did not carry the same weight as the testimony of the Christians. For instance, twice as much was demanded of Muslim witnesses as was required of Christians. The testimony of the latter witnesses became increasingly important and was considered sufficient to find a Mudéjar guilty, even in the absence of evidence. If a Christian testified, then the testimony of Muslims was often considered to be insignificant. The extreme difficulty of obtaining the testimony of Christians if a faithful of Christ murdered a Mudéjar made it very difficult to obtain a guilty verdict for that kind of crime (the same problem arose in the House of Islam when the roles were reversed). Some municipal criminal codes of the Iberian Peninsula, moreover, allowed Christians to acquit themselves by simply swearing they had not committed the murder.

In judicial proceedings where the dominated were permitted to testify in the courts of the dominators, they were required to swear on their own God. In order to give those oaths greater legitimacy and seriousness, they had to be sworn on their own holy books and in some cases in their own religious buildings or in the presence of respectable coreligionists.

Penalties

In the House of Islam, if a Muslim killed a dhimmi, he was not executed but had only to pay a reparation fee to the relatives of the victim. In cases where there were two murderers and one was a Muslim and the other a Christian, the latter could be sentenced to death, while the former had to pay half of the compensation normally prescribed. The sums prescribed in those cases clearly show the difference between members of the different faiths. A dhimmi man was worth the same as a Muslim woman, which is, to say, half what a male believer in Islam was worth. The relationship between the value of a male and that of a female was the same for dhimmis, and therefore the sum owed for a Christian woman corresponded to half the amount for a Muslim woman and a quarter the amount for a man who was a faithful of Islam. If a Muslim killed a dhimmi unintentionally, he did not have to pay the legal compensation but instead was forced to fast for two months or else free his slaves. If the victim was a slave, there was no punishment or penance. If it was not possible to determine with absolute certainty who had committed a crime, but there was still strong suspicion against a Christian, his community was often held responsible and was therefore required to pay a fine.

The situation was largely similar in Christian kingdoms. If a Muslim was found guilty, the monetary penalties were higher (usually, doubled) than those called for in the judicial proceedings in which a Moor was the victim. In response to complaints about the fact that believers in Allah were punished less severely in Islamic courts in the thirteenth century, King James of Aragon decreed that Muslims found guilty of a crime against any Christian should be tried according to the body of law that demanded the highest penalty.

The punishment for anyone who killed a Muslim was lesser than that pre-scribed for the murder of a Christian. According to a 1075 law of the Spanish town of Najera, the compensation to be paid for the killing of a Muslim was roughly equivalent to the price of a donkey. In the years that followed the con-quest, in some areas, there was never any distinction drawn between Moors and Christians. In the legislation in use in the royal courts of Castile starting at the end of the thirteenth century, it was clearly stated that the amount of the sum to be paid was calculated according to local customs, but that in no case could the principle be violated that a Moor was worth less than a Christian. In the king-dom of Jerusalem, extremely severe punishments were ordered for Muslims who beat Christians, and repeat offenders were to be hanged. No punishment was called for, however, if the roles were reversed.

The dominated in the courts of the dominators

The rules described above make it clear what disadvantages the dominated faced in the courts of the dominators. Considering the significant economic relevance of many of those subjects and the necessity of keeping internal peace, the Mus-lim and Christian rulers did not wish to give the impression of any attempt to oppress them. Rather, they aspired to providing equal justice for all and therefore wished to protect the faithful of another religion from the abuses of those who thought they could take advantage of their status as second-class subjects. The magistrates and their underlings were expected to scrupulously adhere to pro-cedure, even in the presence of extremely execrable crimes and acts of violence against the dominators. In legislation concerning cases involving members of the different faiths of the kingdom of Jerusalem, the need was felt to emphasize that Muslim subjects were human beings just like the Christians, and that they were therefore to be treated in an equitable manner. The Christian sovereigns of the Iberian Peninsula, moreover, created a system of control that, to the extent pos-sible, prevented abuse through the replacement of unjust and corrupt magistrates or else by balancing their opinions with those of legal experts not involved in the dispute. In the kingdom of Aragon, this latter approach was adopted at the request of the Muslim in the case, if he felt that his Christian adversary was too powerful. In accordance with that rule, in the second half of the fifteenth century, the viceroy added a legal expert from Valencia to the trial, which concerned the property of a plot of land disputed by the Cavalier Perot and the Mudéjar Abrahim, because the latter, unlike the Christian, was a modest, ordinary man, with no protections in high places. Judges and lawyers were removed if they were suspected of having personal interests or if they had family ties with the Christian involved. Muslim subjects could likewise appeal to the court of the king, a right that was often invoked in Spain with a reasonable degree of success.

Practice was, however, often quite different from theory, and there was certainly no shortage of cases in which there had been instances of intimidation and unscrupulous magistrates had shamelessly favored their coreligionists. The penalties against dishonest public functionaries, moreover, were not always applied. Sentenced to death in absentia for having ordered a Muslim to be hanged in spite of the fact that he had been commanded not to carry out that sentence, an official was subsequently pardoned by King Ferdinand of Aragon. In the Muslim world, kidnapping Christian women was almost never prosecuted and as late as 1889, a Kurdish leader was acquitted of that charge.

This does not mean, all the same, that it was exceedingly rare to have impartial magistrates. In general, the courts of justice were not the place where glaring discrimination took place. If they possessed impeccable written documentation and witnesses belonging to the faith of the dominators, it was not completely impossible for the dominated to obtain justice in the courts of their rulers, especially during periods devoid of tensions, and in fact the dhimmis and the Mudéjars were not afraid to have recourse to those courts.

In a study about early modern Cyprus, it has been found that in a third of the lawsuits brought in Islamic courts, there was a dhimmi involved and that 40% of them were initiated by a Christian or a Jew. At the turn of the seventeenth century in the city of Kayseri in central Anatolia, 27% of the women who brought lawsuits to Islamic courts were dhimmis. Emblematic, in that connection, is the fact that in 54% of the disputes between Mudéjars and Christians in Valencia in the second half of the fifteenth century, the winners were Muslims. Fair verdicts were handed down even during the Mamluk domination in Egypt, characterized by a decided harshening of relations with Christians. In Cairo in 1485, for instance, a Christian woman was accused by her Muslim neighbors of having built a house higher than theirs, an act prohibited to dhimmis. The Christian woman presented a document attesting to the fact that she had purchased that home from a Muslim. Once the authenticity of that document had been established and once the court had verified that the building in question corresponded to the one described in the document, the judge dismissed all charges.

Other examples that took place in various zones of the Ottoman Empire make it very clear that this was no exception. In 1619, in the district of Sofia, a Muslim official's request to confiscate a house and make it the property of the public treasury on the grounds that it was unclaimed and had no owner was rejected, because a Christian woman had stated that she had inherited it from her father, and two faithful of Allah had confirmed her version of events. In 1779 in Damascus, a Christian widow won a lawsuit she had brought against her late husband's Muslim business partner who had refused to pay the woman the inheritance that was due her. Fundamental in this case too was the fact that two Muslims had testified on behalf of the Christian widow. When a Christian man's shop in Candia was robbed by a Muslim in 1672 (which is, we should point out, only three years after the Ottoman conquest of the city), two faithful of Islam testified against the robber. Likewise, on Crete in the early modern period, the Muslim daughter of a Christian woman successfully turned to an Islamic court of justice against her Muslim father who continued to pester and bother her mother, even though her parents were divorced. She too was able to bring Muslim witnesses in her favor.

Thanks to an impeccable body of documentation, in 1860 in Damascus a faithful of Christ won a lawsuit against an insolvent Muslim debtor in spite of the fact that two of the debtor's coreligionists testified in his favor. The honest magistrates, then, chose not to take into consideration the testimony contradicted by clear written evidence. In the absence of documentation and witnesses, however, the judges decided solomonically, as happened, for instance, in the case of a dispute between a Muslim and a Christian over the purchase of a horse. Because neither of the two had provided proof in their favor, the judge ordered that the sum of money be split between them. In Damascus in 1784, a newly converted Muslim had probably presumed he would enjoy special favorable treatment in court and sued his mother, who had remained Christian, for a portion of the assets left in inheritance by his father. The judge, however, sided with the woman. Nor should we think that the dominated parties were always able to find coreligionists willing to confirm their lies against the dominator. For instance, in Damascus in the eighteenth century, a Muslim used two Christian witnesses to prove the falsity of a Christian widow's statement to the effect that her late husband's debt had been paid off. Last of all, there was no shortage of Muslim magistrates who opposed the particularly intolerant demands of coreligionists toward dhimmis like the faithful of Allah of Cordoba, who around the year 1100 wished to cancel the purchase of a house after discovering he would have to share use of the well with the dhimmi neighbors.

Relying upon the justice of the dominators

In lawsuits and cases held under civil law between coreligionists, the hope of receiving a better verdict in the courts of the dominators and of having a greater chance of seeing that verdict applied was rather widespread in both the Christian kingdoms and in the House of Islam. For instance, in Sofia in the seventeenth century, roughly 30% of the cases heard in Islamic courts were between Christians. This phenomenon held true even though both the religious and secular leaders of the dominated group had always tried to persuade the faithful not to seek justice outside of their community. Losing that monopoly profoundly undermined their authority. At the turn of the ninth century, a Syrian patriarch harshly scolded several coreligionists, making it clear to them just how unacceptable it was to present their disputes to Muslim magistrates with the excuse that ecclesiastical law was somehow insufficient. During the same years, in Syria and Egypt, religious leaders threatened to excommunicate anyone who dared to use the Islamic courts. In the Balkans, under the Ottomans, spiritual and monetary penalties were imposed on anyone who did such a thing. In 1788, a Greek bishop stated that anyone who chose to go that route would never again be allowed to make use of ecclesiastic courts. It was further stated that such people would be considered outcasts because they had displayed an utter lack of respect for the Church and their coreligionists. Of course, the weaker the ecclesiastical structure and the community of one's own coreligionists, the less effective such threats proved to be. Well aware of the tensions that these trials could arouse, it was suggested that Muslim magistrates ask the parties at law to agree to be judged according to Islamic law. If one party refused, they were advised not to accept the case.

In the Iberian Peninsula, the Mudéjars usually availed themselves of Christian justice when they thought it would give them a chance against verdicts issued by the courts of their community. This path was followed especially for contested inheritances and insolvent debtors. In those areas, disputes between Muslim communities were also settled in Christian courts because the laws of the kingdom were better suited to solving that type of case. Quarrels about ownership of land often wound up being heard before Christian courts when the parties at law were employed by Christian landowners. The loss of those assets, in fact, would have caused financial harm to their lords and masters. Well aware that royal justice was often more efficient, in some cases, it was the Muslims themselves who turned to it.

The modesty of many of those disagreements in both Christian kingdoms and Muslim dominions indicates just how little respect was felt for the courts of the dominated; in some cases, they were completely absent or they had chosen not to judge the quarrels in which parents and children were involved. Indicative of what happened in Christian lands are the following judicial proceedings drawn from the rich documentation of the kingdom of Aragon.

In the second half of the fifteenth century, several relatives of Fuçey Zignell of Valencia demanded the intervention of a Christian magistrate in order to obtain the payment of his debts and a public officer informed the Moor in question that unless he paid the sum he owed, his property would be seized and sold. Another Muslim demanded that the mulberry trees belonging to a coreligionist be removed from his land. Similar examples can be found in the Muslim courts of the House of Islam. In the archival sources of Cyprus during the first century of Ottoman domination in the early modern period, we find disputes that range from the disagreement between a father and a son over the payment for the sale of a cow to the improper appropriation of assets in an inheritance. Given that women were excluded from any and all inheritance by Bulgarian common law, they often turned to Islamic courts to get their fair share. In the seventeenth century in Sofia, a woman brought a lawsuit against her father, claiming that he had given her only some of the objects left to her by her deceased mother. We should add that the two of them later came to an understanding and requested that the court record it. Another woman availed herself of the Islamic court because a neighbor had refused to transfer ownership to her of a vineyard that her deceased father had purchased from the man's father, and the man claimed in his own defense that the sum for the purchase had not been paid in its entirety. The Muslim magistrate concluded that, since there were no documents to prove the failure to pay, the property belonged to the woman. In another case, a claimant asked for a verdict on the legitimacy of the sale of an ox. According to the buyer, the animal had a defect and he wanted to get a refund, while the middlemen on the transaction insisted that there was no reason for the refund. Cases involving insolvent debtors were fairly common. One man claimed to have made a loan of cash to a coreligionist of his, who in turn denied ever having received such a loan, but two Christian witnesses confirmed that the loan had taken place. In Damascus in the eighteenth century, a woman went to a Muslim magistrate in order to secure the eviction of her elderly mother from her home, because she wished to sell the house, despite the fact that her mother declared that she had been promised hospitality for the rest of her life. Another woman received a favorable verdict against her father, whom she accused of having stolen gold bracelets and cash from her. A widow who wished to recover a sum of money that her late husband had loaned to her father-in-law was likewise successful in her lawsuit.

Christians often turned to Islamic courts in order to record sales contracts, divorces, and in order to certify marriages. Worthy of note is the fact that in Bulgaria in those cases, there was also the possibility of a savings. For marriages, the fee paid to Muslim judges in the seventeenth century corresponded to roughly a third of the fee that was to be paid to the Orthodox Church in the case of a first marriage. The ecclesiastics, moreover, charged a fee twice and then three times as high in cases of second and third marriages and prohibited entirely fourth marriages. According to sharia, the waiting period for widows wishing to remarry after the death of a husband was, moreover, shorter. It was also smart to record marriages in a Muslim court because obtaining certification to remarry in church was quite complicated. In Muslim courts, there was furthermore no requirement of documentation attesting to the fact that there were no hindrances to the marriage, such as consanguinity.

It was not uncommon for a divorce to be announced in church but then certified by a Muslim magistrate. Usually, it was women who wanted a divorce in Islamic courts, probably because they hoped that the legal procedures would move more quickly and that, aside from having greater rights, those rights would be guaranteed to them. Women also turned to Islamic courts for disputes on alimony after the divorce and to add clauses and riders concerning their children from prior marriages. They were also refunded the dowry that had been given to their future husband, something not envisaged by Christian bodies of legislation. Often, they went to such courts in order to appeal against decisions handed down by the Church or else by courts consisting of village elders. Worthy of mention is the fact that ecclesiastical courts accepted a husband's violent treatment of his wife as a justification for divorce, while various Christian common laws did not take violent treatment into consideration because they took it as a given that it formed part of the conjugal relationship. Both bodies of legislation were opposed to any divorce initiated by a woman. This situation continued to be the case in Bulgaria in spite of the fact that the Sublime Porte had forbidden local Muslim magistrates to intervene in those cases. In the Ottoman Empire, in the wake of countless protests from the ecclesiastical hierarchies, it was not until 1764 that patriarchs were given the right to punish directly those who caused problems without first having to appeal to the Sublime Porte, and at the same time, magistrates were commanded to reject dubious marriages. Moreover, they were required to ascertain that spouses really had been divorced.

Marriages and sexual relations between the dominated and the dominators

In the House of Islam, Muslim women were not allowed to marry 'infidels.' The penalties for male dhimmis were very strict and ranged from corporal punishments to the death sentence. The marriage was not valid, even if the man subsequently converted to Islam. The case in which one of the faithful of another religion pretended to be a believer of Allah was considered to be extremely deplorable. In spite of the harsh punishments that it entailed, apparently such unions had actually been formed, especially in areas and historical periods when the monitoring and control had been scanty or absent entirely. The best known case—made particularly thorny by the fact that the woman had converted to Christianity—is that of the mother of two of the martyrs of Cordoba (mid-ninth century). The combination of remote location and less-than-dutiful official produced a notable exception in seventeenth-century Cyprus under the Ottoman rule. In a village, a Christian man, married to a Muslim woman, had problems with the local monks who, on account of his marriage, considered him to be a faithful of Allah and therefore refused him admittance to the church of his own village. That man was not afraid of being punished (or perhaps did not realize that he was liable to punishment) by the Ottoman authorities, and, in fact, worried that he would not be able to be given proper burial in accordance with his own religion, he chose to ask a Muslim public official to certify that he was a Christian. Unfortunately, we know nothing about what happened next, and we therefore cannot say what the authorities' reaction was.

Since this was a way of pointing out the superiority of Islam and its male faithful, men could instead marry dhimmi women, who were then allowed to keep their own faith. Husbands could not prevent their Christian wives from practicing their own religion and wearing the cross at home, where they were also permitted to read the Bible, though not aloud. Nor were those husbands allowed to forbid their wives to attend church or take part in religious celebrations; according to some jurists, though, it was still preferable that women not go to those places or that they get their husband's permission to go there, recommendations that also applied, for that matter, to the female believers in Allah. Christian women, moreover, were to be treated just like the other Muslim wives. This was true even if they were later repudiated (the woman received monetary compensation), but they had no right to an inheritance if their husband died, unless they had converted prior to his death. They were legally protected if their husband unjustly accused them of adultery, but in order to emphasize the fact that they were 'infidels,' in that case the penalty for the husband was lesser than the punishment he would have received if his wife had been a Muslim woman. Those Christian wives were required to follow Islamic rituals of purification after menstruation and giving birth and to abstain from the foods and beverages not allowed to the faithful of Allah. The most intransigent jurists, though, advised against such marriages, pointing out that the wife kept her old habits, habits that were forbidden to Muslims, and the husband would come into contact with them when kissing her or during the sex act. Moreover, it was feared that the mother would give 'impure' things to the children or secretly convert them. That fear was not entirely unfounded. In the tenth century in Sicily, the religious calling of the future saint, John Terista, son of a Muslim father and a Christian mother from Palermo, was in fact the result of his mother's efforts, who had secretly raised him in her own faith. In spite of the negative views of them, this kind of marriage was far from rare, and some Fatimid caliphs and Turkish rulers had Christian wives and concubines. Even the Almoravid leader Bin Yusuf, a rigorous and inflexible faithful of Allah and re-conqueror of Muslim Spain, was the son of a Christian woman.

In theory, the children born into those marriages were supposed to be raised according to Islam, but there were various exceptions when it came to the girls, who were allowed to follow their mother's religion. Evidently unaccustomed to that type of family, an Iraqi visiting Sicily in the tenth century was scandalized when he discovered that they were fairly common in the island's countryside. Similar cases occurred in Andalusia in the ninth century and on the Aegean Islands under the Ottomans. On Crete they were so numerous that, worried about how the children were being raised when the father was absent or failed to come home from the wars, on two occasions the Ottoman authorities ordered that the children be conveyed to the island's capital where they could stay with pious Muslims for a certain period of time.

In Christian kingdoms, the faithful of Christ, however, could not marry non-Christians. There were some exceptions to that rule. A Muslim carpenter in Teruel, having converted to Christianity, was permitted to live with his wife for ten years, so that he might persuade her and their children to do the same. That cohabitation, however, ultimately came to an end because certain of the man's enemies convinced the local authorities that the family was never going to convert. The king weighed in, allowing the couple another year. In another case, the sovereign commanded that a Muslim woman be freed; she had been arrested because she was living with her husband who had converted to Christianity, and the king hoped that the wife might follow her man's example.

In the House of Islam, for men who could afford to own slaves, most of the sexual relations with dhimmis took place with women of that condition, who sometimes played the role of concubines. In the Balkan provinces and in the provinces of Eastern Europe under the Ottoman Empire, various Christian women were, in defiance of the firm opposition of the Orthodox Church, involved in a rather diffuse form of limited-term concubinage; the Muslims paid a sum of money to the woman's father and, at the end of the contract, kept whatever children might have been born to the couple.

In Christian territories, the bodies of legislation tended to prohibit any form of concubinage with believers in Islam, including female slaves. In the thirteenth-century laws of Castile known as the *siete partidas*, the practice of concubinage was allowed only if the Christian men were married. Until the thirteenth century, having a child with one's Christian master often led to the emancipation of both mother and child (usually the baby was automatically considered free and Christian if the father was a faithful of Christ). These practices were subsequently subjected to heavy restrictions and the principal obstacle consisted of the requirement that the master had to admit his paternity. Many denied it and attributed it to other coreligionists whom, of course, they claimed not to know.

The fear of contamination, the fear that excessively intimate relations might occur between dominators and the dominated and the desire to emphasize the inferiority of the other led Muslims and Christians to prohibit or strictly limit sexual activities between members of different faiths outside of the bonds of marriage and those particular forms of concubinage.

In Islamic territories, the death sentence was called for in cases of Christians who had raped a Muslim woman or had had consensual sexual relations with one. If a Christian man purchased a female Muslim slave with intention to engage in such relations, he was to be executed and all the members of his community given canings. The only way to avoid that penalty was to convert and forthwith marry the woman. On occasion, clemency was afforded someone committing this crime for the first time, but repeat offenders were punished without mercy. In the eleventh century in Egypt, two Christians were caught twice with two Muslim women. On the first instance, the men and women were caned and marched through the city, while on the second occasion, the women were subjected to the same treatment, but the men were sentenced to death.

In Christian lands, the first prohibition concerning sexual activities between members of the two religions was established by the Church in the kingdom of Jerusalem in a council that took place in 1120. The punishment for men, both Muslims and Christians, was castration, whereas consenting women were to have their noses cut off. If the woman was a faithful of Allah and a slave and if she belonged to another Christian, then along with castration, the punishment included exile. There is no sign of such laws in the secular legislation of that kingdom, and we are therefore unable to establish whether they were ever actually applied. In the Iberian Peninsula, the punishment for males was not particularly strict. According to a collection of laws, the man and the woman were forced to walk through the streets, naked, and were whipped; the Muslim woman was then usually sold into slavery even if she was a prostitute. Nearly all the bodies of legislation called for no penalty whatsoever for males. Since those women were sold into slavery, and there was an opportunity to attain economic advantages from that transaction, there were even Christians who had reported their Muslim female partner in order to win a reward. In 1357, just a year after giving a monastic community all rights over the Muslim females residing on the lands of that same monastery who were guilty of that crime, the king of Aragon was forced to add the clause that this was not true in cases where it had been the monks themselves who engaged in sex acts with those women. The sovereign had clearly discovered that the monks had exploited those women for a twofold 'benefit,' first physical, then monetary. In Portugal, the attitude toward such infractions was looser. Muslim women were, in fact, merely fined. If their communities wished to execute them as adulteresses, their families could win their absolution by making an appeal to the king.

In Christian kingdoms, consensual sexual relations with the faithful of a different religion were considered far more serious if the guilty parties were Muslim men and Christian women. According to the majority of the bodies of legislation of the Iberian Peninsula, the Muslim men in such cases were to be quartered, while the Christian women were to be burned at the stake. In Castilian laws from the second half of the thirteenth century, the punishment for men was death by stoning; if the women were virgins or widows and that was their first offense, then half their property was forfeit. If there was a repeat offense, all their property was confiscated and the guilty woman was sentenced to death. Fines and dismissal from office were the punishments for magistrates who failed to prosecute cases of that crime or to punish the offenders adequately. In the kingdom of Aragon, it was not allowed to pardon those crimes, a circumstance that highlights just how deplorable they were considered to be.

The idea that a Muslim could have 'carnal knowledge' of a Christian female was considered to be such an abomination that a mere rumor would be sufficient to prompt the execution of those suspected. The frenzy that such an act could arouse occasionally led to the death of innocent victims. In Spain in 1311, having learned of rumors circulating about relations between her and a Muslim man, a young Christian woman fled her city. The man, instead, was caught and immediately burned at the stake. The young woman was later captured whereupon it was determined that she was a virgin, which meant that both she and the believer in Allah were innocent. When she learned that word had gotten around that she had had two daughters by a faithful of Islam, a Christian widow fled to the Muslim kingdom of Granada and there converted to Islam in order to escape the death sentence. The ecclesiastics contributed significantly to keeping tensions high where that type of infraction was concerned. Among the various sinful activities that had caused a crop failure and famine, according to a council held in Valencia, were the illicit contacts between Christians and non-Christians.

The Mudéjars were well aware of just how serious that crime was, to the extent that they used it to eliminate rivals within their own community. Along with the list of accusations leveled against the leader of the Moors of Teruel, his enemies added that his grandson had had sexual relations with a Christian woman and that his daughter had had them with a faithful of Christ. The Mudéjars of Zaragoza tried to rid themselves of a Christian official they disliked by claiming that he tolerated sex among members of different faiths (in that case it was quickly proven that the charges were false). In order to prevent abuses, it was, however, very difficult to sentence a Muslim male for such a violation. Some Muslim communities ensured that two eyewitnesses were necessary, and that one of them had to be a believer of Islam.

The possibility that their own women might have that type of relations with 'other' men was considered intolerable by Muslim subjects as well. In the Christian kingdoms of the Iberian Peninsula, the Mudéjar communities often demanded that women found guilty always be sentenced to the harshest possible penalties. The Moors of Valencia won an agreement from the king that women stained by the shame of that crime could never avoid punishment by paying a fine instead. Often, it was the Muslim men themselves who handed over the guilty women to the Christian authorities. For Muslim women, too, there were exceptions and they or their families were in some cases allowed to pay a fine. For instance, in 1494, a Muslim man of Onda paid a heavy fine to prevent his unmarried daughter, found in a bedroom with a Christian man, should be subjected to twenty-five lashes.

If paying a fine was not allowed, then the only way for women to avoid their terrible fate was to convert. In particular situations, it was possible to obtain a royal pardon if it could be shown that they had been the victims of terrible mistreatment. Fatima avoided punishment by telling King Peter IV of Aragon (1336–1387) that she had been raped at age nine by her Christian master, who had then bestowed her as a bride upon a faithful of Allah. She had then left him when he lost all his property through his reckless behavior, and in order to earn a living she had had sexual relations with numerous Christian men.

In spite of the very severe laws, the presence of a great number of Muslim and Christian prostitutes in the Iberian Peninsula ensured that such relations occurred nevertheless. In most cases, the laws were not applied to the letter when it came to male Moors caught with those women, especially if the accused were capable of paying heavy fines. In 1360, near Zaragoza, two Muslims, charged with having engaged in sexual relations with two Christian women, were released because certain irregularities were found in the investigation; the payment of a substantial sum of money had certainly contributed to the favorable outcome in that case. In Catalonia, eighteen Muslim men, caught in a field with a Christian prostitute, avoided the death sentence by paying a very heavy fine. If the guilty party was unable to pay, then he would be sold into slavery. Neither the sovereigns nor the large landowners wished to lose invaluable laborers on that account. The high number of criminal complaints of this kind to be found in the archives of the kingdom of Aragon and the very small number of sentences handed down are clear evidence that these charges (and other less grave ones) were actually meant to extort money or simply hinder the activities of an enemy. The situation was probably quite similar in other parts of Spain. For instance, in Navarre, it was not until 1367 that a person was executed for the first time for that crime. The few occasions in which the death sentence was applied had to do, especially with persons who were deprived of the protection of their lords and masters and of their community. Their execution, for that matter, reminded the Muslims of their inferior status and of the risks they were running if they tried to escape their condition.

It is worth pointing out that the crime in question was not considered particularly serious throughout Christendom. In Portugal, the penalty was merely monetary (though it was quite a sizable sum) and it was not incurred at all if the woman was a prostitute. A believer of Allah, who was working as a pimp for several Christian women, was ordered into house arrest for a year, a sentence that was later reduced to a fine. The different atmosphere in that area concerning the crime in question is clearly illustrated by the way in which a Muslim justified his actions. He was from Lisbon, and, while he chanced to be in Évora, he was caught in a Christian woman's bed. He stated that he had wound up in that house because, at night, unfamiliar with the Moorish quarter of that city, he had been unable to return to his own home. That does not mean, however, that the authorities in that country were completely indifferent to that problem. At the behest of 'men of good repute,' who stated that Christian women, married and unmarried, were visiting the Jewish and Muslim quarters to engage in sexual relations with non-Christian males, in 1366 the king of Portugal prohibited all Christian women from going to those places. In Lisbon, they were only allowed to transit through certain streets in those districts and always in the company of coreligionists. In 1469, in Évora, an elderly widow was permitted to sell oil in the Jewish and Muslim quarters, only by virtue of her advanced years and good reputation.

In order to limit that sort of interaction, it was decreed in 1311 in the kingdom of Aragon that there must be no conversation between Christian prostitutes and Muslim men. Subsequently it was forbidden to pimps and 'women of ill repute' to frequent public baths, places that were evidently considered particularly well suited to this sort of transaction. In order to make this sort of encounter more difficult, the Moors of Valencia asked the authorities repeatedly, but with little success, to expel these women from their quarter. Christian women were not considered guilty if the Muslims had pretended to be Christians. The prostitutes were well aware that it was their responsibility to identify who was and who was not a faithful of Christ. The fear that they would report their Muslim customers only when they were under threat of being prosecuted themselves was so widespread that the magistrates in charge of questioning them were instructed to do their best to trick the women into falling into self-contradictory statements. There was no shortage of public functionaries who used the women to extort money from the Mudéjars. These men, moreover, might be tangled up in struggles among Christians who accused believers in Islam in the service of their adversaries of such a crime in order to harm those adversaries.

Much as is true of any sex acts outside of marriage and of concubinage, prostitution is not permitted by Islamic law and is punished either by whipping or stoning. In spite of this, Muslim and dhimmi prostitutes were present in the House of Islam, especially in the large cities of the Ottoman Empire. Only rarely, however, were Muslim customers and Christian prostitutes sentenced according to the demands of sharia; it was preferred to levy cash fines and the women were usually simply expelled from the neighborhoods they lived in. The law was instead applied in cases where the roles were reversed, but, considering the great risk and the relative ease with which they could be caught, Christian men only rarely frequented those Muslim women. An increase in the application of those laws seems to have occurred in the nineteenth century, when, as a result of the agreements between the Ottoman Empire and the Western countries, numerous non-Muslim subjects of the Sublime Porte fell under the jurisdiction of the European powers and therefore could no longer be tried in an Islamic court.

The end of the differences?

It was not until the nineteenth century in the Ottoman Empire that measures were taken to put an end to any religion-based differences. This was not a linear process, and the changes were not immediate. To prevent the outbreak of independence movements like the one in Greece and faced with the necessity to develop a more efficient army, bureaucracy, and system of taxation, on November 3, 1839, the sultan issued the edict of *Tanzimat* (reforms), presenting it as a return to the good governance of bygone times. Using a fairly vague language, the ruler invited non-Muslims to become full-fledged citizens of the empire and established the principle of equality between dhimmis and believers in Islam. Everyone, therefore, had to pay taxes to the state, without distinction (Muslims had not been required to pay any annual taxes since the end of the sixteenth century). Everyone was subject to the same secular laws, which would soon replace religious laws (both Islamic and non-Muslim laws), and the court councils would have to be mixed from here on. Everyone would have the same right to obtain positions in the public administration, and, moreover, all subjects would now be liable to military conscription, though former dhimmis could secure exemption by paying an established sum of money. Some of the above-mentioned differences, however, were only modified. In fact, in order to build new houses of worship in places prevalently inhabited by Muslims, Christians still had to obtain authorization from Istanbul.

The edict immediately aroused widespread discontent. The only reason they did not culminate in violent protests on the part of the Muslims is probably because the majority of the reforms were never actually put into practice by the provincial governors and their officials, who were generally opposed to those regulations. The non-Muslim members of the commissions were often explic-itly informed that their presence was not needed. In retaliation, in many courts of justice, the faithful of Islam began to be favored shamelessly. Crimes against Christians increased on account of the almost complete immunity enjoyed by Muslims on those occasions and the absence of validity accorded to the depo-sitions of Christians in the courts. In 1851 in Thessaloniki, the testimony of a Christian in a criminal trial was admitted for the first time, but it took another ten years before it was given any real value in comparison with the depositions of Muslims.

Harsh criticisms were leveled against the rules concerning military service. The faithful of Islam emphasized that only ex-dhimmis would take advantage of the exemption, and therefore the only ones defending the empire would be the faithful of Islam. At the same time, they forcefully emphasized that they would never accept to report to non-Muslim officers. According to ex-dhimmis, the payment for avoiding service in the army was, instead, just a new form of jizyah. In practical terms, until 1908, the army was made up exclusively of believers in Allah. In some areas, moreover, the prohibition against constructing new reli-gious buildings continued to persist. One case was emblematic—that of a small Egyptian town with 4,000 Christians that in 1860 possessed not a single church because the local authorities refused to permit the construction of one.

Resistance to the reforms is also clearly underscored by what happened in connection with the edict handed down in 1829, which, with the aim of putting an end to distinctive markers among males, required the adoption of the same head covering for all secular men; the fez was meant to take the place of the tur-bans of different colors. The faithful of Allah, and in particular those belonging to the working classes in the cities, were not pleased with that reform, which visually placed them on a par with the 'infidels' and instead decided to wear fez-zes of particular colors and shapes. Under the pressure of the Muslim population, dhimmis placed tassels on their fezzes to indicate their religion (blue for Jews and black for Christians). Contrary to that edict, the grand vizier ordered dhimmis to replace their fezzes with kalpaks, large sheepskin hats often worn by Armenians in the service of the Ottoman public administration.

On February 3, 1856, another edict was issued, requesting that the reforms be implemented and inviting public officials to look into all the immunities and privileges enjoyed by non-Muslims in order to prevent discrimination among the subjects of the empire. This edict, too, did nothing to end the differences between Muslims and non-Muslims. The state structure was not organized to attain any such result and lacked the financial resources that would be required to apply those reforms. Many governors and public functionaries, moreover, failed to put many of those recommendations into practice; the open refusal of the gov-ernor of Damascus to do so, for instance, was particularly emblematic.

In 1876, the sultanate became a constitutional monarchy, and in the constitu-tion it was clearly stated that all subjects were to be considered Ottoman citizens with equal rights and obligations. Although religious freedom was guaranteed,

Islam was nonetheless declared the state religion; anyone who wished to work in the public administration had to be able to speak the 'Turkish of the Ottomans.' It was attempted to create a multireligious and multicultural state and the motto featured in the propaganda of that period was 'equal and diverse.' Without economic incentives for all Ottoman subjects and a strong sense of loyalty to the empire, these remained, however, illusions, especially in the provinces of the Balkans and Eastern Europe, where the processes of independence had already been underway for years. The attempt of the reformists to put a sultan who was favorable to them on the throne failed and the new ruler, Abdül Hamid II, suspended the constitution and the parliament. In order to strengthen the state, he proposed a form of powerfully politicized Islamism and, in the meantime, blocked the process of implementing the reforms. That process got slowly and painfully back underway in 1908 with the advent of the government of the Young Turks, but, as we shall see in the last chapter, what happened during and after the First World War prevented the realization of that dream.

2

Conversions

Forced conversions

The adoption of the 'true faith' of all the human beings represents a fundamental objective for both Islam and Christianity, and to obtain the conversion of the faithful belonging to the rival monotheistic religion was, therefore, a much-appreciated result because it confirmed the truth of one's own faith and the fallacy of the adversaries' religious belief. In general, the subjects were allowed to convert to the religion of their rulers. Christians and Muslims shared the principle that this had to happen voluntarily, and the use of any form of coercion was, therefore, forbidden. On the basis of this principle, some Muslim religious leaders managed to convince two Ottoman sultans, Selim (1512–1520) and Ibrāhīm (1640–1648), not to implement their plan to Islamize the Balkan provinces of the empire by force. However, both sides did not always follow this course of action, especially in times of war.

During their conquest of the Maghreb in the twelfth century, the Almohads, for example, offered the Christians living in Marrakech either to convert to the Islamic faith and remain or to leave that region. After the taking of Tunis around 1160, an Almohad leader ordered instead to kill all the faithful of Christ and the Jews who refused to adhere to Islam. Probably with the intention of teaching the Christians a lesson and weakening their morale, after the battle of Hattin in 1187, Saladin forced some prisoners to choose between life, if they converted to Islam, and death; all preferred to be executed. Sometimes, it was an angry crowd proposing to the Christians to become Muslims to avoid being lynched. In the sixteenth century, after drinking too much, some Egyptian Christians insulted a Muslim leader. One of them was taken by a large group of Muslims and forced to choose between converting to Islam or being burned alive. The unfortunate man decided not to die, and the crowd celebrated the event by parading him through the streets of Cairo in the typical headgear of Allah's believers.

During the early modern period, Muslim pirates immediately circumcised the majority of Christian children they captured during their raids on the western Mediterranean to present them with a forced choice. Their young age meant that they quickly forgot their previous lives and could, therefore, be transformed into devout believers of Islam, willing to serve their leaders and the Ottoman Empire loyally.

The Ottomans created a much more explicit system for converting young Christians to Islam, the devshirme. In order to secure a pool of faithful servants and soldiers, the sultans periodically forced their Christian subjects—especially those from the Balkan areas that did not surrender to the Ottomans immediately—to hand over intelligent and healthy children between eight and fifteen years of age who, after having become Muslims, were educated to that end. Without wanting in any way to minimize the cruelty of this system and the trauma it caused, it must be pointed out that it was a formidable means of social and economic ascent for those individuals. It was, therefore, not uncommon to see Christian parents offering their children to recruiters in the hope of providing them with a better future and of receiving help from them if they obtained prestigious positions.

Christians, too, used coercive methods for converting Muslims to Christianity. In the second half of the tenth century, during the Byzantine reconquest of some parts of Syria, imperial troops carried out numerous massacres against the Muslim population, after which only those who had accepted the Christian faith were allowed to remain in their homes. The population of Haifa underwent a similar treatment when it surrendered to the Crusaders in 1100. However, the most striking example of such a choice was not given to the faithful of Islam during war operations. In 1502, most of the Muslim subjects of the Iberian Peninsula were enjoined to choose between adhering to Christianity or abandoning the land where their ancestors had lived for centuries. As will be seen in chapter 6, the majority of them decided to remain and become Christians. Preventing that edict, applied a few years earlier to Jewish subjects, in 1500 all Muslims of Palencia and Murcia accepted baptism in the hope of getting a better treatment. In retaliation for this measure, two early-sixteenth-century Egyptian rulers also issued a similar edict against their Christian subjects, but the order was never implemented.

In times of peace, forced conversions were rare and took place at times of great tension between the faithful of the two religions, such as those that occurred in the Near East at the beginning of the eleventh century under the Caliph of Cairo, Al-Ḥākim, a ruler known for having persecuted his co-religionists as well. Some cases also occurred in Morocco in the ninth and tenth centuries. In Spain, after the Christian occupation of Granada in 1492—the last Muslim kingdom in the Iberian peninsula—the attempts to establish peaceful relations with the local believers of Islam were ruined by the brutal and oppressive methods of

Cardinal Cisneros, who obtained adherence to Christianity through the use of various coercive methods (including torture).

When forced conversions took place during riots against Muslim subjects, however, they were perceived as a challenge to the authority of the sovereigns who, in those situations, were not ready to turn a blind eye and consider the change of faith irreversible. In 1263, on the occasion of an attack by a crowd of Christians against an Islamic community during which some Muslims were killed and some were forcibly baptized, the king of Aragon ordered both to punish the murderers and to declare those changes of faith null and void.

The phenomenon of forced conversions was more common during the repression of revolts, when people did not go too subtle, the laws were not respected, and the rulers vented their resentment in various ways on the dominated belonging to another religion. For example, this happened around 1770 in southern Greece after a failed attempt at insurrection. In the period following long and bloody campaigns of conquest, conversions usually took place for fear of being mistreated or drastically losing their standard of living. The fact that the neo-converts were one-third of the people mentioned in the Muslim courts of Cyprus in the years immediately following the Ottoman occupation of the island in the early modern period indicates that the conversion rate there was higher than in more easily obtained areas. During the Christian conquest of Sicily in the second half of the eleventh century, the Muslim governor of Castrogiovanni instead agreed to surrender and be baptized together with his family in exchange for the recognition of his marriage to his wife, who was a blood relative of his, and the concession of an estate in Calabria.

This expedient was also used during indiscriminate repression of riots and attacks carried out by crowds or irregular militias hoping, sometimes to no avail, to escape death or slavery. This happened in 1300 when the sovereign of Southern Italy decided to sell all the Muslims of his kingdom; the conversions that took place on that occasion were not taken into consideration. On the contrary, those of Granada's Moors were considered valid when their revolt was suppressed in 1499. The fact that the conversions had taken place in the days following the failure of their insurrection and that they amounted to about fifty thousand highlights the climate of oppression and terror created at that time.

In the Ottoman Empire, during the 1895–1897 attacks and the 1915 deportations of the Armenians, many of the latter (sometimes entire communities) requested to become Muslims. Faced with the stalling of the Ottoman authorities, who decided to examine the requests individually after the re-establishment of order to ensure the genuineness of the conversions, many males asked to be circumcised (some performed the operation themselves) hoping to speed up the process of approving their change of faith and to be able to hide their identity from the attackers. With the intention of perfecting their camouflage, some Armenian villages transformed their churches into mosques, where the inhabitants went to pray in the manner prescribed by Islam; couples remarried according to the Muslim custom. In those years of great instability and terror, the phenomenon of the abduction of young Christian women, who were then subjected to strong pressure to adhere to the Islamic faith, reached its peak in rural and mountain areas. In those cases, the shame for the loss of their virginity and the certainty of leading a marginalized life in their community of origin also influenced their choice; almost all of them refused to return to their families.

Conversions for social and economic reasons

In times of peace, the majority of the adhesions to the faith of those in power gradually took place both in the House of Islam and in the territories governed by the faithful of Christ. An exception was the behavior of some Syrian and Iraqi Christians of Arab origin who welcomed the warriors of the Arabian Peninsula as liberators from persecution by the Persians and Byzantines. This factor and their common descent and language led many of them to convert from the very beginning.

There were various motives unrelated to religious beliefs that led people to adopt the faith of the ruler. The first advantage was undoubtedly not to be considered a second-class subject anymore. This, first of all, allowed the neoconverts to maintain or improve their social and economic status. In the House of Islam, the recurrent prohibitions on the use of Christian personnel in the public administration, sometimes followed by requests for money to regain one's place, constituted a further incentive to convert for those individuals. The edict issued by the caliph around 717, in which such prohibition appeared for the first time, added that those who adhered to Islam could keep their work at court and in the public administration. Promotions and awards, especially for senior officials, were another push in that direction. Many Coptic public officials who followed that path secured prestigious positions.

The same phenomenon occurred in the Balkans under the Ottomans. An Albanian who had adhered to Islam managed to become a grand vizier and pointed out that the Ottomans had wisely chosen the poorest peasants who did not believe in the true God, had made them true believers, and made them victorious officers and distinguished governors and that he was one of them. Emblematic was the decision that, in a period characterized by the expulsion of Christ's faithful from the public administration, the Andalusian Christian, Qumis ibn Antonian, took in the second half of the ninth century after being hired as assistant to a Muslim official because the latter could no longer travel due to an illness. Qumis ibn Antonian worked so well that, on the death of his superior, the emir of Cordoba said that he would immediately entrust him with the vacancy if he changed his faith, which he did.

Starting from the mid-fourteenth century, the economic status of the Mudéjars and the rights granted to them began to decline. This process did not spare the members of their elites, and some of them chose to deny their faith in order to obtain a position and, thus, maintain a high social status. However, their numbers were much smaller than the Christians who converted to Islam for the same reason in Egypt in the Middle Ages and the Ottoman Empire.

During the first centuries of the Ottoman Empire, cash prizes were also awarded to those who adhered to the Muslim religion, a practice especially widespread under Sultan Muhammad IV (1648–1687). Knowing how much he appreciated the conversions of Christ's faithful, particularly when he was the promoter, his courtiers very likely organized such adhesions to Islam during his travels to lands inhabited by many Christian subjects such as the Balkans and Eastern Europe. For example, while hunting in Bulgaria, Muhammad IV met a peasant and, having discovered that he was a faithful of Christ, invited him to accept the 'true faith,' but the peasant refused his invitation. The sultan's officers then revealed to him who the hunter was, and the man immediately converted. He received a cash prize and good employment. Since the use of Muslims in the administration and courts of the Christian kingdoms was extremely rare, this phenomenon did not often occur in the territories governed by the faithful of Christ.

Economic constraints could be another reason for conversion. Although the jizyah was calculated on the basis of the dhimmis' income, for a nonspecialized worker that tax corresponded to about ten percent of his salary (for the poorest it could reach thirty percent). Being imposed on males from the age of nine to ten years, its weight was significant on large families. For those who fell ill and could not work, the situation became catastrophic. Fundamental, therefore, was the presence of a well-organized and, above all, rich ecclesiastical hierarchy that took on the burden of paying that tax for its faithful, especially for the less well-off. At a time when the support of their husbands and relatives and the assistance network of the Christian churches were lacking, it was not unusual to have widows, often with dependent children, converting to Islam in order to obtain some form of assistance that the Ottoman rulers often guaranteed.

Aware of the strong economic and psychological pressure that tax exerted on the poorest of their faithful, religious leaders tried to create subsistence networks and to raise awareness about these problems among the wealthiest co-religionists. On various occasions, there were disputes among the ecclesiastical hierarchies over the use of the goods available to the churches. In Egypt, there was strong opposition to centralized management of funds, arguing that paying for the jizyah of the poor should always be a priority. There was no lack of those who instead criticized that system, claiming that it 'bought their religion.' Not surprisingly, in times of economic crisis, the number of conversions increased significantly. The serious weakening of the Christian Churches under Muslim rule in certain areas and in certain periods led to a greater Islamization of those territories because of the lack of assistance both from the spiritual and economic point of view. Well aware of the connection between these factors, in 1252, the vizier of Cairo, a former Copt, ordered the doubling of the jizyah with the intention of gaining the sympathy of the sultan. In fact, he did not only aim at filling the state coffers, but probably also hoped to obtain a considerable increase in conversions to Islam.

During the Mamluk era, the increasingly pressing requests for donations to pay for the jizyah of the poorer co-religionists and the frequent imposition of extraordinary taxes pushed many members of the Christian elites to adhere to Islam to maintain their economic status. In the Egyptian countryside, many Christian peasants also associated, sometimes erroneously, new taxes with their religious status, and therefore, many of them changed faith when this happened. One of the most famous cases took place in 1220 when an injunction was issued to pay a large sum of money on palm trees. Their bewilderment was very strong as soon as they discovered that everyone had to pay it regardless of their religion.

Adherence to Islam was also favored by the absence of a clergy motivated and able to enjoy the respect of its faithful. The rapid Islamization of northern Albania was, for example, also due to the fact that the local population recently converted to Catholicism and that most of the Church hierarchies were foreigners and left the country when the Turks arrived. Among the reasons for the rapid decline in the number of Christians in Northwest Africa were the fragility and poverty of its Churches weakened by centuries of disputes.

Conversions to take advantage of the laws of the rulers

Among those who had committed a crime, it was quite common to believe that by converting they could receive a more favorable verdict with the legal system of the rulers or could take advantage of their status. According to Islamic law, if a dhimmi adhered to the Muslim faith during a trial with one of his coreligionists, he could no longer be prosecuted. If, instead, he made that decision after the sentence had been passed, the verdict was valid only in civil law cases. The situation became more complicated if the injured party was a Muslim because it was fundamental to ascertain the genuineness of the conversion. For instance, according to a ninth-century Andalusian law expert, the genuineness had to be determined in order to decide what punishment to inflict on a newly converted Christian accused of raping a Muslim. If his conversion was sincere, he only had to pay a settlement to the woman; otherwise he had to be executed.

Since this type of assessment was extremely questionable, it left ample room for decisions influenced by the personal convictions of the judges and external pressure. In times of great tension, these requests were often subject to the mood of the crowd, soldiers, and rulers. In Cairo in 1417, a Christian, who had converted after being discovered together with a Muslim woman, was stoned together with his mistress. Imprisoned for having rejoiced at the death of many Islam's faithful in a clash with a Christian ship, in 1440 a Copt was convinced by the vizier to change his faith in the hope of being freed. The Muslim religious leaders and the population protested so strongly that the conversion was declared null and void, and the neo-convert was executed. Arrested for theft, in 1485 a Christian from Damascus adhered to Islam, thinking he would thus avoid punishment for that crime, but the city's governor ordered his hand to be cut off anyway. Equally useless was the conversion in 1522 of a Copt condemned for falsifying coins. A group of soldiers impaled him.

Given the difficulty and sometimes the impossibility for Christians to obtain a divorce, becoming Muslim could be a way, especially for women, to escape an unhappy marriage. According to Islamic law, if a Christian woman converted but her husband refused to do that, she had the right to separate and keep her children. In Cyprus, in the seventeenth century, an Armenian woman appeared before an Islamic court and, after stating that her husband treated her cruelly, she joined Islam. Since her spouse had refused to do the same, the couple was ordered to separate. To make sure they had custody of the children, those women had them converted. At the end of the nineteenth century, the children of such couples were allowed to choose their religious faith once they reached adulthood. For example, Mary of Santorini converted with her children, and the Cretan Sofia took the same step with her youngest daughter in 1707. In this case, it is also recorded that the woman took a name, Ayşe, more in keeping with her new faith. This certainly occurred with all converts with names connected to the tradition of the dominated.

Some of the newly divorced and newly converted women immediately married a Muslim, which indicates that it was also a way to marry a man with whom they had fallen in love or who had promised them a better standard of living. In Cyprus, in the early modern period, there is the case of Mary who went to an Islamic court with her husband Loize and, as it was established that she had not been forced, her adhesion to Islam was made official. Her spouse was asked to do the same, but he refused. She then married Mustafa. In another case, a Christian man named Karcire accused a Muslim named Musa of having kidnapped his wife Çako. Musa, however, replied that the woman had changed her faith and assumed the name Fatma and that Karcire had refused to take that step. Musa had then married Fatma. Called to court, the latter confirmed what her new husband had said. In the period of Tanzimat, a newly converted woman married to a Muslim, of whom she had grown tired, could instead, without any problem, tell a commission of inquiry that she had been forced to convert and then admit that she had made up that story in order to have the chance to return to her family and her original faith and save face.

Although it was rare, there were also Christian men converting to Islam to marry a Muslim woman. In Egypt, some Copts adhered to Islam to get a quick divorce because, according to Coptic law, a woman could not be married to a faithful of Allah. Disagreements between spouses about whether or not to adhere to Islam led to separation as indicated by the case of a newly converted man who, faced with his wife's refusal to follow his example, asked for a divorce. A man, on the contrary, took that step because it would have been easier for him to try to have back his beloved wife who had run away and married a Muslim. That was also a way to remarry for those who had had the misfortune of being widowed several times as an Albanian had done, because he had lost three wives and was not allowed to have a fourth one to look after his young children.

Similar reasons can be found among Muslims in Christian kingdoms as well. Some cases are recorded in Sicily toward the end of the twelfth century where, on the occasion of disagreements between parents and children and between wife and husband, it could happen that the offspring and the wife converted to Christianity. According to a Muslim traveler who passed through the island in those years, the fear that this could happen was so widespread among his Sicilian co-religionists that they tried to avoid any quarrel with a consequent damage to parental and husband authority.

Conversion to escape slavery

Another strong motivation for adhering to the rulers' faith was the desire to escape the condition of slaves or prisoners. Christian women who had been captured by Muslim pirates and managed to return to Christian land in early modern times reported that they had become Muslims by marrying Islam's faithful only to avoid remaining slaves. These unions were not uncommon, since many Muslim men believed that unlike their lazy female co-religionists, those women were hardworking and helpful wives. For those who could not or did not want to spend money to get married, taking a renegade former slave was also an economic advantage, since no money had to be paid to the woman's family and it was not obligatory to organize parties and banquets for relatives, friends, and neighbors.

The intensification of Muslim piracy in the western Mediterranean between the sixteenth and eighteenth centuries led many Christians captured during raids to change their faith. The terrible prison conditions, the impossibility for many of them to be redeemed, the opportunity for the soldiers to continue to carry out their work, and the hope of social ascent favored those decisions. In general, however, the difficulty in finding a sponsor for their conversion and sometimes the absence of any prospect of employment as freedmen prevented conversions from taking place on a large scale. Since the dhimmis could not have Muslim slaves, the few Jews and Christians who could afford to have slaves preferred to choose them among the African 'pagans', hoping that they were unaware of that opportunity.

Much more complex was the situation in the Christian kingdoms. In theory, a Christian could not be a slave of a co-religionist, and the Muslims who converted to Christianity had to be freed. The spread of such demands and the economic damage to their owners and slave traders, who protested vigorously against that rule, led Christian rulers to place a number of obstacles in the way of those wishing to take that step. For example, in the kingdom of Jerusalem, the masters did not allow their slaves to be baptized and prevented them from listening to Christian preachers. In Spain, a waiting period was established to prove the genuineness of conversion, and the former slaves had to compensate their masters. In southern Italy, on the other hand, it was clearly emphasized that becoming Christian did not imply that one would automatically achieve freedom.

In 1237, the pope tried to resolve the impasse by stating that if some slaves wanted to change their faith, they could do so, but this would not change their servile condition. For fear that this rule would be changed and probably to justify the fact that being non-Christian meant being different and therefore deserving slavery, the majority of the owners refused to let their slaves be baptized. The pontiff then threatened to excommunicate those behaving in this way. Yet, the fact that the threat had to be repeated on several occasions suggests that it had not been a good deterrent. To remedy these problems, it was established in the municipal laws of Valencia that if the slaves were baptized without the consent of their masters, they would remain in the same status as before. To resolve any controversy, the king of Aragon finally decreed that whatever way the slaves were baptized, only their owners could decide to free them.

Since it was not permissible for a believer of Christ to be a slave of a non-Christian, this rule was not considered valid if the master was a Jew. At the urging of the Jewish community, concerned about the economic damage caused by that measure, it was established that the Muslim slaves who converted to Christianity had to compensate their masters and, if they did not have the necessary sum, had to be sold to a Christian. If this did not happen within three months, they were considered free and nothing was due to the Jewish owner.

Conversion due to pressures from and disagreements with family and employers

For Christians orphaned at a young age and adopted by relatives who had converted to Islam, it was very difficult to maintain their original faith, especially if they were female. This situation was not unusual in the recently conquered territories in the Mediterranean and the Balkan peninsula where it was not uncommon for families to have both Christians and Muslims. Emblematic in this regard is the case of Magdalene of Sibenik, who fled to Venice in 1647 at the age of fifty. She told that she had been born of Christian parents and baptized. Orphaned as a child, she was entrusted to Muslim relatives of her father who had given her a Turkish name. At a young age, she was married to a believer of Allah and had lived according to the Islamic religion. She maintained that she wanted to be Christian again.

Although they were rarer and involved many more dangers, cases of Muslims converting to the Christian faith within their own family occurred in the House of Islam. In the early modern period, in Crete, a girl named Ayse lived with her Christian mother. One day, a certain Ahmet from Istanbul met her, said she was the daughter of his deceased brother Muhammad, who had converted to Islam together with his daughter, and accused her of apostasy. The girl declared that Ahmet had the wrong person and that she was the daughter of another man. With the help of some witnesses from Istanbul, Ahmet proved himself right. When her father died, all of Ayse's relatives were Christians, and she wanted to become one of them. It is not known whether she was later executed for having repudiated Islam.

It is, on the other hand, known that in Cordoba, in the mid-ninth century, Flora, the daughter of a Muslim man and a Christian woman, who, having been orphaned by her father as a child and raised according to her mother's faith, was sentenced to death. She was put in crisis by her Muslim brother, who, offended by his sister's choice to live openly as a faithful of Christ, had tried to convince her to confess her Islamic origins. Inspired by the behavior of many Christians in her city, who had been executed for having condemned Islam, Flora publicly confessed that she was a renegade.

As has already been noted, in some areas of the House of Islam, Christian women married to Muslim men could keep their religion. The lives of these women, especially those of low rank and who no longer had ties with their family of origin, must not have been easy because of the considerable pressure to which they were subjected. Many of them gave in and converted for quiet living, thus becoming the target of criticism from their co-religionists. That was, for example, the fate of most of the young Christian women of Mytilene. When the Ottomans conquered that Greek island, in 1462, Sultan Muhammad II allowed the soldiers of the local Turkish garrison, who had complained about the monotonous life in Mytilene, to marry the local Christian women. If the latter did not want to do that or their relatives were against that union, the Muslim soldiers could take them by force. The sultan hoped that this would also promote the spread of Islam, and he was right.

In the texts on the early modern neo-martyrs, there are several examples of Muslims employers offering better working conditions and economic advantages to young Christian workers living far from their families, without friends of their faith and employed if they converted. The young men later regretted their adherence to Islam, returned to the Christian faith, and were executed for apostasy. These accounts should not be taken literally because they were written both to warn Christians of the dangers posed by Muslims and to offer them models of perfect behavior to follow. At the same time, this does not mean that some aspects of those stories did not reflect real situations.

This is confirmed by Ottoman archive sources dating back to the period following the Tanzimat edict when, under strong pressure from European states, the Ottoman authorities began to conduct more thorough investigations into the conversions of Christian children and young people. Indicative of what might have happened is the case that emerged in Ioannina in 1848 where a Muslim notable was accused of having unduly convinced a ten-year-old Christian servant of his to change faith. The boy testified in front of the local authorities that he had not been forced and that he had 'left the false faith and embraced Islam' and converted to 'the purity and brilliance of Islam.' Probably suspicious of those expressions, unusual for a boy of that age, of low social background, and almost illiterate, the magistrates decided that he should be sent to Istanbul for a rigorous investigation. Since he had stated that he had not been subject to any coercion, he was for the moment left to his master, who two days later reported that the boy had escaped. The story had obviously taken a turn that was not desired by the parties involved, and one or both of them had obviously decided to end it in that way.

Other episodes of those years highlight how even the kidnapping of Christian children by Muslim neighbors to convert them was not an absurd invention. In Thessaloniki in 1844, a ten-year-old Armenian girl suffered that fate after, with her father's permission, a Muslim neighbor had taken her to a public bath. Not seeing her return, her parents asked the Muslim woman where their daughter was, and she answered that the girl had converted and that they had to leave. Since the local magistrates did nothing, the case was brought to Istanbul on the intervention of the Armenian patriarch, but nothing is known of its outcome.

However, it could also happen that some young people joined Islam to escape an unbearable situation either a Christian master or authoritarian parents had created. This was the situation from which a Cypriot girl named Mary, sent by her mother to work with a faithful of Christ, wanted to leave, in the seventeenth century. That she received some money after her conversion had undoubtedly been an incentive to take that step. Instead, she wanted to escape an authoritarian father and live legally with her Christian lover the Mudéjar girl, who, after fleeing with him in 1498, joined Christianity, thus rendering null and void the accusation of kidnapping her parent had made.

Conversions of churchmen

Much coveted by the Muslim authorities for their propaganda potential and feared by Christians for their detrimental effect on the morale of their communities were the conversions of clergymen. Often, that choice was taken by people involved in disputes with the ecclesiastical hierarchies and, therefore, constituted a way of escaping a situation considered untenable and, in some cases, was used as a form of revenge against a powerful adversary. The most famous example in premodern times was that of the Egyptian monk Ibrāhīm who, following a bitter quarrel with the patriarch of Cairo in the second half of the fourteenth century, joined Islam to escape the punishment imposed on him.

In the Ottoman Empire, the most sensational case was that of the Armenian bishop of Sis, Harutyun Achabayan, who became a believer of Allah in 1886 and moved with his family two years later to Istanbul, where he worked for the Ottoman administration as a press officer; he was assigned the task of controlling publications in Armenian due to his language skills. A bitter dispute with the Armenian patriarch of Istanbul about the leadership of Cilicia's Armenians was probably at the origin of that choice. However, according to Armenian sources, Harutyun Achabayan had divorced a woman with whom he was in love and whom he then had married to one of his collaborators; having then got her pregnant, the prelate became a Muslim to marry her. According to the same sources, he continued to profess Christianity with his family secretly and baptized his children. One of them was later arrested for remaining a Christian and tortured to make him deny his faith, which he did not do. Ottoman documents instead report that the son declared himself a Christian to avoid military service.

In the early modern times, for the Ottomans to obtain this kind of conversion was so coveted and had such a symbolic importance that in numerous biographies of pious Muslim men, it became a widespread rhetorical theme aiming to highlight how Islam was the only true faith in a period of strong Turkish expansionism. The best example is found in a very popular fifteenth-century work. It narrates how a representative of the sultan attended the annual competition on the knowledge of the Bible among the clerics of a city in Macedonia. The winner, who was appointed leader of his community, was a young priest. Knowing this, the sultan invited him to his court and emphasized that in that way his intellectual gifts could be fully appreciated. In the meantime, the young man decided to obey the vision in which he adhered to Islam and placed himself at the service of the Ottoman ruler.

Conversions due to fascination for the other's religion

Finally, there was no lack of Christians who—attracted by the absence of a complex liturgy, the rigor of the worship of God, and the presence of mystical forms among Muslims—genuinely adopted Islam. The brotherhood of the Mevlevi dervishes, created in Anatolia in the thirteenth century and opposed to the rigidity of traditional believers, inspired considerable interest among Christians in search for a spirituality not conditioned by formalisms. The remarkable flexibility and inclusiveness of those dervishes also allowed the disciples to maintain their original religion or certain Christian customs and facilitated their adherence to Islam. The little importance given to the differences between monotheistic religions was such that sometimes the creator of that group advised against conversion. Not all dervishes, however, had that kind of mentality, and the Ottoman leaders often took some dervishes with them in their campaigns of conquest in the Balkans as missionaries.

There were also some very rare cases of Christ's faithful living in Christian lands, who, strongly attracted by the Muslim religion, moved to the House of Islam to embrace the Islamic faith. The most famous was the Spanish Franciscan Anselm Turmeda, who fled to Tunis around 1400, where he abjured and became the author of anti-Christian treatises.

Procedures for conversion

To avoid forced conversions, not based on spiritual motivations or taken lightly, some Muslim jurists established that one could change one's mind after a short time and that saying the profession of faith did not necessarily mean being converted. In theory, the young age of those who made that choice should have led to accurate investigations. In reality, these principles were very rarely followed, and in the case of males, an attempt was made to circumcise the newly converted as soon as possible in order to confront them with an irreversible change. Obtaining the conversion of a Christian was considered such an important success that one did not think too much about the means and circumstances that had produced it. Even in the eighteenth century, conversion of ten-year-old boys to Islam did not cause any problems among Muslims. Although the sources for Christian kingdoms are less detailed, the situation in them should not have been too different.

In the Ottoman Empire, the willingness to certify the authenticity of conversions through a very specific procedure emerged after the edict of Tanzimat, a period when the Sublime Porte wanted to avoid providing the European powers with reasons to criticize its backwardness and the way it treated its Christian subjects. The changes that took place in those years also provided them with the opportunity to make their protests more incisive. It was, therefore, established that those aspiring to adhere to Islam should have a sponsor with the task of guiding the aspirant to conversion through the whole process. This person had to be highly respected and highly virtuous and to have no interest in the conversion. In the presence of a commission, made up of Muslim religious leaders and witnesses, the candidate had to declare that he had taken that decision of his own free will and without having been subjected to any pressure, to be capable of understanding and wanting, and to have reached puberty. He was given an Islamic name after the formula of adherence to the Muslim religion was pronounced. This procedure was then repeated in the presence of a commission, made up of the secular authorities of the area, parents or relatives and the local Church leader, who were allowed to try to change the decision of the potential neo-convert. If the latter confirmed his wish, the certification of the conversion had to be signed and sealed by Muslim officials and the local Christian authority. They were ordered to follow the rules scrupulously and not to execute them hastily.

In order not to provoke violent protests by Muslims and Christians, it was also recommended that neither the conversions nor the negative results of the request be publicized. Everything was left in the hands of the local authorities who, often being contrary to the Tanzimat edict, did not put these indications into practice. On several occasions, it was the guarantors who created problems because they were often rich local notables who sponsored the conversion of young people in their service. Since the attainment of puberty was visually established and therefore questionable, his determination was often a point of contrast between the faithful of Islam and those of Christ. It was only after various pressures from the Christian Church hierarchies that the minimum age for changing faith was raised to fifteen years for both sexes and to twenty in 1913. There were also disagreements between the Muslim and secular religious authorities.

Living as neo-converts

As has already been observed, both Muslim and Christian rulers stressed that no one could oppose or create obstacles to the choice to convert. To this end, shortly after the conquest of Valencia in 1238, the king of Aragon decreed that no tax should be imposed on Muslims' baptism. Rights to their inheritance were also guaranteed even if their family members did not follow their example. At the end of that century, the sovereign of Aragon declared it illegal for the Mudéjar communities to prevent the granting of real estate to former co-religionists on the pretext that it was illegal to hand it over to Christians. To highlight the power of God and His saints and to make such conversions acceptable to Christians, some accounts from that period attributed this decision to Mary's intervention. According to one of those texts, a Moorish woman was baptized after the Virgin had resurrected her child. The converted Mudéjars, however, lost their status as servants of the king, and therefore constituted a financial damage for the Crown. Although the Church condemned this practice, until mid-thirteenth century, many Christians discouraged their conversion by confiscating the property of those taking that decision.

In the House of Islam, to underline how dhimmis' adherence to Islam led to a break with the previous world, the right to inherit from one's nonconverted relatives was not valid. The latter, in turn, were not allowed to inherit the property of those who had become Muslims. If in one family the parents and some of their children adhered to Islam while the others remained Christian, the latter had no right to inherit. These prohibitions were also valid in the event that a family member became a Muslim after the death of his relative. For not cutting ties with the Christian community completely and at the same time to overcome those prohibitions, exemplary is the strategy a Coptic family adopted during the Mamluk era. Only the head of the family, an official of the public administration, adhered to Islam. At his death, his brother, a newly converted scribe, sold (in reality donated) to his sister-in-law what he had inherited when his brother died. That the woman then married a co-religionist confirms that the choice of her first husband did not exclude her from the Coptic community. These cases certainly created a lot of discontent among Muslims.

As the following story shows, however, the Copts who became Allah's faithful did not always manage to have the solidarity of the former co-religionists, especially when disagreements occurred and there were economic advantages. In the fourteenth century, Ibn Mukanis, a newly converted man working in the public administration, hired a modest Christian instructor, named at-Tāj, to teach his children to read and write. Knowing that he was about to be arrested, Ibn Mukanis went into hiding but, probably due to some disagreement, his employee had him arrested by revealing his hiding place to the soldiers. Fearing that his employer was released and wanted to punish him, at-Tāj became a Muslim. His sponsor was an emir, and at-Tāj placed himself at his service as a soldier, thus improving his standard of living.

The prejudices against converts were very strong both in the House of Islam and in the Christian kingdoms. There was a widespread belief that their choice was not genuine. In the Muslim territories, the definitions that recalled their origin were quite common. In Egypt, they were often referred to as 'Copts,' and this identification was also used sometimes for their children and grandchildren. Suspicions were heightened, especially when adherence to Islam took place after a conquest and on the occasion of repression and popular violence against Christians. For example, during the very violent riots of 1354 in Egypt, in addition to expelling Christ's faithful from the administration, the authorities forced Christian relatives of those who had changed faith and held public office to become Muslims. They were also forced to attend the mosque and pray on Fridays.

In the Nile's land, however, these injunctions were not always implemented. A Muslim writer of those years maliciously observed that Christians converted en masse at times when their afflictions increased and their earnings decreased. The tone of the protests increased if the new Muslim was entrusted with an important position. Although they themselves were converts, in 1555, a group of Ottoman soldiers sent a letter of vehement protest to the vizier complaining that an 'ignorant infidel, who had joined Islam the day before and whose breath still smelled like pork' had been placed at their command. An Ottoman officer expressed very vividly his opinion on the neo-converts, stating that 'a pig remains a pig even if its tail is cut off.'

If powerful adversaries criticized one's conversion, it was possible to lose the position one had acquired, an eventuality made extremely bitter when that was the only reason for the change of faith. This happened to the already mentioned Qumis ibn Antonian, the Andalusian Christian who had become a follower of Allah when faced with the prospect of obtaining a prestigious position if he joined Islam. Calling him a Christian, son of Christians, one of his Muslim rivals convinced the Andalusian ruler that it was not honorable to give a neo-convert a position that should be given to a believer of Islam of noble lineage. At his death, an attempt was made to deprive his relatives of their inheritance by claiming that Qumis ibn Antonian had died a Christian. Only the intervention of a venerable Muslim religious leader, who testified to Qumis ibn Antonian's great attachment to Islam, prevented his memory from being tarnished.

Even worse could be the fate of the neo-converts and their heirs in times of severe economic crisis and other emergencies, particularly when they held prestigious positions and had a high economic status. Extremely tragic was the end of the Damascene who held important public offices and was a rich grain merchant, who was said to be the son of a neo-convert, and to practice Christianity secretly. During the terrible drought of 1397, he found himself passing by chance in a place where a crowd of Muslims had gathered to ask Allah to stop the calamity. His appearance was considered a provocation, and the insults were immediately followed by the stones that killed the unfortunate man. With the intention of sending a message to the authorities about the use of that kind of people in the public administration, his body was burned in front of the governor's palace. The fact that some neo-Christians in Spain continued to frequent their former co-religionists and put their Moorish clothes back on when they went to visit them or attended their parties contributed to the climate of suspicion toward them. As proof of the existence of such tension, during the anti-Muslim riots in the Valencia region, in 1276, they too were attacked.

In those years, the king of Aragon stressed several times that the neo-converts had the same rights as other Christians and that they should not be harassed. According to a famous Spanish intellectual of that period, many Mudéjars would have adhered to Christianity if Christians had behaved honorably toward those who decided to take that step. Since the majority of neo-converts who owned a house could not move out, they remained in a hostile environment. Outraged by the harassment to which the former co-religionists subjected them, the Aragonese rulers imposed a heavy fine on those offending them and calling them turncoats. At the same time, Dominican preachers were allowed to visit them periodically and to correct any errors of faith; those refusing to listen to their sermons were punished. A dispute over the request by a Moorish tax collector to make some neo-Christians pay taxes on the houses they owned in the Muslim quarter of Sagunto indicates that there was sometimes a tendency to consider those people as if their status had not changed (particularly when this involved the loss of income).

In many cases, the convert was considered a traitor and treated as an outcast by former co-religionists, and sometimes attempts were made to punish him. Toward the middle of the fourteenth century, the relatives and the wife of one of the children of the Lleida Mudéjar community leader who had become a Christian in order to gain a position at the royal court took revenge on him by ending all relations with him, kidnapping his children, and refusing to pay him a sum due to him. In a Balkan province of the Ottoman Empire, a Christian convert and her two daughters were killed by her relatives.

The new converts and their descendants sometimes behaved like zealots and persecuted former co-religionists, especially when there were reasons for revenge of economic and social or ethnic-cultural nature. Infamous were some Cretan neo-converts who came from the countryside and were employed in the Ottoman garrisons stationed in the cities, where it seems that they often vented their resentment toward the wealthier urban classes. In the early modern period, excellent pirates, especially those of low social extraction, proved to be the Christians, who, after being captured during raids in the Mediterranean, had denied their faith and had had the opportunity to carry out piracy with the Muslims. In general, the faithful of Christ who moved to the House of Islam and converted to escape persecution and justice and to rebuild their lives or have the opportunity to regain the social and economic status lost in their homeland also demonstrated to be loyal officials and soldiers.

The failure of the uprisings in some parts of Europe in 1848–1849 led some Italian, Polish, and especially Hungarian patriots to take refuge in Ottoman territory. Some of them adhered to Islam to make sure that the Porte would not give in to pressure from the Austrians and the Russians to surrender the rebels and to have the chance to enlist in the Ottoman army and fight against their oppressors. The best known was the Polish Joseph Bem, who, after playing a leading role during the uprising in Poland in 1830 against the Russians, was among the leaders of the Hungarian uprising against the Austrians in 1848. He became a

Muslim along with 256 of his followers, took the name Murad, was appointed general of the Ottoman army, and died at the end of 1850 fighting against rebels in Syria, where he had been sent waiting for the waters to calm down. In the following century, his second life was forgotten, and the Poles and Hungarians celebrated him as the symbol of the struggle against Russian oppression.

Rarer, on the contrary, are the examples of Muslims who converted to Christianity after moving to a Christian land, perhaps because the chances of obtaining a prestigious position in that case were much fewer. Among the few exceptions—favored by the fact that in the Mongolian Turkish world, there were various forms of syncretism because adopting a new religion did not mean eliminating the previous one but adding something to it—there is the case of a Muslim Turk who, after having been a shaman at the Mongolian court, moved to the Byzantine Empire, adhered to the Christian faith, and became an imperial official.

Crypto-faithful

The discussion so far highlighted how varied and numerous were the reasons not dictated by religious convictions to convert to the rulers' faith. This particularity and the circumstance that concealing one's religious belief in life-threatening conditions was admissible or at least tolerated by the faithful of both religions—especially Muslims—meant that many newly converted people continued to practice their 'true religion' clandestinely. The most striking example concerned the Spanish faithful of Islam who were forced in the early sixteenth century to choose between becoming Christians and leaving their homeland. The fact that almost everyone had preferred the first option produced the well-founded suspicion that their decision had not been sincere and, as will be examined in another chapter, led the king of Spain to implement a drastic plan to solve the problem of those false Christians.

Although there were no cases comparable to what happened in Spain, examples of crypto-faithful were not lacking in the House of Islam. In late medieval Egypt, Christian authors wrote about co-religionists who had adhered to Islam while continuing to follow their religion secretly, with the aim of justifying conversion during periods of strong tension between Muslims and Christians, providing an easy way to maintain their religious faith and consoling the Coptic community for which such writings were composed. In this regard, it is relevant that in the fourteenth century, the Coptic Church instituted a secret ceremony, a sort of rebaptism, through which apostates, repenting of their adherence to Islam but not ready to die for that reconsideration, were secretly readmitted into the Christian community. According to the biographies of the 're-baptized,' they subsequently became monks in places sheltered from the Muslim authorities or died after reconciling with their relatives who had remained Christian. Probably, some of them continued to pretend to be believers in Islam.

The rumors circulating among Muslims about these people obviously contributed to increase suspicions about the neo-converts. The higher the office one of them obtained, the higher the number of insinuations about his true faith. The most famous case in the Ottoman Empire concerned the Grand Vizier Sokullu (d. 1579), who drew attention to himself when, after restoring the Patriarchate of Pécs (Hungary), he gave its leadership to two of his Christian relatives. According to some gossip, he secretly went to mass and had a special predilection for Easter celebrations.

The fear that the Christian wives of Allah's faithful secretly baptized their male children and secretly practiced Christianity with them was not entirely unfounded, especially in cases in which those women married Muslim men to escape slavery. According to the report a Cretan informant sent to the Venetian government around 1687, a senior Ottoman officer, commenting on the losses suffered by Muslims in Hungary at that time, revealed to him that it would not be a problem for him to change sides because his mother, a Christian, had secretly baptized him and raised him to the Christian faith. For the time being, however, he preferred to do nothing because his son was in the army and would be punished for his treason. Similar rumors circulated about other Ottoman military officers stationed in Crete. Various crypto-Christians revealed their true faith to western travelers, for example to an Italian archbishop in Albania in 1610 and to a German nobleman in northeastern Greece at the end of the eighteenth century.

In 1839, the edict of Tanzimat established equality among the subjects of all religions, thus ending the need to keep one's faith secret because apostasy was no longer a crime. Consequently, there emerged cases of families, and sometimes entire communities, who, theoretically Muslim, had nevertheless practiced Christianity clandestinely, often for over two centuries. Such examples increased from the Crimean War (1853–1856), when the British Empire and France appointed themselves as the protectors of the Ottoman Empire's Christian subjects. However, it was above all the possibility for the former dhimmis to avoid military service by paying a tax that favored those revelations.

The Ottoman tendency not to conduct accurate investigations, if appearances were respected, had created a favorable terrain for this phenomenon in previous centuries, especially in remote areas and communities in which solidarity among their members was very strong. It was discovered that these people had two names, one official, Muslim, used for contacts with the outside world, and one private, Christian, used with family and friends who shared that practice. They married twice, the first in the 'Muslim way,' and the second, secretly, in front of a priest. Usually, they married members of those groups; however, there were examples in which the Muslim wives had been secretly converted to Christianity.

There had also been a precedent. In 1832, when asked to do military service, the members of the Albanian community of Shpat revealed that they had always been Christians and had pretended to be Muslims in order not to pay the jizyah. This situation was extremely embarrassing for the Ottoman authorities and was silenced perhaps to avoid the outbreak of a revolt like in Greece or because they were about to prepare the edict of Tanzimat. It was probably also intended to avoid, as much as possible, that whole communities would follow that path as a result of the reform. A few years after the edict, the population of a Bulgarian village, who had declared to be crypto-Christian, was transferred to Anatolia for punishment and, according to a Bulgarian source, half of the inhabitants perished from ill-treatment and illness during the journey.

A sensational case emerged after the 1856 reform when some members of a group living in the mountains near the east coast of the Black Sea, the Hemsinli, known as 'half Armenians' for having always spoken Armenian, declared that their ancestors had been converted by force between the seventeenth and eighteenth centuries and that they had always continued to be faithful to Christ. Some inspectors were sent from Istanbul to examine their request. However, some Muslim religious leaders from a nearby area, known to be religiously zealous, publicly stated that if those people were considered Christian, they too would ask to be recognized as believers of Christ because their ancestors were Orthodox Greeks. Fearing a scandal, the officers left and everything was silenced.

An even more striking episode occurred in 1857 in a mountainous area of the eastern Pontus region called Kromni. Known for having always spoken Greek, the inhabitants of that zone affirmed that their forefathers had adhered to Islam in the seventeenth century and had always practiced Christianity secretly. They wanted to declare themselves faithful to Christ since 1839, but their religious leaders advised them to be cautious and see how the situation evolved. Still in 1843, there was the case of an Armenian executed for apostasy. The stir caused by that revelation was remarkable because it was not a marginal group and many of them were wealthy. Over the centuries, they had managed to maintain a very strong sense of solidarity. Their preachers were Orthodox Greek priests, they did not give their daughters in marriage to the faithful of Allah, but took Muslim women as wives, who were allowed to approach their husbands only after they had been baptized and instructed by their mothers-in-law.

Seventeen thousand of them revealed that they were Christians, and no one in that region, characterized by a strong presence of the faithful of Christ, was surprised. This was a well-known secret, but the local authorities had never intervened because, working in the rich silver mines of the area, they had been considered useful for the prosperity of that area. In addition to the new situation created by the edict of Tanzimat, their choice to come out into the open was due to the desire to avoid military conscription. The exemption from it, which they had hitherto enjoyed thanks to the high profits from their work, was in fact no longer valid because in those years the mines had become unproductive and had, therefore, been closed. The problems arose when they presented their case in Europe. Not liking such publicity, the Porte granted them the status of Christian converts, forcing them to do military service. They were also required to bear both their Muslim and Christian names in official documents, thus exposing them to the stigma of the faithful of Islam and those of Christ. The local authorities did not allow them to pray at the graves of their dead in Muslim cemeteries.

Subsequently they were obliged to have only the Muslim name, which led to numerous attempts to falsify the documents.

The twenty thousand or so miners from that region who moved to the Ankara region at the end of the nineteenth century, attesting that they were faithful to Christ, met with a much worse fate. The situation in those years was different because the sultan of that period was religiously intransigent, and the 1876 constitution had been suspended. In the tense atmosphere created by the massacres of the Armenians in the 1890s, their status did not go unnoticed. They were called 'the people of the two cults' and accused of manipulating birth records to make their numbers appear smaller. The governor of that region ordered them to bear Muslim names and send their children only to Muslim schools, appointed preachers to instruct them in the Islamic faith, and exiled their leaders. He also recommended that a careful investigation be conducted into their requests to be recognized as Christians. According to the investigations, their aim was to avoid military service, and they were kept in a sort of limbo by not registering them either as Muslims or Christians. Finally in 1905, they were officially considered Muslims, but after the Young Turks took power in 1908, they were registered as Christians. Although they had declared themselves believers in Islam so as not to leave their homes, in 1923–1924 they were deported following the agreements between Greece and Turkey on the expulsions of Muslims and Christians living in their territories.

Apostates

For both Muslims and Christians, converting to the faith of the other was considered a very serious crime punished with death and with the confiscation of all the assets of the 'traitor.' Rather than to their co-religionists, this prohibition was mainly addressed to the neo-converts, who were thus reminded that they could not have second thoughts about their decision. Some sensational episodes in the Christian kingdoms of Islam's believers, who had pretended to deny their religion and had succeeded in obtaining important court appointments, contributed to increase the suspicions toward those people and sometimes provided an excuse to the zealots to attack the sovereigns who had proved too inclined to accept the other.

At the beginning of the twelfth century, the King of Jerusalem, Baldwin, baptized a Muslim and gave him his name. The latter then made a very good career, but in 1110, he was executed because it was discovered that he had provided information to the Allah's faithful of a neighboring kingdom eager to reconquer Jerusalem. The case of Philip, a eunuch who became Christian at a young age and was raised at court under King Roger II (d. 1154), caused a sensation in Sicily. Esteemed by this sovereign, he held prestigious positions among which was the command of troops during a military campaign in northwest Africa. Although Philip returned victorious, his benevolent treatment of the Muslim elite in that area created some suspicions about the genuineness of his adherence to Christianity. In 1153, he was arrested and accused of secretly remaining a follower of Islam, secretly attending mosques, sending offerings to Muhammad's tomb, eating meat on Fridays, and hating Christians. With great sorrow, narrates a contemporary chronicler, the king sentenced him to death. After being tortured, Philip was dragged through the streets of Palermo by horses and then burned, to offer an example to the neo-converts and the Muslim population of the kingdom of Sicily.

This episode can be taken as a model of what usually happened in areas characterized by a high percentage of subjects having a faith different from that of the rulers. As long as this situation persisted, the need to maintain internal order led the rulers not to investigate too much in matters of faith and not to listen to extremist co-religionists. Therefore, an approach that could be defined as 'do not ask, do not tell' prevailed. The atmosphere changed when, thanks to immigration and conversions, the percentage of dominators increased significantly.

In Sicily, Philip's case represented a watershed in the attitude toward the 'new Christians' and the Sicilian Muslims. In fact, it favored the wide diffusion of feelings of hatred toward them, especially for those who held prestigious positions at court and in the public administration. The first attack against the palace eunuchs and Palermo's faithful of Allah happened a few years after the execution of Philip. This, however, does not mean that the practice of using eunuchs and Muslim personnel disappeared immediately. The Sicilian sovereigns still considered them useful and continued to employ them, but the rumors and attacks did not stop. In 1167, the rumor began to circulate that the court eunuch Peter, the queen's main counselor and minister, was only outwardly a Christian, but in reality he was a follower of Allah. Not wanting to end up like Philip, Peter fled with some members of his entourage to the Maghreb.

The arrival in Sicily in those years of people not accustomed to the presence of Islam's faithful in a Christian kingdom and at the same time in search of fortune produced a struggle between factions in a period characterized by the weakness of central power. During her regency, Marguerite, a noblewoman of French origin, surrounded herself with a group of compatriots led by Stephen. The latter's decision to eliminate the taxes imposed by the court notaries for drawing up some documents and to conduct a careful investigation into the existence of false Christians among the palace staff provoked strong hostility among the palace eunuchs. Stephen, however, did not stop and resorted to violence.

First of all, he ordered the arrest and torture of the commander of the royal prison, who died as a result of the treatment suffered, on charges of raping a Christian girl and creating a Muslim sanctuary in that prison. He was a close friend of the court eunuchs and had played an important role in the repression of the violent riots against the king and the faithful of Islam in 1161. Stephen then had one of the most important of those eunuchs arrested on the pretext that he was preparing his assassination. Indicating that not all Sicilian Christians had such suspicions and such strong hatred for the royal palace eunuchs and for the faithful of Allah and that not all of them appreciated the abrupt methods of the 'French' and their heavy meddling in the politics of the kingdom, there is the circumstance that there was also a bishop among those arrested for the supposed conspiracy against Stephen. When the French imposed taxes on Catholic Christians—usually paid only by Muslims and the Orthodox Christians—violent riots broke out against them. Besieged by an angry crowd in the cathedral of Palermo's bell tower, Stephen obtained safe conduct with the promise to leave southern Italy. Internal peace was then restored, and the climate of tension between Christians and Muslims cooled down. No court eunuch, however, ever again managed to have the same power and influence as his predecessors.

Although the atmosphere in the Iberian Peninsula did not reach the atmosphere sometimes created in Sicily and although there were no sensational cases like that of Philip, there were various investigations to discover false converts also in that area. As will be seen in Chapter 6, the problem became extremely pressing from the beginning of the sixteenth century when all Muslims chose to adhere to Christianity. In those years, the Inquisition was very active with regard to those 'new Christians.'

False converts were also unmasked in the House of Islam where extensive and detailed investigations of those cases were not, however, constantly conducted. In areas and periods characterized by a tenuous presence of Christ's faithful and zealous Islamism, however, it was difficult to hide the true faith professed. For example, in Marrakech, at the beginning of the twelfth century, under the intransigent Almoravids, it was discovered that a neo–convert had a Bible, a cross, and pieces of dry bread with a symbol in his home. He was, therefore, accused of practicing Christianity in secret and condemned to death. This accusation, combined with that of having plotted with foreign powers, was used in Egypt to eliminate an adversary. In the 1020s, the presence of a caliph in Cairo with little interest in government affairs put power in the hands of a triumvirate. Soon there were disagreements among them, and one of the three was deposed with the accusation of having invited the Byzantine emperor to conquer Egypt. The man professed his innocence but was equally executed. To confirm his guilt, his enemies said that after his execution, it was discovered that he was not circumcised and had, therefore, always been a Christian.

With the edict of Tanzimat, apostasy ceased to be considered a crime in the Ottoman Empire. In the early years of its application, the lack of clarity on the part of the Porte and the opposition of many local officials and members of the court to that reform created confusion as to how to proceed in those cases, and this led to some newly converted people returning to their original faith being executed; the last to be sentenced to death was an Armenian in 1843.

Alongside the order not to impose any punishment on apostates, the central authority decreed that they should be sent to Istanbul immediately and recommended that they be given as little publicity as possible. The cases of apostasy were mostly connected to conversions under pressure or through coercive methods and, therefore, had the potential to create strong tensions between Muslims and Christians. The tendency was, therefore, to try to save the face of both communities by quickly removing the 'renegade' from the area of residence and then to attribute that decision to his inability to understand and want or lack of education. Removal was not always possible, and those cases created disagreements between local Muslims and Christians. There was no bloodshed, but, if the apostate was a woman, the desire to defend her religion was added to the duty of men to protect the honor of their community. It, therefore, sometimes happened that a crowd of Islam's faithful had taken away the Christian candidate for apostasy, declaring her a Muslim by popular acclaim. In large cities strongly inhabited by Christians, such as Thessaloniki, however, the attitude was beginning to change, particularly in the face of violent reactions. Consequently, it happened that the city governor saved a woman who had returned to Christianity from the wrath of her husband who was looking for her to shoot her.

Reactions to conversions: the 'neo-martyrs'

In Muslim territories, the conversions of Christian subjects to Islam provoked strong disapproval of those who remained faithful to Christ and sometimes led some people to state openly that Muhammad's was a false religion or to deny their adherence to Islam. Aware that the punishment for their gesture was death, those persons wanted to ask for forgiveness for their acquiescence toward the rulers and at the same time to show Muslims how strong the Christian faith was and to invite their co-religionists not to abandon it. In many cases, the preference was to forget that those following that path could not in reality be considered martyrs because they had gone against the Gospel precept that one must escape persecution and not seek death.

It is significant that the first examples occurred about seventy years after the Arab conquest of the Middle East, that is, in a period in which in various areas (especially in Syria and Palestine), many believers of Christ had adhered to Islam in order to maintain or improve their social and economic status and not to be subjected to the growing discrimination regarding dhimmis. It is not by chance that some of those individuals, recognized as martyrs by the Eastern Churches, were Christians who repented of having become Muslims.

Exemplary in this regard is the story concerning Gelasius. His father had converted and then convinced his wife and their seven children to do the same. With his mother's help, Gelasius decided to return to his original faith and went to the monastery of St. Saba, near Bethlehem, where he was baptized, became a monk, and took the name Bacchus. Knowing that his mother and his brothers were in Jerusalem, he visited them to convince them to imitate his example. However, one of them refused and denounced him to the Muslim governor who condemned Bacchus to death for denying Islam.

Only on one occasion did the faithful of Islam execute a fair number of people and in a short space of time. This occurred around the mid-ninth century, in Cordoba, the capital of Muslim Spain. The widespread adoption of the language, culture, and customs of the rulers (a phenomenon perceived as a prelude to join

Islam) by their co-religionists, the high number of Christians who had converted until then, the absence of a strong condemnation of this situation by the Spanish ecclesiastical authorities, and the spirit of emulation induced about fifty people to insult Islam publicly or, if they were neo-converts, to apostasize.

The background of those persons and the reasons leading them to take this step open some windows on what was happening at that time and on the pressures and mistreatment to which they and probably many other Christians in other periods and areas had been subjected. In addition to extolling their behavior, the writings about their actions aimed both to demonize the Muslim rulers and to discredit the Andalusian Christ's faithful collaborating with them. The first was a monk who, while shopping at the market, was harassed by a group of Muslims who asked him insistently what the Christians thought of Christ and Muhammad. He immediately emphasized the divinity of the former, saying that he did not want to say anything about the latter. Having been cornered, he expressed unflattering judgments about the prophet of Islam. At first there was no reaction, but when the churchman returned to the marketplace, those Muslims stirred up the crowd against him, accusing him of having insulted Muhammad. Brought to a judge, after denying this, the monk repeated what he had said about Muhammad and was executed.

Many of those who were later sentenced to death for having offended the Muslim religion and Muhammad were young people who, driven by strong idealism and a probable generational conflict, refused to accept the compromise situation in which their families had placed them. Isaac, for example, belonged to a wealthy Christian family, had received an excellent education in Arabic, and worked in the Muslim administration. Suddenly, he decided to abandon that life and become a monk at a monastery of which his uncle was abbot. After three years of ascetic life, he returned to Cordoba and, pretending to convert, declared that Islam was a false religion and was therefore executed. His uncle and five other monks imitated him and met the same end. A girl, whose original name is not known, was the daughter of Muslim parents who had recently converted to Islam or children of converts. She was baptized by a nun who was a relative of hers and took the name Leocritia. She left her father's house and took refuge at the home of Eulogius, an advocate of the new martyrs and who was the newly elected bishop of Toledo. Denounced by their Muslim neighbors, they were arrested. Since Leocritia had repudiated Islam and Eulogius, during interrogations, had called the Muslim faith a false religion, they were both sentenced to death.

Wishing to maintain the status quo and avoid tensions with the Muslims, the ecclesiastical hierarchies of Muslim Spain, strongly criticized by the supporters of the neo-martyrs for their collaboration with the administration of the rulers, not only did not consider those people as martyrs, because they had voluntarily sought death, but blamed their behavior. Probably, most of their co-religionists shared this condemnation, especially those who at the time were banned from the court by the emir of Cordoba who became angry at the behavior of those

Christian 'fanatics.' The latter were instead venerated as champions of the faith in the territories under Christian rule where many of their remains were brought.

In the following centuries and during the Ottoman period, there were other believers of Christ who acted in that way, but they were isolated cases. Although the deaths occurred over a longer period of time, the only other example comparable to what happened in Cordoba occurred in Egypt in the second half of the fourteenth century during the Mamluk domination. Unlike those in Cordoba, those who made that choice were considered martyrs by the Coptic Church, and many of them were in contact and supported by the Patriarch of Cairo, Matthew. According to his biographer, God granted him a natural death shortly before he was arrested, thus sparing him the humiliation of being punished for his role in that movement.

Unlike those in the ninth-century Andalusia, both officially and unofficially, Egyptian Christians were under attack at that time and many of them were converting to keep their jobs in the Muslim administration and for fear of being victims of violence. The modus vivendi established in Egypt in previous centuries no longer existed, and the Coptic Church itself was the target of anti-Christian campaigns. Those who had sought death by denouncing Islam had, therefore, to be honored for their exemplary behavior. Their biographies also included the condemnation of the Copts with 'two hearts,' that is, those who had corrupted themselves because of their great familiarity with the Muslims and their customs, considered the antechamber of conversion. The first to be executed were bishops and monks from small towns and monasteries located in remote places. This form of resistance was, therefore, initially put in place by those who had not been contaminated by the pressures of the secular world. Their sacrifice later aroused a desire for emulation even among the laity. As already observed for those in Cordoba, their cases are particularly noteworthy because they shed some light on practices and reveal tensions within the families of converts.

Michael's father had, for example, adhered to Islam together with his son to whom the name Muhammad had been assigned. The young man then retracted his decision and refused to answer to his Arabic name before the court. When he reported what his name was, he quoted Muhammad's name in the Coptic version, thus implicitly refusing his adherence to Islam, and was, therefore, sentenced to death. Hadid's grandfather had converted to Islam, while his father was a Christian (which was obviously illegal). This was discovered, and Hadid was declared legally Muslim. Having refused invitations to declare himself a believer in Allah, he was executed. In another case, a man provocatively opposed Muslim officials by going to them on horseback, thus challenging the ban on dhimmi riding.

As it had happened in Cordoba, even under the Mamluks, the judges, aware of the problems raised by those people, were reluctant to impose the death penalty immediately and gave them the opportunity to recant, but no one did so. Christian texts would obviously never have reported the story of a failed martyr. The only exception is, in fact, recorded in a Muslim work, according to which in 1380 in Damascus—therefore, far from the heart of the Mamluk dominions—a

Christian, after having adhered to Islam, having married a faithful of Allah, and had several children from her, decided to deny his new religion before a judge. Probably convinced by his wife, he regretted his gesture and recanted what he had said to another magistrate belonging to a legal school that admitted such a recantation. In addition to presenting an example different from those mentioned in Christian texts, this case is also relevant because it illustrates how Allah's faithful sometimes had different approaches to apostates. In the Ottoman Empire, with the edict of Tanzimat, those gestures obviously did not have the same meaning anymore and the insults to Islam were no longer punished with the death penalty. In those years, in Thessaloniki, an 'out-of-time' aspiring martyr was in fact condemned to forced labor for his repeated offenses against the Muslim religion.

Rates of conversion and return to the faith of the ancestors

So far we have seen how various were the reasons leading the conquered to adopt the faith of the conquerors. The conversions took place both individually and in groups that varied from a few dozen to hundreds of people. For the premodern period, there are no reliable data and, therefore, only very vague estimates can be made about the percentage of converts. In general, in the areas easily conquered by Muslims such as the Near East, Middle East, and the Iberian Peninsula, the process of conversion was slow in the first 80 years and accelerated in the following 150 years. By the tenth century, the faithful of Islam had become a large majority everywhere in the House of Islam, and in the areas mentioned above their percentage ranged between 75% and 90% of the population. The rate of conversion was largely due to the greater or lesser solidity and wealth of the Churches and the Christian secular elite and the more or less oppressive attitude of the authorities and the Muslim population. The largest minority of Christ's faithful was in Egypt, while the smallest was in northwest Africa, where Christians almost completely disappeared.

In the following centuries, the percentages did not change significantly, but in the land of the Nile under the Mamluks, there was a new acceleration that caused the number of Egyptian Christians to fall by about two-thirds; at the beginning of the sixteenth century, it amounted to about 8% of the population. Except for some areas along the Black Sea and Armenia, the Islamization of Anatolia was faster than that of the Near East and Middle East (at the end of the fifteenth century, Muslims accounted for about 92% of the population). The majority of the populations of the Balkan areas conquered between the fourteenth and fifteenth centuries by the Ottomans remained mainly Christian until the second half of the sixteenth century (at the end of the previous century, the faithful of Christ were about 97%). According to the census carried out between 1520 and 1530 in the Ottoman Empire, 80% of the Balkan populations were Christian, about 60% of Allah's faithful were converts, and the rest were immigrants. However, the inhabitants were not equally distributed. Eighty-five percent of the Muslims resided in ten of the twenty-eight Balkan provinces and in none of them were they the majority. The most Islamized area was the district of Istanbul where the faithful of Allah were 46% of the inhabitants. They exceeded 50% in nine cities including Sarajevo, founded by the Ottomans and almost devoid of Christians. In Thessaloniki, they were more in number than the faithful of Christ (25% and 20% respectively), but thanks to emigration from the Iberian Peninsula, the Jews made up the majority of the inhabitants (54%). In Istanbul in 1478, 51% of the population was Muslim and 31% was Christian. In the second half of the seventeenth century, two-thirds of the residents of Athens were Christ's faithful.

Not even the Christianization of Sicily and the Iberian Peninsula was a rapid process and, in addition to conversions, the immigration of Christians to those areas made a considerable contribution. In Sicily, the percentage of Muslims became lower than that of Christians about sixty years after the conquest of the island (1080s/1090s). In 1300, in the southern parts of the Iberian regions occupied by the Christians for over a century, Muslim subjects constituted a significant minority (about 30%), while in the Valencian region, definitively subjugated for just over fifty years (1230s/1240s), they were still the majority. In the following two centuries, economic and central power crises, the immigration of Christians, and conversions contributed to changing those percentages quickly. In Navarre and Portugal, the believers of Islam were reduced to 2–3% of the population.

Whatever was the reason that induced their ancestors to adhere to the religion of the rulers, the majority of subsequent generations followed the creed chosen by their predecessors with conviction, and not many were ready to give it up immediately when their land was regained by their ancestors' co-religionists. For example, after taking over Cyprus and Crete in the second half of the tenth century, the Byzantines, to their great disappointment, discovered that the descendants of the Cypriots and Cretans, who had converted to Islam following the Muslim conquest of those islands in previous centuries, did not join Christianity en masse. A churchman, known for his holy conduct of life, complained a great deal because his proselytizing work failed in that period. The same disappointment was often experienced by various preachers in the Spanish territories taken away from Muslim rule between the twelfth and fifteenth centuries. As has already been pointed out, in the Ottoman Empire after the edict of Tanzimat, there were several cases of people declaring themselves crypto-Christian, but mass conversion to Christianity, strongly feared by the Porte and hoped for by the Europeans and Christian missionaries, did not take place, a sign of the difficulty in secretly transmitting the Christian religion to subsequent generations in many areas and above all an indication that faiths, traditions, and convictions cemented over the centuries could not be dissolved with a simple stroke of the pen.

3

Working

Public administration

The Arabs' occupation of the Middle East was characterized by the small number of conquerors, and their inexperience in the field of governance in areas marked by the presence of large cities and accustomed to many centuries of sophisticated administration. Thanks to the local population's scarce resistance to the Arabs' conquest and the rather peaceful behavior of the new rulers, significant changes in the social and economic structure of those regions did not occur. Its preservation was essential to obtain high proceeds from taxes, to maintain internal order easily, and thus to be able to allocate economic and military resources to the expansion of Islam. Although there had been some protests among the most intransigent Muslims, the new rulers, therefore, decided to keep the existing administrative staff who had immediately proved to be in favor of the new regime. The language of the bureaucracy (i.e., Greek) did not change either.

In those years, Christian scribes and doctors were a regular presence at the caliph's court. The need for experienced officials was such that Christians were employed even in settlements created by the Arabs. For example, in Palestine, a Christian from Jordan was appointed superintendent of the Ramla palace and mosque. They were also used as tax contractors, an extremely lucrative business. Upon learning of the great culture of a Christian named Athanasius, Caliph Ab al-Malik (646—705) appointed him to be his brother's tutor. Thanks to the position acquired by the father, the sons of Athanasius had the task of providing wages to the soldiers, thus getting very rich because they kept a large percentage of the salaries. One of the best known of these characters was John of Damascus (d. 749) who, like his grandfather and father, held prestigious positions in the caliphal bureaucracy. These men were respected by co-religionists, were usually pious, lavished huge gifts on their communities, and protected them from abuse.

At the beginning of the eighth century, however, the situation changed. Believing that there were enough Muslims in possession of the knowledge necessary to administer and govern, the caliphs and many members of the Muslim élite began to maintain that the dhimmis should no longer hold important public offices except if they would convert. Perhaps the new atmosphere contributed to John of Damascus's decision to abandon his job and to become a monk. The governor of Egypt— the territory with the highest percentage of Christians in the House of Islam—replied to the caliph to fear that all the dhimmi officials would become Muslims in order to keep their jobs with a consequent drastic decrease in the tax revenues that were obtained from the jizyah's payment. Observing that the conversion of all humankind to Islam is the goal of every good Muslim, the ruler ordered him to obey his will.

In various parts of the House of Islam and especially in Egypt, that directive would have however provoked effects so deleterious to the public administration and to the society that it was not put into practice. Despite the immigration of Arabs, the conversion of a part of the Egyptians to Islam, and the adoption of Arabic as the official language, the presence of Christians with those tasks did not change significantly in the following 250 years. The Christians in that area also quickly adapted to the new situation and learned the language of the rulers. The same thing happened in Syria among those who used Syriac, a language quite similar to Arabic. According to a late-tenth-century Muslim geographer, in the Syrian-Palestinian area, all scribes were Christians, and everywhere, the dhimmis held prestigious public positions.

When Egypt was occupied by the Fatimids, who were Shiites and were therefore considered heretics by Sunni Muslims, the new rulers increased their collaboration with the numerous local Christians to strengthen their power in that area. This happened mainly in the first period of the government during which the Fatimids did not assign any relevant office to Sunni subjects. Under the first three Fatimid caliphs five viziers, that is, the highest office in the court, were Christians. The Fatimid rulers also found it very advantageous to employ Christians because, being easy to fire them, they hoped to have more loyal officials. It has been hypothesized that the high number of dhimmis with those duties was also due to the fact that the great economic opportunities of the Fatimid era discouraged the more educated and capable Muslims from seeking a job that was not well paid and sometimes risky, but the sources at our disposition prevent us from expressing a positive or negative evaluation about this supposition.

Although it was theoretically forbidden for the dhimmis to hold positions that placed them above a believer in Islam and to carry out activities involving the writing of verses from the Koran, in Egypt, some Christians held the offices of tax collectors, chiefs of the court secretariat, and as it has been already observed, some were even appointed as viziers of the caliph. The first Christian vizier was particularly appreciated for his remarkable knowledge, previously acquired from other positions in the public administration, and for the excellent results he achieved. As a bitter irony of history, it was a Christian secretary who prepared the draft of Caliph Al-Ḥākim's order to destroy the church of the Holy Sepulcher. During the Fatimid period, Christian dignitaries were considered equal to Muslim dignitaries and could participate in ceremonies, events, and public holidays. In addition to using them in their administration, the Fatimid caliphs employed churchmen as ambassadors to their co-religionists (for example, the Byzantines). Most of those who held important positions came to a tragic end, but this depended more on the struggles for those offices than on the fact that they were Christians. Their religious faith certainly made them more vulnerable, however, it is significant that many Muslims and Jews with those duties also suffered that fate.

Some episodes dating back to the twelfth century highlight the lack of scruples among some of the Christ's faithful and, at the same time, underline how widespread their use in Egypt was. To take revenge on a Muslim boatman who had refused to give him a free ride, a Christian official forged a document to damage him. Others bribed the court astrologer (a co-religionist) to report to the caliph the prediction that, if he placed a faithful of Christ, whose description corresponded to one of them, at the head of his administration, agriculture, and fishing would flourish. The ruler followed his suggestion.

To have so many dhimmis in those positions created discontent and envy among Muslims and provoked protests unheard by the authorities. This frustration was also expressed in short works in verse, a literary genre very popular in the Muslim world. With poisonous irony at the end of the tenth century, an Egyptian Muslim author invited the vizier to convert to Christianity because, as those times showed, Christianity was the true religion. Referring to the favorable attitude toward the faithful of Christ, the writer also suggested that he should pray to the Trinity: the vizier was the Father, the caliph was the Son and the commander of the army was the Holy Spirit.

Christian officials were often accused of nepotism, being corrupt, and getting enormously rich at the expense of the Allah's faithful (those crimes were, however, often attributed to Muslim officials as well). According to these detractors, Christians were characterized by the arrogance with which they treated the believers of Islam, an unacceptable behavior for dhimmis. In the mid-twelfth century, a writer asked the vizier to depose the 'arrogant' Christian treasurer and humiliate the faithful of Christ by ordering them to shave their beards. In those years, a Muslim secretary of the caliphal court instead composed a sort of manual to be used in the chancellery of his lord in which it was pointed out that the dhimmis should not be trusted; therefore, no office should be assigned to them in the public administration. According to another author of that period, a Christian had accumulated an incalculable wealth with his mischief and was so shameless that he exhibited the great number of coins he possessed.

The worst Christian official of that period was a character nicknamed 'the Monk.' His victims were not only Muslims, but also his co-religionists, the first to be struck by his greed. Accusing every Christian secretary of misappropriation of public funds and promising to fill the state coffers, he obtained the position of chief superintendent of tax collection. Having obtained all that was possible from the Christian officials, he turned his attention first to his Muslim colleagues and then to all the wealthy. His lavish conduct in life, some outrageous abuses (the worst of which would have been the embezzlement of money intended for orphans), and the increasingly widespread rumors that his behavior toward Allah's believers was a kind of retribution for the Muslim conquest of his land finally attracted the attention of the caliph who ordered his execution. According to the very detailed list of the crimes committed by 'the Monk,' he had in particular distinguished himself by the scandalous waste and the accumulation of things he had never used: three hundred unused mattresses and piles of clothes were found in his house.

The end of the Fatimid rule in Egypt (1171) corresponded to a progressive worsening of the economic conditions in that country and an increase in resentment for the use of Christians in public service. Their status became extremely difficult under the Mamluks when there were periodic expulsions of Christian officials, but sometimes they managed to regain their place after some time by paying a large sum of money. In 1301, a Maghreb traveler was astonished at the important positions Christ's faithful held in the land of the Nile and their wealth, pointing out that this was not the case in his country. In the fourteenth century, another writer observed that, although Egypt was the largest and most famous country among all Muslim territories for its culture, it was the only place where Christians worked in the public administration.

This situation continued with some temporary disruptions until the fifteenth century when, following rumors of mistreatment of Muslims in neighboring Ethiopia, a sultan ordered an investigation into the behavior of Egyptian Christians. Having discovered that they did not respect the prohibitions on clothing, he ordered them to apply those rules to the letter and never again to use 'infidels' in government offices. The Christian secretary of the vizier was beaten, and after being stripped of his clothes, he was paraded through the streets of Cairo in the company of an officer who shouted 'Here is the compensation due to Christians employed in government offices' and finally imprisoned. Egyptian Christ's faithful offered large sums to the sultan to revoke these measures, but the ruler was adamant. According to the author of that story, he had thus defended Islam because the presence of Christians with those duties represented a tremendous evil. In order to obtain their services, the faithful of Islam were in fact obliged to be kind to them and sometimes to humiliate themselves. The measures the sultan adopted, the writer points out, were comparable to a second Muslim conquest of Egypt because, thanks to them, 'he exalted Islam and humiliated the infidels, and nothing is more meritorious in the eyes of Allah.'

Although to a lesser extent, also in the Iberian Peninsula, which was easily occupied by the faithful of Islam, Christians, both laymen and churchmen, were employed in the Muslim administration and court between the eighth and tenth centuries, particularly in the first decades after the occupation. Like their colleagues in the Middle East, Iberian clergymen took part in diplomatic missions to European Christians. One of the best known was Bishop Recemund, who went to the court of the German King Otto as ambassador of the caliph of Cordoba in mid-tenth century. In Andalusia too, officials were victims of tensions between the dominators and the dominated and court intrigues. In reaction to the movement of the so-called Cordoba's martyrs, around 850, the ruler expelled all the believers of Christ from his palace. A few years later, a monk was called to the court to translate a letter from Arabic to Latin for the king of the Franks, which aroused the envy of the Christians who had returned to serve the lord of Cordoba. Accused of passing secret information to the Franks, of having induced a co-religionist to offend Muhammad, and of heresy, the monk decided to flee to a Christian land. Here, he composed a work in his defense in which he harshly criticized the behavior of the Andalusian court's clergymen. Since it is an apologetic text, written without fear of retaliation, the work cannot be considered a 100% accurate description of what really happened. His accusation that one of those churchmen handed over to the Muslim ruler an accurate census of his diocese's Christians so that they would all pay taxes gives, however, an idea of what kind of collaboration the Andalusian clergymen provided.

As for Sicily, whose complete conquest took about eighty years of campaigning and harsh sieges, some rare news suggests that it was not impossible for Christians to have occupations of that kind. For example, a letter from a Calabrian abbot addressed to a Sicilian emir had been translated by that ruler's secretary, called 'excellent and most Christian.' Although the rules for the dhimmis forbade it, two Christians, father and son, were employed in Palermo as palace doctors at the end of the tenth century. In addition to various Egyptian rulers, it is known that Christian physicians also worked for Ottoman pashas and viziers. Remarkable was the itinerant career of George (c. 1080s–c. 1151), a Christian from Antioch. Having distinguished himself in Syria for his skills in the field of public finance, he was hired to administer the treasury in Tunisia. Although George had achieved excellent results, in the early years of the twelfth century, he feared losing his office because of his employer's death and therefore fled with his family to the Normans in Sicily under whom he held prestigious positions.

During the early stages of expansion in Greece and the Balkans, the Ottoman sultans allocated the conquered territories' control to nobles and military officers who in return were to supply troops to the army. It was not unusual that there were Christians among those local rulers, but they gradually disappeared with the consolidation of the conquests. Instead, the system of assigning the collection of taxes and the resolution of disputes among Christ's faithful to Christian notables survived for a long time, a task that was carried out with the collaboration of the priests. In practice, the Christian elites often governed at the local level, sometimes coming into conflict with the Muslim authorities.

The most successful Orthodox Christian in the first period of the Ottoman Empire was Michael Cantacuzenus (d. 1578), nicknamed by his adversaries as the 'son of the devil.' Descendant of a noble Byzantine family, he skillfully exploited his ability in making friends with sultans and viziers (connections also achieved by paying out of his own pocket the construction of several ships for the Ottoman fleet) to become the most important customs official in the second half of the sixteenth century. The Phanariots, Istanbul's Orthodox Christians, acted as diplomats and interpreters for the Ottoman government. Some of them managed to gain considerable influence at court, and in the eighteenth century, they obtained the governorship of two north-eastern principalities of the empire, Wallachia and Moldavia, inhabited mainly by Christians. A large sum had to be paid to the sultan to obtain those positions, but the investment was largely repaid owing to the proceeds from the control of those areas' finances. In order to fill the coffers of the empire and to satisfy the elite of the Phanariots, those offices were assigned and revoked quite frequently. The members of the most influential family, the Maurocordatos, obtained them six times between 1710 and 1821.

In the territories recently taken from the Christians, the Ottomans also had to use the services of Christian translators to communicate with their new subjects, while in areas whose occupation had led to widespread destruction, such as Cyprus and Crete, it was necessary to hire local chief architects. Between the end of the eighteenth century and the nineteenth century an Armenian family, the Balyans, distinguished itself on the latter profession to the point that the Ottoman sultans employed several of them. The Balyans skillfully and in an extremely original way mixed various oriental and Baroque styles and left their mark on Istanbul, erecting a wide variety of religious, public, and private buildings. The first of them, Master Krikor (1764—1831), was so appreciated by the sultan that, besides considering him a personal friend, he granted him and his family tax exemption, permission to ride horses in Istanbul, and that only the grand vizier could administer justice against him. In Izmir, the most Christian city of the empire, Orthodox Christian architects built the most important buildings of the second half of the nineteenth century and the beginning of the twentieth century. An Armenian businessman, Anton Misrilan, was responsible for the extremely rapid construction, in 1853, of the building that symbolized Beirut's remarkable economic and architectural expansion in the nineteenth century. Unlike the previous ones, the Anton Bey Kahn was a completely outward facing edifice with a beautiful facade provided with a private dock that allowed the immediate transfer of goods inside the warehouses and, above all, equipped with modern offices where the major shipping and banking agencies and post offices of the city were located.

In the nineteenth century, in Aleppo and Damascus, the Christians returned to be employed in customs after almost two centuries of Jewish control of those positions. Following the Greek War of Independence, the Orthodox Christians of the empire were no longer considered reliable, and many of their positions were assigned to the Armenians, little used until then as officials. In those years, the ruler of Egypt used several of them, and two of those sent to study in Europe became his ministers of Foreign Affairs. Taking advantage of the opportunities offered to non-Muslims during the Tanzimat period and the increased welfare of many of their co-religionists, some Armenians made excellent careers in various sectors of the civil service, including higher education.

Exemplary, both for the successes he achieved and for how it ended, was the career of Gabriel Noradukyan (1851—1936). Son of a baker, who worked at the sultan's palace and whose family was from a village in northeastern Anatolia, Noradukyan was first educated at home and then studied at the French Institute of St. Joseph in Istanbul. Using his intellectual talents, he was then able to perfect his education in law and political science at the most prestigious academic institutions in Paris. Returning to Istanbul in 1875, Noradukyan was appointed as professor of law and shortly afterward Secretary of the Ministry of Foreign Affairs. He always maintained strong ties with the Armenian community and, in 1894, became president of the Armenian National Assembly. In an attempt to create peaceful relations between Muslims and Armenians, which had deteriorated greatly due to the massacres against the latter in the late nineteenth century, the government of the Young Turks gave some Armenians the opportunity to hold high-level positions, and Noradukyan became Minister of Commerce and Minister of Foreign Affairs between 1908 and 1913. Following the worsening situation of his co-religionists, which degenerated completely in 1915, he fled to Europe where he became an active member of organizations that assisted Armenian survivors of the 1915—1917 massacres and deportations and advocated the creation of an independent Armenian state in Anatolia. At the beginning of the twentieth century, members of Beirut's wealthiest Christian families also held high positions for the Sublime Porte. Among those of the Melhamé family were two ministers, a senator, and a state councillor, while a Sursock was secretary of the Ottoman embassy in Paris.

Although much less common than in the House of Islam, the use of public officials and court dignitaries belonging to another faith was not entirely absent on Christian lands. In Constantinople, there is evidence of the use of entire Muslim families in the early tenth century at the court of two emperors. In the kingdom of Jerusalem, the prohibition for the faithful of Islam to reside in the capital and the fear of connivance with their neighbors meant that the Muslims were not employed at the royal court. That kind of prohibition did not exist in the Christian kingdoms of Southern Europe, and although it did exist, that fear was not comparable to that in the 'Holy Land,' and therefore, Muslims were sometimes used in the public administration and as court personnel.

This happened in Sicily, especially in the first decades after the conquest of the island by the Normans, when the small number of Christians and people with those skills made their use necessary. In that period, it was also possible to offer positions in Palermo's royal palace to Muslim intellectuals from the House of Islam. The most famous was the geographer Al-Idrisi (c. 1100—c. 1165) invited by King Roger II to build a great planisphere and to write a work describing it. As will be seen below, the Muslim subjects excelled in the field of construction, and various Spanish sovereigns ensured the services of the best in their courts and assigned the position of chief architect and master carpenter to the most capable.

Some Mudéjars were also employed to create new craft activities on a large scale. Worthy of note in this regard is the case of Zalema, Muslim master carpenter of the king of Navarre, sent twice to Zaragoza in the second half of the fourteenth century together with a Christian official to hire dyers and learn how to build textile mills. The expenses for the expeditions were high, but the mission was successful and Zalema was promoted to 'Master General for all carpentry work throughout the kingdom.' A master carpenter was held in such high esteem by another sovereign of Navarre that he was brought by the king to Paris in 1405. Some particularly skillful tailors, and jewelry makers also managed to obtain official positions in the palaces of the Spanish kings.

Farmers, craftsmen, workers, and shopkeepers

The Muslim and Christian rulers never placed serious obstacles in the way of the enrichment of the dhimmis and the Mudéjars, especially those having highly specialized skills, and actually, they encouraged it. In addition to the general benefit that this brought to the economy, such a policy had an extremely practical implication, since the sovereigns could, in fact, without any problem, demand forced loans from those subjects who therefore constituted a good source of income. The same result would have been more difficult to achieve with their co-religionists. Therefore, the richer the dhimmis and the Mudéjars were, the better for their rulers.

Except in urban areas, in both Muslim and Christian lands, the majority of the subjects belonging to another religion were farmers, and their status and living conditions did not change significantly after the conquest of their land. Taxes and tributes to be paid to the new masters remained largely the same as before. According to the testimony of a Muslim traveler passing through the kingdom of Jerusalem in the twelfth century, the economic treatment received in the countryside by some of his co-religionists was better in Christian land than in the neighboring territories under Islamic rule. In the Christian kingdoms of southern Europe, there was a progressive transformation of many free Muslim farmers into land-bound servants. This was, for example, the situation of those residing in the vast estates of the Sicilian monasteries and churches in the second half of the twelfth century. In the Iberian Peninsula, however, relations between Christian lords and Mudejar farmers, similar to those of modern share-cropping, continued to be widespread. Similar contracts were also established in the Islamic world.

The progressive weakening of the Ottoman Empire from the end of the seventeenth century caused an increase in the tax burden on the subjects with their consequent impoverishment, particularly in rural areas, but this was a phenomenon affecting farmers of all faiths. The same conclusions apply to the request of free labor services to farmers by landowners. Following the edict of Tanzimat in 1839 in Bulgaria, Christian peasants refused to make them for their Muslim lords, who had privatized the lands the Sublime Porte had granted to them, and demanded full ownership of those estates. This provoked various uprisings that contributed to Bulgaria's independence movement. It should be remembered, however, that for similar reasons in the Middle East in the nineteenth century, there were various uprisings of peasants of all faiths.

Following the saying 'no Moro, no oro' (no Moor, no gold), the Iberian Christian landowners quickly learned not to create strong discontinuities with the agricultural production system created in the Islamic era. There were adaptations and some changes dictated by the new type of market and distribution systems, but there were no profound changes especially in the countryside, often characterized by intensive and profitable horticulture that was supported by a sophisticated irrigation system. In the Iberian Peninsula and Sicily, the increase of land destined to cereal and livestock farming was a rather slow process that became more rapid with the disappearance of Allah's believers from those lands.

Just as it had happened in agriculture, the role of dhimmis and Mudéjars in craftsmanship, regional trade, and retail did not change significantly after their land's conquest. The suppliers of raw materials often belonged to the faith of the other, as did the users of their products. For example, in Castile, Christian cattle breeders supplied Muslim butchers, and no one had anything to say about it. As a result, dhimmis and Mudéjars maintained a relevant position in the economy of the places where they lived and could not therefore remain excluded from the society.

For many years, in the Christian kingdoms of the Iberian Peninsula, the Muslims had almost the monopoly in various activities related to the high-level building sector (the manufacture of bricks and ceramic tiles, plaster and stucco work, and carpentry). Their skill was fully recognized not only by the sovereigns and nobility but also by ecclesiastical institutions. Numerous palaces and churches—still existing today—were largely built by those craftsmen and masons and had typical Mudéjar decorations. They often directed the construction and, sometimes, acted as supervisors of Christian labor. The most beautiful edifices were built in the twelfth century in Sicily where, however, the collaboration of craftsmen and masons of the 'Byzantine school' was quite important. The Palatine Chapel in Palermo and the churches and cloisters of Monreale and Cefalù are vivid and splendid evidence of those workers' skill and refinement.

When the Mudéjar style went out of fashion, the believers of Allah were able to adapt to the new demands and continued to be of great importance in those activities. The large number of colorful panels adorning late medieval churches and portraying people of various social classes, animals, caricatures, and monstrous creatures were in fact mostly painted by Mudéjars despite their representation being banned or strongly discouraged in Islamic art. Muslims also made the elaborate ceilings of the aristocratic residences. The information in our possession indicate that this choice was dictated by the great skill of those craftsmen and builders, not by the fact that they were a more economically advantageous option. The Muslim skilled labor was certainly not less expensive than the Christian one.

In the Christian kingdoms, the faithful of Islam also had a role of primary importance in the production of luxury fabrics, particularly silk, and in the processing of leather and the production of shoes and paper. One of the most elaborate and luxurious garments was the cloak prepared for the King of Sicily Roger II's coronation. In Spain, the skill of a silk maker was such that he was exempt from royal taxes for the rest of his life. Extremely appreciated were the refined products of the Mudéjar goldsmiths. Very important was the Muslims' role in the production of weapons intended primarily for the royal armies. Thanks to the widespread use of Arabic in their business and to the fact that the majority of that specialized labor force worked with family members, the faithful of Islam managed to keep their knowledge 'secret.' The Christians' use of Muslim slaves in those activities and the possibility of studying their artifacts, however, led to a slow erosion of Allah's faithful's monopoly in almost all those sectors.

Although they did not have the same prominence as the Muslim craftsmen had in Spain, in the Middle Ages, some Christians made a name for themselves in the House of Islam, mostly in Egypt, where some types of fabrics they produced and architects were famous. Many of the Andalusian Christians the Almoravids deported to Morocco in the twelfth century had skills acquired in their native land that the Moroccan rulers put to good use. In fact, in Marrakech, those Christians provided a valuable contribution to the construction of a huge and sophisticated hydraulic system to bring water to the city from a nearby mountain. In the sixteenth century, the majority of the artists and craftsmen serving the court of the Ottoman sultan were Muslim, but some of them were Christians from recently subjugated areas. For example, a Westerner from Egypt named Bastyian was hired for his skill in making seals and cutting diamonds. Russians and Ukrainians were among the manufacturers of muskets while two Christians captured in Tabriz were skilled in building shields. Christ's faithful were also those who in the sultan's palace at the end of the sixteenth century created the sophisticated and intricate geometric figures typical of Ottoman decorative art.

In those years, the weavers of the flourishing Angora wool industry in Ankara were Orthodox Christians as were, together with the Armenians for several centuries, the majority of the silk workers, especially in Bursa. Between the eighteenth and nineteenth centuries many northeastern Greeks were specialized in the spinning and manufacture of red cotton whose threads were greatly appreciated in Holland and England. They were so successful in Austria and Germany that in various villages and towns of that area many people spoke German, and a local shopkeeper named Mavros found it more convenient to be called Schwartz. Describing one of those villages in 1800, a European traveler wrote that it looked like a Dutch village. Although the mechanization of the textile industry had made some of those activities obsolete, others survived because of the high quality of their products. In the nineteenth century, one village produced a highly sought-after silk, and half of its production was exported to Vienna.

In contrast to the previous period, around 1645, the majority of the skilled labor in the main shipyard in Istanbul was made up of Greeks mostly from the Aegean islands and Crete, where the war between the Ottomans and the Venetians was in its infancy. Left unemployed because the Serenissima had greatly reduced shipbuilding in Crete, these workers had moved to the capital of the empire offering their services for such a low wage that they replaced the local laborers.

Although Christian craftsmen also had to face the competition of the European products in the nineteenth century, they and the retailers benefited from the wealth created in those years. Suffice it to say that, in 1850, there were forty Orthodox Greek trade guilds in Istanbul, each with about 350 members. Although they carried out a wide variety of activities, the presence of the Greeks was particularly high among bakers, shoemakers, furriers, tailors, and clothing sellers.

In addition to these jobs, the Armenians excelled in more sophisticated and lucrative occupations such as goldsmithing, diamond working, and jewelry (in 1806 sixteen of the seventeen best jewellers were Armenians; the other was a Greek). They also distinguished themselves in watchmaking (one of them was employed at the sultan's court shortly after 1860), in the production of weapons, carpet weaving, carpentry, and luxury furniture. In the nineteenth century, the Kemhajian family was the first to open a large plant in the latter sector. Much sought after were the ceramists, descendants of Armenians, who had migrated from Persia. They were always ready to adapt and develop new techniques to the point that their products were in high demand both in the Ottoman Empire and in Europe. Thanks to the discovery, in 1623, of the Zildjian family's founder, an Armenian alchemist who produced an alloy with which thin sheets of metal could be made that could emit musical sounds without shattering, this Armenian family monopolized the manufacture of cymbals used by believers of all religions for almost three centuries. In the nineteenth century, they became very famous in Europe, and all the best musicians and composers demanded that only the instruments made by the Zildjian be used in the performance of their works.

In the nineteenth century, the activities of the Christians in Istanbul, Thessaloniki, Izmir, and the other main urban centers of the empire were so flourishing that they attracted a constant flow of young co-religionists from rural areas who, after being employed as apprentices for a few years, hoped to open a workshop or business or to take over that of their employer. The increased well-being of many Christians undoubtedly increased the opportunities among the low-ranking co-religionists to obtain good employment. However, there was also the other side of the coin that is typical of the economically booming periods. In the cities, there were considerable increases in house prices and rents and the cost of living that only rich craftsmen and tradesmen could sustain, since the wages of unskilled labor were not adjusted to inflation. Many members of the working class, both Christian and Muslim, were therefore forced to live on a daily basis at levels slightly above subsistence level. Several Christians became rich at that time, but the majority of them were among the less well-off. The data in the register of the jizyah Aleppo's Christians paid in 1848—1849 are significant: 154 of them paid the tax reserved for the rich, 1262 for the middle class, and 2259 paid the lowest amount. In Bursa's textile factories, owned by the faithful of Christ, an unskilled Christian labor force worked, mostly women (especially young girls, widows and orphans), was paid very little per day, and employed seasonally. During economic crisis periods, they were the first to be laid off, and if it was not harvest time, very few of them managed to get another job.

Merchants and businessmen

The Muslim subjects of the Christian kingdoms did not participate in the trade with the Eastern Mediterranean and the Middle East; however, until their movements were drastically restricted, they took part in mercantile activities between the Iberian Peninsula, Sicily, and the Maghreb, where their linguistic knowledge was extremely useful. They were also present in regional and local trade networks. In the Middle Ages, Christian merchants residing in the House of Islam played a more modest role. Almost completely absent from the large merchant network of the Islamic world, they sometimes acted as intermediaries and agents of their Western European co-religionists. More important was their presence in regional and local markets, especially in Egypt under the Fatimids, where it was not uncommon to see wealthy Christian merchants. According to a Persian traveler, a Christ's faithful was rich enough to provide grain for six years to all the land of the Nile.

The situation did not change significantly in the early modern period in the Ottoman Empire. However, the Orthodox Greek merchants from Cyprus and Crete, who replaced the Venetians after the Ottoman conquest of those islands, and those from Izmir, Thessaloniki, and Istanbul, who actively participated in the flow from the Balkans and Anatolia of products and food needed to support the central administration, court, and army, played a significant role in the Eastern Mediterranean. They also supplied luxury goods to Muslim traders who then sold them to members of the Ottoman elite. In Syria that function was mainly performed by the Armenians who used Aleppo as a hub for trade between Iran, Iraq, and the Mediterranean. Thanks to them, between the sixteenth and seventeenth centuries, the Armenian community in that city became so rich that the Armenian archbishop of Nis in Cilicia was persuaded to move to Aleppo and to build the church of the Forty Martyrs there, after a rich donation was given to the city authorities. In the eighteenth century, several Syrian Catholic merchants successfully moved to Lebanon and Egypt.

The wealth, the range of action, and the number of Christians involved in commercial activities increased considerably from the end of the eighteenth century. As a result of the concomitant weakening of the Ottoman Empire, the industrialization of Europe, an increasingly Eurocentric world economy, and the advent of steam ships, which greatly facilitated transportation, Christ's faithful assumed a major role in trade both within and outside the Ottoman Empire. The business volume of Orthodox Christians in the area between Epirus and Thrace increased considerably and concentrated on the production and export of products in high demand such as tobacco and processed cotton.

Whether flying the Ottoman flag or those of Russia, Great Britain, and the Habsburg Empire, many of the ships circulating in the Black Sea and the Mediterranean had Greek captains and crews. For example, the agent of a wealthy Austrian merchant arrived in Thessaloniki in the summer of 1776 aboard a ship flying the Russian flag with a Greek captain from Izmir and a crew of Greek and Ragusan sailors to buy tobacco from local Christian merchants and send it to Trieste, from where it would then be sent to the markets of the Habsburg Empire and Northern Italy. Within a short time, the Orthodox Greek traders joined the European agents and opened offices in Crimea, where many of their co-religionists had moved in those years, and in the main European cities. Their importance was such that Greek became the lingua franca in the eastern Mediterranean. From the end of the 1830s, those changes also involved Anatolia and especially the Syrian-Palestinian area. The most visual symbol of this was the exponential growth of merchant activities and the size of port cities in Lebanon, Syria, and Egypt. An exemplary case was Beirut which grew from a town of seven thousand inhabitants into a very lively center with a hundred thousand inhabitants at the end of the nineteenth century. Also remarkable was the development of Izmir and Thessaloniki, thanks to their ports being suitable for steam ships.

With the elimination of restrictions and taxes applied to foreign merchants, various parts of the empire opened up to European merchants, who bought raw materials and sold finished products. Not knowing the local markets, languages, and customs, foreign merchants relied on indigenous intermediaries, mainly Christians and Jews. Typical of what was happening at that time is the description of the commercial network's functioning in Anatolia of a British company based in Izmir. His representative explained to the headquarters of the company in England that an agency had been set up in a small inland town where two Orthodox Christian brothers sold and bought on his behalf. Iron utensils, sugar, coffee, and indigo were sold on credit to local farmers and were later paid for with crops. The agricultural products were then either sold in other parts of the Ottoman Empire or exported. Many of Christ's faithful in those areas were able to benefit greatly from the new market economy by using the capitulations, which allowed the European consuls to grant them licenses that placed them under their protection. Intended for a few people that system grew enormously and, to the great scandal of the Muslims, several tens of thousands of Christians and Jews obtained those certificates. With legal and economic privileges guaranteed by the capitulations, they acted as agents of both the economic interests of foreigners and those of their Muslim partners. At the same time, Christians and Jews managed to remain competitive in the new economic system.

In those years, Christians usually preferred to engage in trading goods rather than in their production. In the sectors in which they had an important position, however, they tried to cope with the new economic scenario. Emblematic is what happened in Bursa, famous for the production of silk and manufacture of silk garments, made with artisan methods mostly by Christians. Competition with cheaper clothes from Europe and high state taxes were fatal for this activity during the first decades of the nineteenth century. However, Europeans were interested in the manufacture of raw silk, and in the 1840s, various factories with European machinery for the production of silk threads were created with European and native Christian capitals. A good number of those factories belonged to local Christ's faithful. However, Orthodox Christian businessmen refused to invest in industries largely managed by the Ottoman authorities because they did not want to engage in an activity over which they did not have full control. The diseases of the mulberry trees and the opening of the Suez Canal with the consequent import of silk from the East subsequently greatly damaged that industry. Thanks to the high demand for agricultural goods and the fact that it was considered a safer investment, in the second half of the nineteenth century, many Orthodox Christians businessmen used the profits from trade to buy or rent the most fertile lands in Anatolia, i.e., those located near the coast that had been little exploited until then. In particular, they concentrated on products that were easy to trade and guaranteed high yields such as mulberry trees, sugar cane, tobacco, and grapes. Toward the end of the century, this process moved toward the more inland areas. Most of the Muslim peasants had no capital for this type of investment, and the faithful of Christ bought some of their land which was then cultivated by either co-religionists, who had migrated to those territories, or seasonal Muslim workers.

Doctors, other high-level jobs, and entertainers

Heir to that of classical antiquity, Islamic medicine enjoyed such a great respect in the Middle Ages that the faithful of both religions widely used Muslim doctors in the Christian kingdoms of the Mediterranean, especially in the fields of surgery and obstetrics. In Spain, also popular were Mudéjar midwives and 'barbers,' who were greatly appreciated for their remarkable ability to perform small surgical operations. The fact that aristocrats and kings often resorted to them indicates that their quality and not economic convenience dictated their use. For example, the best doctors whom, in the second half of the fourteenth century, the king of Aragon, Peter the Ceremonious, could find for himself and his son, were Muslims. At the end of that century, the sovereign of Navarre granted a lifetime exemption from taxes to a believer of Allah and his family for having cured the court falconer of a very serious illness.

Even churchmen recognized the superiority of Muslim doctors. Significant, in this regard, is the case of the Spanish Cardinal Cisneros (1436—1517) who, after condemning the use of Moorish midwives, had to resort to the cures of a Muslim physician. According to a Christian chronicler, in the second half of the twelfth century, influenced by their wives, the nobles of the kingdom of Jerusalem despised western medicine and relied on the cures of Jewish, eastern Christian, and Muslim doctors. He added the malicious observation that they were poisoning all the aristocrats of the kingdom. A Christian doctor in the Holy Land admitted, however, that a Muslim colleague had cured the brother of a bishop whose illness he and other doctors could do nothing about.

However, the case of a European medical expert who cured an Allah's faithful in the kingdom of Jerusalem, whose sight Muslim and Eastern Christian physicians had concluded as lost, indicates that not all Western doctors were inferior to their Muslim colleagues. In the House of Islam, Christians took advantage of the opportunity to acquire excellent knowledge and high-level internships in that field and became esteemed doctors. As has already been mentioned, some of them also managed to become court physicians. Complaining about the low cultural level of his co-religionists, a Muslim geographer, at the end of the tenth century, polemically observed that almost all doctors in Egypt and Syria were Christians. The same thing happened in 1700 in Istanbul where out of twenty-nine surgeons, there were twelve Orthodox Christians, eight Jews, four Muslims, four Western Europeans, and one Armenian. Various Christian doctors were present in Syria in the thirteenth century, and some of them collaborated with their Muslim colleagues, while others were the object of hostility from Islamic believers in that area.

In view of the special relationship between the doctor and patient, both in the House of Islam and in the Christian kingdoms, there were religious leaders who, among the prohibitions, issued to separate the faithful from the infidels; they included some prohibitions concerning the use of the 'infidel' physician. During the Almoravid period in Andalusia, this practice was strongly discouraged while in the Maghreb, Muslim women were strongly advised not to use such doctors stressing that the medicine of Christ's faithful was not safe. At the beginning of the thirteenth century, in Europe, the Church forbade Muslim doctors from treating Christians; however, in the secular legislation this prohibition started to appear in a later period. In Spain, one way to hinder the practice of medicine for Islam's believers was to make it extremely difficult for them to obtain a doctor's certificate, which became obligatory from the fourteenth century onward. However, since it was a matter of having to choose between life and death or between being maimed or living healthy, the recourse to the doctors of the 'infidels' continued to take place in more discreet forms.

During the nineteenth century, the desire to modernize the Ottoman Empire and the expansion of the middle class among Christians went hand in hand with an increase in their literacy, especially in urban centers, and many of them had the opportunity to acquire a higher education. Many believers in Christ therefore became lawyers, pharmacists, doctors, and architects. Some had the opportunity to study in Europe, especially in the fields of agriculture and veterinary medicine, and then made use of their knowledge throughout the empire. They were among the first to open schools in the capital and other cities in those fields. Some of the most intelligent and well-prepared even managed to be employed as university lecturers. There was great demand for teachers and journalists to meet the increased demand in the fields of education and culture. As a result, there was a remarkable impulse in the production of newspapers, books, and other printed material. Significant is the case of Izmir which, being around 1900 a city mostly inhabited by Christians, had ten Greek, three Armenian, two French, and one Turkish printing presses. More and more open to novelties from Europe, the Armenians were the first to have photographic studios in the empire. The Viken brothers were the pioneers in that field acting as court photographers and photographing the most important Europeans visiting the capital in those years.

In Sicily, under the Normans and especially in the Christian kingdoms of the Iberian Peninsula, Muslim musicians, singers, dancers, and acrobats were so popular that they were present in most festivals, from those celebrated in the villages to the most refined ones in the palaces of the aristocracy. The best ones were hired permanently at the royal courts, and if a particular type of entertainer was needed or one wanted to hire a very famous one, the kings did everything they could to get them. Wanting to offer his guests a show worthy of his palace, in 1409, the king of Aragon commissioned an official to hire the famous Muslim dancer Nesma, her husband, an acrobat, and some Mudéjar dancers, specifying that he would have to oblige them if they refused his offer. In 1474, on the occasion of the coronation of the Queen of Castile Isabelle, believers of Islam performed sword dances. In Palermo, in the twelfth century, Muslim drummers and players of wind instruments were always used in events of that kind. In spite of repeated prohibitions in the Iberian Peninsula, Muslim musicians were a regular presence in the churches and processions of Corpus Christi, during which they were also employed as extras.

Rather widespread were contracts such as the one stipulated in 1498 between the city authorities of Elpina and Mahoma, hired for a year to dance and play the tambourine on Sundays and during the main Christian holy days. He was allowed not to work on Fridays even if there were celebrations on that day and to perform during his free time at the wedding feasts of Christians, Muslims, and Jews. In the fifteenth century Ali, on the other hand, took advantage of his fame in playing the trumpet and his diplomatic skills to be appointed by the king as the official representative in relations between Muslim farmers and the aristocracy of Navarre.

The faithful of Christ never had such a role in the House of Islam. In the nineteenth and early twentieth century, Christian and Jewish musicians, however, cheered the clients of some of Istanbul's cafes and taverns during the nights of Ramadan and the guests of Muslim weddings in Jerusalem; moreover, in the theatrical performances, the female parts were entrusted to non-Muslims. It is noteworthy that in this period the Porte was greatly opened to European-style modernization, and Christians were the most enterprising in the field of Western-style entertainment organization. In fact, it was an Armenian who founded one of the most famous theater companies in Istanbul that was acclaimed for its performances in Turkish during Ramadan. Another Armenian opened the first opera house in the capital while in Izmir, at the beginning of the twentieth century the Orthodox Christians controlled almost all of the city's movie theaters.

Working for and with the other

The previous pages highlight how, thanks to the excellent quality of the services offered, Mudéjars and dhimmis often worked for their dominators, who spared no expense in securing their services. The less sophisticated a job is, the more people are able to do it, but despite this, it was not unusual for Christians and Muslims to have at their service Mudéjar and dhimmi unskilled workers. This aspect emerges in particular from the accounts concerning the neo-martyrs of the Ottoman era about the experiences of Christ's faithful, usually young, in the service of Islam's faithful.

In the seventeenth century, Nicholas was employed as a baker in Sofia; in the eighteenth century, a man worked as a fisherman near Adrianopolis; and in the early nineteenth century, a group of boys was in charge of the camels of a merchant from Ephesus. Similar information can be found in the description of a violent robbery irregular Muslim troops carried out against a bakery in Thessaloniki in 1734. Among the victims were two believers of Islam, the owner and the baker, and a Christian shop assistant.

Attracted by the great expansion of Izmir in the nineteenth century, many inhabitants of the nearby islands moved there to serve the rich Muslims and Christians of the city. Sometimes radical ideas about purity emerged and attempts were made to prohibit the use of employees belonging to the other religion. For example, in Aleppo, in 1770, the confectioners' association prohibited its members from having dhimmi employees. These were, however, rare exceptions.

Both in the Muslim and Christian territories, neither wealth nor poverty were directly connected to the religious faith of the first- and second-class subjects. There were, therefore, members of the first group who, driven by necessity, accepted to be employed by the second. In the Middle Ages, in the House of Islam, there were some cases of Muslims who had low-level occupations, such as stableman, muleteer, and servant, under wealthy Christian employers, and the Almoravids forbade this in Andalusia at the end of the eleventh century. In the House of Islam, rich Christ's faithful used Muslim nannies, a practice not forbidden by Islamic jurists, who nevertheless recommended women not to carry out this activity in the Christians' homes. In the eighteenth century, in Aleppo, it was not uncommon for the faithful of Islam to work for those of Christ.

In the nineteenth century, there were some Orthodox Christian landowners in Anatolia who had no problem in hiring seasonal Muslim workers; they just had to do their job and were not too expensive. In some cases, they gave their land to cultivate to the faithful of Allah with whom they shared the profits. In the large port cities of the Ottoman Empire, it was not uncommon to see young Muslim apprentices employed by Christians (e.g., shoemakers), and the porters of all religions paid no attention at all to the faith of their clients. During the nineteenth century, in the Ottoman domains, many Western companies were active in various economic sectors (trade, banks, railways, and the production of textiles and food). Some of them were of considerable size and employed many Ottoman subjects, but the way in which they were recruited created a very tense atmosphere between the Christians and the faithful of Allah. The managers were, in fact, always foreigners; middle managers and qualified jobs were assigned to Christians and Jews, while Muslims were given the less specialized and therefore less paid jobs. In times of crisis, there was also a tendency to distrust the latter and to hire as little of them as possible. In turn, in the Christian kingdoms of the Iberian Peninsula, some believers of Islam used unskilled Christian labor, and sometimes attracted the attention of legislators. At the end of the fifteenth century, the Muslim constructors of Burgos were, for instance, threatened with a severe penalty if they continued to use Christian women as assistants in mixing plaster.

For those who were not used to working for that kind of employers, it was humiliating because they were in a position of inferiority toward second-class 'infidel' subjects. It was even more humiliating to be refused a job request, and this could lead to violent reactions. For this reason, in the eighteenth century, a Muslim from Aleppo even murdered a fellow Christian citizen. Such working relationships created difficulties, especially in the countryside, when the faith of the rulers changed. The annexation of the Thessaloniki region to Greece in 1912 put Christian farmers at the service of the faithful of Islam between two fires: to renounce their occupation, often the only one available, or to endure the threats and mistreatment of the gendarmes. The definitive solution to that dilemma came about ten years later when almost all Muslims were expelled from Greece.

On various occasions, the faithful of the two religions found it convenient to collaborate. In the Andalusian countryside, the scarcity of water and the complex system of irrigation canals, created during the Muslim domination, induced the believers of both faiths to collaborate in order to have the best yield from that precious resource for the fields. Consequently, the councils that regulated its use were formed by Muslims and Christians. This spirit of collaboration emerged especially during the harvest period, and it was quite common for neighbors of different religions to hire guardians to control everyone's fields. In construction and crafts, Muslim workers often carried out their duties alongside Christians.

In the main cities, there were various trade associations formed by members of the two faiths. In the seventeenth century in Istanbul and in the nineteenth century in Thessaloniki mixed guilds were about one third and one fourth respectively (in 1838, in the capital of the empire the percentage reached 50%). In the eighteenth century, for example, the silk weavers' guilds in Istanbul, Damascus, and Aleppo had those characteristics. In 1723, there were at least three of that kind in Sofia. Their leaders were always Muslims, even when the members were largely Christians; the latter were usually second in command. Some examples of mixed guilds can also be found in the Christian kingdoms of the Iberian Peninsula. In the late Middle Ages, however, they became increasingly rare, and sometimes attempts were made to create obstacles to Muslim colleagues to eliminate economic adversaries. The same thing happened with the use of Muslim labor in large projects, particularly those related to military campaigns. At the end of the fifteenth century, during the preparation of an expedition against North Africa, the Valencian rope-makers obtained that the Mudéjars were not to be employed in the preparation of the equipment, stating that they were allies of the enemies and were ready to provide them with weapons and information.

In the Middle Ages, there were a few cases of Christian and Muslim business partners. In the fourteenth century, in the Spanish town of Borja, believers of Christ and Islam ran an inn together; the fact that it was located in the Jewish district probably made that co-ownership possible. From the seventeenth century onward in the Ottoman Empire, Muslims participated more and more in the merchant activities of Christians as financers and sometimes as owners of ships used by Christian merchants and maneuvered and guided by Christ's faithful. It was quite normal for Christian businessmen to associate with or have the patronage of a powerful Islam's believer to be protected, especially when the clients were Muslims. In Cairo and Crete, it was quite common for soldiers to provide that protection. In turn, the faithful of Islam, who granted loans to Christian businessmen, made sure to have the support of soldiers to obtain the prompt payment of the debts. The collaboration between Muslim businessmen and Catholic Christians in Aleppo was very fruitful and of high level. At the end of the eighteenth century, the majority of both faith's elites invested together in various sectors, and economic competition was more among power groups than between members of different religions. In the nineteenth century, these collaborations intensified, and Muslims played an important role in the economic boom of various parts of the Empire, but it was usually the Christians who led the negotiations, and thus gave the impression that they were the only ones getting rich.

Slavery

Widely used in Antiquity, Christians and Muslims employed slaves among whom, thanks to military campaigns and piracy, the adversaries belonging to the other monotheistic religion were strongly present. Another source of slaves were the courts, which often turned the most severe punishments into slavery. In Spain, the believers of Islam who were guilty of having caused damage to a Christian and unable to compensate him were considered his slaves until they repaid him. The Mudéjars could also become 'fiscal slaves,' that is, they could serve Christians until they had paid a loan without losing their property and rights and could not be sold. Between the fifteenth and sixteenth centuries, the Ottomans instead installed numerous prisoners captured during the Balkans' occupation in lands owned by the Porte and Ottoman generals, assigning them plots, seeds, and tools and demanding half of the crops; they could, however, be sold together with the estates in which they had been placed.

Except for those destined in early modern times to row in galleys, to build public works (which was quite common in north-west Africa) and the Muslim slaves of Mallorca used in the countryside, slaves were not employed in large numbers as cheap labor, but were often used with rather specialized tasks in agriculture, construction works, and craftsmanship and as servants in houses and courts. In the Muslim ones, men were utilized as eunuchs, while some women were used as concubines in harems. During the Ottoman period, slaves could buy their freedom by paying their masters a certain amount of money or producing a certain quantity of goods. In this way, the owners ensured themselves very efficient workers. Some former slaves used that system and became successful entrepreneurs.

On conquering Tyre in 1124, the Christians instead allocated almost all the Muslim female prisoners to the production of textile products. Muslim slaves were also employed in Christian lands without Muslim subjects, such as northern Italy. Their strong presence in the kingdom of Aragon in various artisan and industrial activities led some guilds to impose certain limits on their use, evidently because they provided cheaper labor than Christian workers and therefore damaged many of Christ's faithful. Much appreciated and therefore expensive were the educated slaves. In Spain, in 1296, a Muslim doctor was sold for fifteen times the price of a common slave, while in 1263 some Christians in Acre rejected the Muslims' offer to exchange prisoners on the grounds that their slaves were very valuable because they were all artisans, and it would have been too expensive to replace them.

In the Iberian Peninsula there was a widespread use of Moorish slaves who were copyists and translators from Arabic. The famous theologian Ramon Llull (c. 1232–c. 1315), eager to learn that language, was given a Muslim slave to teach him Arabic. The Moor was probably a good teacher because Llull wanted to keep him even after he had tried to assassinate him. Taken prisoner in 878, the Syracusan Christian Anne put her intellectual skills and medical knowledge at the service of a Seville's Muslim savant who wanted to have clarifications on some medical terms present in a work written in Greek. Passionate about chess, in 1292, the king of Aragon ordered to look for experts in that game among the Muslims captured that year. Slave Moorish trumpet players were widely used in the courts and by the city and religious authorities of the Iberian Peninsula. Some Christian masters considered their slaves so valuable that they created a kind of insurance on them so that they could be compensated in case of escape.

There was no lack of persons not having any scruples about owning foreign co-religionists. Around 840, the Sicilian Helias fell into the hands of Muslim raiders, was then sold to a Christ's faithful, and taken to North Africa where he was bought by a rich Christian tanner from that area who freed him a few years later. In the 1720s, in Thessaloniki, a Ukrainian slave girl, who knew how to sew, embroider, weave, and cook very well and wished not to have a Muslim master, was bought by a French merchant with the proceeds of the lottery organized among his countrymen present in the city. Similar examples can be found among Muslim subjects in Sicily and in the Christian kingdoms of the Iberian Peninsula, but in their case, there was a greater tendency to free slaves. This practice was hindered in the fifteenth century by imposing that the sum to free the slaves had to be collected in the House of Islam or an exchange with Christian prisoners had to be organized.

In Europe, the use of slaves ended at the end of the eighteenth century, while in the Ottoman lands the utilization of slaves, especially enslaved Christians, decreased more and more in the nineteenth century and, despite various prohibitions concerning the slave trade, legally disappeared only with the end of the empire. When the sultan was deposed at the beginning of the twentieth century, his harem was closed, and the court slaves were freed.

Fighting for the other

Muslim rulers never allowed Christian subjects to serve in their armies. As we have seen, one of the most important prohibitions for the dhimmis was to have no weapons. In the convulsive post-conquest period of the Near East, however, it happened that in 645 the Copts, who felt persecuted by Constantinople authorities, helped the Arabs to repel a Byzantine attack against Alexandria. Events of this type were, neverthless, rare exceptions; moreover, that news is reported by a late source on which there are suspicions of forgery. Given that it is unlikely that the Arabs quickly learned the art of naval warfare, and that in the second half of the seventh century, the faithful of Christ in the coastal areas of the Middle East had not converted en masse, it is possible, however, that the crews of the large Muslim fleets that began to circulate in the Mediterranean at that time were mostly made up of former Byzantine subjects, eager to give their contribution in naval expeditions against their former rulers.

In case of extreme necessity, the Muslim leaders, especially the Ottoman governors, gladly accepted the military collaboration of their Christian subjects. For example, in 1735 there were Christians of Nazareth among the troops led by a Bedouin leader against his Muslim opponents in Nablus. In 1743, during the Persian invasion of the Mosul region, the Ottoman commander of the city enlisted the Christians from a nearby village and then rewarded their valor in the defense of Mosul by allowing them to rebuild the churches the enemies had destroyed. At the end of the 1830s, in order to put an end to the Druze uprising in Lebanon against the military conscription, thousands of rifles were handed over to the Christians of that region. The rebellion was suppressed and the restitution of the weapons was requested, but the episode greatly increased the tension between the two communities.

Some Muslim leaders employed foreign Christian warriors in their armies. Taking advantage of the lack of cohesion between the small Christian kingdoms in the North of the Iberian Peninsula, between the ninth and tenth centuries, the believers of Allah obtained troops from them on various occasions as a part of the tributes they had to pay. In the second half of the tenth century, the famous vizier Al-Mansur used them in his campaigns against his Christian adversaries. The same thing happened with the Ottoman Turks on the Balkan peninsula and in some parts of Eastern Europe between the end of the Middle Ages and the beginning of the early modern period. These contingents were usually assigned the task of ravaging the enemy territory before the arrival of the regular army.

In the Balkans, it was not unusual to have fortresses garrisoned by Christian troops under the command of Turkish officers. Many of those soldiers converted to Islam. There were, however, moments of tension between the members of the different faiths. For example, considering his Muslim comrades' jokes about Jesus intolerable, in the fifteenth century, a Christian Bulgarian soldier insulted Muhammad and then paid with his death his instinctive reaction.

Quite common was also the use of Christian warriors for a limited period. In the Iberian Peninsula, the golden age for those adventurers was the eleventh century—years in which the caliphate of Cordoba shattered into numerous principalities often fighting among themselves and against the Christian kingdoms of the North of the peninsula. The most famous was Rodrigo Diaz, better known as 'El Cid,' who distinguished himself for serving both Muslim and Christian rulers, fighting against their enemies regardless of faith, and for having created an independent dominion in Valencia after taking the city from his Muslim employer. A similar behavior occurred in Sicily when the political unity of the island's Islamic believers broke down. Invited around 1061 by the governor of a Sicilian city to defeat a rival, the Norman leader Roger of Hauteville soon discovered how weak that Muslim was and therefore decided to conduct an independent campaign to conquer Sicily.

Although they presented themselves as the champions of pure and rigid Islamism, the Almoravids and Almohads used Christian soldiers in the Maghreb against their Muslim adversaries and to suppress revolts. Knowing their loyalty and perhaps wanting non-Muslims to perform a thankless task, the Almoravids also employed them as tax collectors. The chaotic situation created in Egypt in the 1060s and in the 1070s, with the arrival of the Turks, led the caliph of Cairo to take a drastic decision. In order to eliminate his opponents, he asked the intervention of one of his cities' governor, named Badr, a former Armenian Christian slave converted to Islam, and successfully opposed the Turks. Times were extremely difficult, and the caliph did not give importance to the fact that there were many Christians in Badr's army, especially Armenians. The choice turned out to be right, and order was restored. Thanks to those Armenians and others who had fled their lands occupied by the Turks, Badr and his descendants succeeded in obtaining the position of vizier.

The considerable size of the empire and the impossibility of having regular troops everywhere forced the Ottoman authorities to use Christ's faithful with police duties to fight banditry in remote areas and mountain passes. Used mainly in areas of Greece inhabited predominantly by Christians, this system allowed the residents to carry weapons and guaranteed them a wide autonomy. In other parts of Greece, Christ's faithful, called armatoles, were enlisted to keep internal order during war campaigns requiring the deployment of local Muslim garrisons. However, this system had the disadvantage that at the end of the war the majority of the armatoles were dismissed. Not wanting to carry out other activities, some of them placed themselves at the service of the private militias of local lords, while others joined the gangs of outlaws, thus fuelling internal disorder.

Except for one episode in which the ruler of Tyre summoned all available men, including Muslims, to defend himself from an attack by the Venetians in 1264, the Christians of the kingdom of Jerusalem never allowed believers of Islam to serve in their army. Too great was the fear that they would spy or take sides with their enemies. Only those who had converted were allowed to fight among the Christian ranks as archers on horseback.

There were no such qualms in Europe. Apart from expecting the Muslim subjects of the inhabited centers, located in the recently conquered border areas of the Iberian Peninsula, to climb the walls together with the Christians to defend the community from attacks by marauders of any faith, the Christian rulers often used Muslim subjects in their armies, especially in their wars against their Christian rivals. Both Frederick II in Italy and the kings of Aragon and Castile had Allah's faithful in their personal guard. They distinguished themselves above all by the use of the bow and crossbow. The sovereigns of Navarre employed them as artillerymen in the fifteenth century, while the Portuguese allowed the Muslims to serve in the cavalry of their army.

Islamic soldiers often proved to be excellent and highly motivated warriors, probably, because in addition to having the opportunity to improve their social and economic status, this was the only time when a Muslim subject could without any problem use weapons against a believer of Christ. During the French attack against Catalonia in 1285, the king of Aragon sent Islamic believers to repel the invaders. On that occasion, the Muslim lancers and crossbowmen of Valencia were highly praised by the sovereign for their skill in the use of weapons and their courage. After the conquest of Sicily at the end of the eleventh century, Roger of Hauteville forbade any attempts to baptize the faithful of Allah serving in his army, thus contravening the papal invitation to do so. This measure was intended not to create discontent among his Muslim subjects and to guarantee the presence of soldiers well-disposed to fight the Christian enemies of the Norman leader. In Italy, too, those faithful of Muhammad proved to be excellent and brave warriors and succeeded in raising their social and economic status. The enemies of the rulers who used them accused them of having allied themselves to the Muslims to destroy Christianity. Taking advantage of the fact that many Mudéjars were allowed to possess weapons, the aristocrats and even Iberian military orders used Allah's believers in clashes with Christian rivals.

In the absence of Muslim subjects, some Christian kingdoms and potentates in the Mediterranean had no scruples about employing Muslims in conflicts with their Christian enemies. For example, in southern Italy, in the ninth century Neapolitans, Gaetans, Salernitans, and Beneventans used Islamic contingents from Spain, Sicily, and North Africa, while in the fourteenth century the Genoese and the Catalans of the Duchy of Athens used Turkish warriors. The same thing was done by the Byzantine sovereigns. Turkish warriors served in the army of the future emperor Alexius Comnenus when he took Constantinople toward the end of the eleventh century; since Alexius Comnenus allowed his army to sack the city, the Turks did not hesitate to plunder churches and convents. In the fourteenth century, the personal guard of Emperor John VI Cantacuzenus was mainly composed of Turks; they were so appreciated that the sovereign ordered to let them practice their religion undisturbed. At the end of the eighteenth century, during the campaign in Egypt, Napoleon, on the other hand, had little success in his attempt to enlist Egyptian Muslims to fight against the Ottomans despite having tried to make them believe that he had converted to Islam. He took some of them with him on his return to Europe, and Goya portrayed them in a painting depicting the uprising of the inhabitants of Madrid against the French in early May 1808.

In the Middle Ages, it was not uncommon in border areas to use Islamic believers to avenge an offense. Extremely bloody was an episode in which an Armenian, who had been humiliated by the Byzantines, was involved. Much more serious consequences were the invitations to intervene addressed to the faithful of Islam by Byzantine rebels. Refusing to recognize the legitimacy of the new Byzantine emperor, in the 820s, Thomas the Slav placed himself at the head of numerous dissidents, who with the help of the Muslims even managed to besiege Constantinople. Much more serious and longer lasting effects produced a few years later the request for help to the Muslims of Tunisia by the Sicilian Euphemius, who wanted to seize power in Sicily. His allies in fact began a series of campaigns to subjugate the island.

The familiarity with weapons of the Christian subjects in some areas of the House of Islam and especially of the Mudéjars meant that, in addition to gangs of criminals, formed by members of the same religion, there were also some made up of Christ's and Islam's believers. As was the case in the regular armies, more attention was paid to skills and efficiency than to religious faith. In the Iberian Peninsula criminal groups of that type kidnapped Christian children whom they circumcised and then sold them. The leaders of those gangs were both Muslims and Christians. For example, in the kingdom of Aragon there was 'Garcia el Moro' at the end of the thirteenth century among the first and at the beginning of the fourteenth century, Sancho de Ravanera among the second. The latter proved to be extremely loyal to his men in trouble regardless of their religion to the point of conducting a raid against a prison in 1322 to free a Muslim member of his band.

4

Sharing beliefs and spaces

Beliefs and holy sites

Islam has strong connections with Christianity and Judaism because Muhammad had not 'created' a new religion but considered himself as the last prophet of God. While denying his divine nature, Muslims believe that Jesus was a prophet and have great respect for Mary, John the Baptist, and the main characters of the Old Testament. It should also be remembered that popular devotion among Muslims, Christians, and Jews shared many characteristics. In times of need, many of them preferred to ask for help from prestigious intermediaries who, having also been human beings, could better understand the difficulties of life and help to find a remedy. The requests essentially concerned the problems of the present, for example, the health of family, friends, and working animals and the fertility of people and of the earth. Obviously, the more prestigious was the saint or prophet, the more likely it was to see the entreaty granted, which took on a special force if it was made in places strongly connected with those people. These peculiarities therefore facilitated the existence of sacred spaces for all the faithful of the three monotheistic religions where they sometimes prayed together.

Closely related to biblical accounts, Palestine and Syria have a remarkable abundance of sacred sites. Much visited by Muslims, Christians, and Jews were (and still are) the Hebron tombs of some patriarchs of the Bible. In that area, there was a spring that was said to be the place where Adam and Eve hid after being expelled from Eden. Along the roads on Mount Lebanon, there were several piles of stones believed to be the altars on which Adam and his sons Cain and Abel had made sacrifices. Also popular was the throwing of stones against the tomb of Absalom, the rebellious son of David, located near Jerusalem. On the western outskirts of Damascus, it was believed that God had created Adam from clay, while around that city there was the 'cave of blood' in which Cain had killed his brother. The spot where Saint Paul had received his vision was instead marked by a simple pile of stones just outside Damascus.

Another famous site was the church near Nablus where the head of John the Baptist would have been buried. According to others, that precious relic had been kept in the main church of the Syrian capital. It was then demolished by the Muslims and the main mosque of the city was built on its site. However, the spot where the head was located was marked with a special column that had become sacred for both Christians and Muslims. Particularly devoted to this saint, an Ottoman sultan donated a large quantity of candles in 1699 to illuminate the site. In a monastery near Damascus, there was an icon of Mary considered miraculous by members of both faiths.

Many Allah's faithful and Jews attended Christians' celebrations at Joseph's Prison, located in a suburb of Cairo. Near Acre, there was a spring where it was believed that God had given Adam an ox to help him plow the land. Muslims had built a mosque there, and when the Christians conquered the area in the twelfth century, they added an altar. The faithful of the two religions shared that sacred space and prayed there together. In some places of the Christian kingdoms of Spain, there were the tombs of Christian saints and famous Muslim ascetics and the faithful of the two religions went there to worship their 'champions' without any problem.

In the House of Islam, Muslims did not fail to promote in various ways the relevance of some of those sites to their faith. With the clear intent of creating a physical and spiritual link with the patriarchs' tombs in Hebron, the belief that a cave in the vicinity of Gaza associated with Muhammad's grandfather led to the cave beneath those sepulchers became widespread among the faithful of Allah. In one of the most famous of them—that of Moses—with a skillful propaganda move aimed at underlining the goodness of the new government, one of the first Mamluk sultans, Baybar, had a mausoleum built there in 1269. That initiative probably also had the objective of making the importance of the site for Muslims equal to that for Jews and Christians, exercising a certain control over pilgrimages and perhaps revitalizing an economically depressed area. The Ottomans continued this approach, expanding the mausoleum and sponsoring the spring pilgrimage in particular. The success of these initiatives was such that even believers of Islam from India participated.

In the early modern period, the Ottomans made a more explicit attempt to exercise control over a special place for the faithful by cutting in two the rock on which the footprints of Christ were believed to have remained when he ascended to Heaven from the Mount of Olives. The left one therefore remained there in a small chapel, while the other was taken inside Jerusalem. In a village near Hebron, a mosque was built in order 'to take possession' of the so-called bed of Abraham, a large rock where the patriarch was believed to have rested. Since it was in a Muslim religious building, the dhimmis were forbidden to pray there. Many believers of Islam went there after having seen the tombs of the patriarchs. The most important process of appropriation of a sacred place with the exclusion of the faithful of the other religions took place with the Mosque of the Rock in Jerusalem. Inside there is a rock that, according to the Muslims, bears the im print left by Muhammad at the beginning of his nocturnal ascension to heaven, a circumstance making Jerusalem the third most important city for Islam. The Christians instead believed that the footprint was that of Christ, while for the Jews it belonged to Abraham.

There were also people whose great fame transcended a particular location. Exemplary is the case of Mary for whom, as has already been observed, the Muslims had a great veneration. Having conquered Jerusalem, the caliph went to pray on Golgotha and at the tomb of Jesus's mother. When a Turkish general learned that he had unconsciously crossed a frozen lake in northern Greece, he thanked Mary for the danger he had escaped and ordered a chapel and then a monastery to be built there. At the end of the seventeenth century, in a village in northern Lebanon, the faithful of Islam allowed new Christian arrivals to build a chapel in her honor. In 1735, both for his own devotion and to ingratiate himself with the Christians of Nazareth who militated among his troops, a Bedouin chief, before going into battle, went to the church of the Virgin in Nazareth and, prostrating himself before the door and rubbing his head in the dust, asked Mary for victory and promised to supply oil to the church for the rest of his life if he were victorious. The presence of the faithful of Islam in the church of the Nativity in Bethlehem was so common that a niche facing toward Mecca was made for them.

In many areas of the House of Islam, the faithful of Allah participated in the celebrations for the assumption of Mary. On that day, the tents of the two religions' faithful mingled on the slopes of the Mount of Olives in Jerusalem. In the evening, Christians and Muslims went together to the chapel of the Virgin Mary bringing votive offerings and praying, the former using the rosaries and the latter amulets with the initial verse of the Koran.

Not even the very high tension between Christians and Druzes in Lebanon in the nineteenth century and the bloody massacres perpetrated in 1858–1860 by the latter against the former put an end to the Druzes' veneration for the mother of Jesus. After the carnage carried out in 1860 in the most famous Marian shrine with the accompaniment of the bells of that site rung in contempt of the faithful of Christ, the Druzes did not dare to go there for three decades but continued to send votive offerings through Christian acquaintances.

Muslims had an even more special veneration for Saint George, the knight slayer of a dragon and savior of a virgin. Believing that he protected them from all evils, many of them kept an image of him at home, sometimes with a blessing from the Koran, and went to pray in the Christian churches dedicated to him. This happened so frequently that in some religious buildings, the direction to Mecca was indicated. In the church of a Syrian village, it could be found praying in front of a painting depicting the saint. Muslim popular devotion often merged this saint with al-Khidr (Hidirellez for the Turks), the mysterious character, who in the Koran teaches Moses the knowledge of God, and the faithful of Allah sometimes told Christians that George was their saint.

In some cases, the fusion of the two characters was used to give a sense of continuity between old and new rulers. In Anatolia, the first Turkish dynasty used bilingual coins depicting Saint George, and many places were associated with al-Khidr and considered sacred even by Christians. This saint was also perceived as a symbol of resurrection and renewal, and therefore his feast day near the summer solstice was so common in Anatolia that the faithful of both religions often celebrated it together. Muslims considered that day so special that their women could participate in the celebrations along with men. Usually the believers of Islam did not attend the ceremonies in churches but took part in the festivities after mass by bringing food. Some Muslims in the rural areas of that region thought it was a sin to work during that holy day and therefore cooked and fed the animals the day before. In the nineteenth and early twentieth centuries, Muslim itinerant farmers serving Orthodox Christians landowners in Anatolia had a special preference for that feast because they were invited and ate very well. In Ottoman times, the dervishes had great admiration for Saint George and other Christian saints, while Sinassos' Christians worshipped a famous dervish by giving him a Greek name. In Bosnia, Muslims celebrated the feasts of Saint George, Saint John, and Saint Barbara, and many of them kept icons of saints in their homes. Although it was a less common practice, some Christians also worshipped individuals clearly related to Islam. For example, many Christians went on pilgrimage together with Muslims to the shrine of Dahi—a companion of the prophet Muhammad (south of Nazareth).

In the House of Islam, the faithful of Christ could not enter the prayer rooms of mosques (a ban still in force in almost all Muslim countries), but the Ottomans did not always enforce that prohibition when they had been churches. In the seventeenth century, without creating any scandal, the custodian of the mosque in a Bulgarian town charged the local Christians who, still having great veneration for their former church, wanted to pray there. In Domuz Dere, a small town in Anatolia, Muslims had appropriated a church dedicated to Saint George, but in the nineteenth century, Christians were allowed access to it to commemorate the saint. According to a western traveler, even the believers of Islam celebrated it and 'did not mix with the Christians any more than necessary.' The dervishes who had occupied the place divided it into various sections, keeping intact the most important parts of the ancient building, including the wall where there was still an ancient icon of Saint George for whom they had great devotion.

Although the church of Saint Helena in Homs (Syria) was transformed into a mosque at the beginning of the sixteenth century, the symbols of the Christian faith were not completely erased and Christians were able to pray there quietly. They did the same thing so often in the former church of Saint George, converted into a Muslim religious building, that they paid half the oil burned in the lamps of that structure. It was widely believed that Sultan Selim's mosque in Adrianopolis was built on a church called the Ascension. For this reason, Christians were permitted to pray there on the feast of the Ascension of Mary, the day on which one half of the place was occupied by Muslims, who prostrated themselves in their prayers, and the other half full of Christians, who with candles in their hands prayed and made the sign of the cross. After the devotions, they went to a spring in the center of the mosque and took water from there, believing that on that day it was blessed.

In Thessaloniki, in the church of Saint Demetrius, transformed into a building of Islamic worship, it was thought that the remains of the saint were still preserved there, and therefore in the nineteenth century, Christians were allowed to visit the sanctuary, and like them the superintendent of the mosque, a dervish, showed great veneration and trust in the miraculous powers of Saint Demetrius. Also at that time, near an Anatolian village, there was a sanctuary dedicated to Nempi Hodja, a pious Muslim religious leader who died in a reputation for holiness, and the local Christian population believed that they could access the grace of Saint Theodore on that site, thus recognizing that some aspects of Christianity had been taken up by some special believers of Allah.

To indicate how different the practices could sometimes be from the rules and prohibitions at the top of the main mosque in Beirut were a cross and a crescent moon. According to tradition, when the Muslims had transformed a church into that building, they placed a crescent moon there, but it had been damaged by lightning on several occasions. At the suggestion of a newly converted to Islam, they put a crescent and a cross a little lower down and the lightning did no more damage. It is not possible to ascertain the truthfulness of this story, which underlines the desire to give some satisfaction to the large Christian community of the city that had been deprived of its main place of worship. It is important to note that the two symbols aroused astonishment only among the Western visitors. The good relations between the faithful of the two religions in the town of Lydda (Israel) allowed for a real cohabitation. A church in ruins dedicated to Saint George was divided into two parts. The Christians took the eastern section where there were the remains of the main altar, while the Muslims took the western part.

Along with those of places and characters, there were also temporal overlappings. Despite their religious authorities' disapproval, on the day of Saint George, the Andalusian faithful of Allah celebrated the feast of Al-'Ansara. On that occasion, Muslim women put decorations in their homes, did not carry out any activities, and put their clothes out at night so that they would soak in dew, a good-omen custom whose origins were lost in the mists of time. After his conversion into a mosque, the basilica of Saint Demetrius in Thessaloniki continued to be a center of worship for the Christians, and it is noteworthy that the feast of the saint (at the end of October) became for the Turks that of 'Father Autumn,' which for soldiers and sailors marked the end of military service and navigation. In Homs (Syria), a popular Sufi commemoration took place during the Christian Holy Week. Thanks to the respect most Anatolian Allah's faithful displayed toward the Christian saints and holy days and in general to their faith and good behavior, in the nineteenth and early twentieth century, various Christians of that area stated that their Muslim neighbors also belonged to the people of God and therefore could access the benefits Jesus, Mary, and the Christian saints provided.

Folkloric beliefs

According to many Muslims and Christians, the places and characters just mentioned possessed thaumaturgical powers. To solve their problems, sterile couples and mothers without milk were advised to spend the night in caves those individuals had frequented. From the 'Cave of Milk,' where Mary would have breast-fed Jesus, Muslims and Christians took some powder with which they prepared potions in the hope of solving their breast-feeding problems. To cure the same problem, those of an Anatolian village drank water from two springs located near a chapel. By attributing miraculous powers to the drops falling from the ceiling of the cave dedicated to Saint Thecla near Damascus, the farmers collected them in a basin to be kept at home. According to an Orthodox Christian in the early twentieth century, near Göbelye, an Anatolian village inhabited only by Muslims, there was a spring dedicated to Mary and Christian and Muslim girls from the region used to go there on Saturdays to light a candle hoping to obtain the protection of Jesus's mother.

During periods of drought, farmers of all faiths took part in propitiatory processions. Without anyone having anything to object, biblical figures were included in rituals prior to the birth of Judaism. The one seen in 1854 in Palestine is emblematic. Faithful of Christ and Allah paraded through their village singing vows and carrying in procession a sort of doll representing the 'Mother of Rain' and placed on a cross. This happened even in areas inhabited exclusively by Muslims.

In Alaşehir/Philadelphia (Turkey), there were the remains of an ancient church dedicated to Saint John, and at the beginning of the nineteenth century, the belief was still widespread among Muslims that at night the spirits of the martyrs, who had died in the name of Jesus, wandered on that place and that the ruins possessed healing virtues for toothache. By placing a lighted candle on its walls, one was sure to have immediate relief from pain. Although it was a less common phenomenon, Christians also attributed thaumaturgical properties to sites connected to Muslim popular devotion. On the outskirts of Konia, there were two rocks believed to be the petrified horses of a famous Islamic religious leader. According to the faithful of both religions, children unable to walk and women unable to conceive healed by straddling those rocks.

In many parts of the House of Islam, believers of all faiths made sacrifices of animals in very similar ways and for very similar purposes that also had their roots in the era before the birth of their religions. Worthy of note is the one performed to obtain the favors of the already mentioned al-Khidr for Muslims, Saint Helias for Christians, and the prophet Elijah for Jews, because it was performed in the same place near Haifa and above all in the same way and for the same reason. All the faithful dipped a finger in the blood of the sacrificed animal and then placed it on the forehead of the person for whom that sacrifice was made to protect him from disease. In various parts of the Balkans under the Ottomans, Muslims performed similar rituals in churchyards.

Additionally, there was no lack of sites and practices, common to the faithful of both religions and not related to the Bible or the saints, but to magical-folkloric beliefs. For example, in Nazareth, there was a column in ruins where women with fertility problems or wishing to ensure a normal pregnancy went to put a thread around it and then put it around their hips. In a land largely characterized by arid or desert areas such as Syria, the Orontes, the main river in the region, had always been considered to have special powers. Once a year, farmers drained the irrigation canals connected to the Orontes to clean them, after which they let the water flow back into them. On the night of the day the barriers were reopened, their women bathed in the canals believed to be made fertile again by the water spirits. In various parts of Anatolia, the custom of sacrificing a goat and placing its head in the foundations of a building to provide it with solidity was quite common.

Fascination with churches and Christian liturgy

Reacting to the austerity of their religious practices and many mosques, there was no lack of Muslims who felt the fascination with churches and symbols and rituals of the Christian religion. In the relaxed atmosphere of the court of Caliph Hārūn al-Rashīd (786–809), a poet magnified the monasteries around Baghdad and extolled the majesty of the great crosses carried in procession and the solemnity of the offering of bread and wine during mass and the beauty of the rites held at baptisms. A Spanish Muslim traveler praised the beauty of the Martorana church in Palermo, which he visited on Christmas night in 1184. As proof of this type of attraction, a Muslim jurist from Seville at the end of the eleventh century advised Muslim women not to attend churches so as not to become prey to licentious Christian clergymen.

Fascinated with the Holy Sepulcher of Jerusalem, in the early modern period, the sufis sometimes gathered there and danced with great pleasure to the sound of the organ European monks had installed there in the seventeenth century. Usually, the custodians and those in charge of the churches followed the precept that the 'House of the Lord is open to all,' but the ecclesiastical hierarchies were not always in favor of the presence of Muslims in their sacred sites and, not being able to prohibit their entry, they sometimes reproached or dismissed the superintendents who invited the faithful of Allah to do so. However, the fascination of various rulers with monasteries, especially in Egypt, was mainly due to the idyllic scenery and the beauty of the gardens of those places. Although the monks were not happy about it, some Fatimid caliphs used them as destinations for outings, venues for their feasts, and bases for hunting expeditions. In spite of this, there were no cases of mistreatments and outrageous gestures against the Christian religion. The caliphs were also often generous to the monasteries by donating property and funds for their embellishment.

Believing that they could benefit from the sacredness of certain Christian holy days and fascinated by their liturgy, many Muslims attended particular Christian celebrations. Very popular was the rite taking place in the church of the Holy Sepulcher in Jerusalem on the Saturday before Easter, the day when it was believed that a miraculous fire lit all the lamps in the building. Many Muslims also considered the blessings given on Palm Sunday to be extremely beneficial. In the thirteenth century, a Turkish sultan took refuge at the Byzantine court with his family, and during his stay, his children took communion without being baptized and he participated in processions and masses on the main Christian holy days. When he returned to his homeland, the patriarch of Constantinople was put under investigation for such behavior, but in the end, it was preferred not to punish him.

In Egypt, several Muslims complained that some co-religionists visited the monks and sometimes took the host. They also accused Christians of wanting to deceive the faithful of Islam who were ignorant by telling them that by baptizing their children they would live a long time. Some did this even before they were circumcised. In Anatolia, at the beginning of the twentieth century, many of Allah's faithful took sick children to monasteries to be sprinkled with holy water. Such practices still exist. A few years ago in a church dedicated to Saint George in Palestine, some Muslim women asked priests to baptize their children to protect them from disease. A faithful of Allah often visited the church of the Nativity in Bethlehem with a Christian friend. The latter also lit candles for the Muslim woman and members of her family, after which the faithful of Allah did the same for her sick relatives and her brother imprisoned in Israel. In the nineteenth and early twentieth centuries, Muslim itinerant laborers, employed by Orthodox Christian landowners in Anatolia, returned to their families on Saint George's Day and, before leaving, asked for the blessing of their employers.

Both in the House of Islam and in the Christian kingdoms, Christ's faithful were generally unwilling to absorb Muslim practices and beliefs. Islam had after all come after Christianity, and the vast majority of the Christians saw no connection between the two religions. In territories far from the centers of Christianity and Islam, inhabited by small Christian communities and characterized by a relaxed religious atmosphere as in the Mongolian Turkish countries, however, it could happen that some Christians adopted some Muslim customs such as polygamy, performing ablutions before entering places of worship, eating meat on Friday, and considering that day a holy day.

In times of weakening of the ecclesiastical structure and loss of prestige of Christian religious leaders, it was not uncommon for Christians in the House of Islam to go to pious Muslim men for spiritual support and protection. For example, in the sixteenth century in Egypt, many of Christ's faithful began to turn increasingly to sufi leaders. In one case, they even asked for the help of a pious Muslim although he was known to be hostile to the dhimmis. He was asked to write a blessing on an amulet to protect children and the sick. When he asked why they had come to him, he was told that they had more faith in him than in their religious leaders, including the patriarch.

Syncretisms

Alongside the sharing of beliefs, places, and times, forms of syncretism between the two religions characterized some Muslim mystical groups, especially some dervishes. According to one of their famous spiritual leaders, who lived in the thirteenth century, exteriority has no importance, and the true devotee is capable of praying in any building of worship. His heart contains all the faith, and there is no difference between the sacred books of the monotheistic religions. The biographers of pious dervishes report that, to obtain conversions to Islam, they often used Christian themes and miracles similar to those of Jesus, such as walking on water, multiplying the loaves and fishes, and raising the dead. A Turkish text about a dervish saint reports that a Christian monk decided to adhere to Islam because he recognized Jesus in that man. According to some Muslim preachers, Christ had the same dignity as Muhammad while others believed that he was the son of God. They displayed such a good knowledge of the Gospels that they were considered Christ's faithful who pretended to be Muslims out of convenience. Some of them were executed for their syncretism.

Those ideas did not remain among those mystics' narrow circles. During an exchange of confidences, the grand vizier of Sultan Suleiman (1520–1566), Rusten Pasha, would have told a Christian ambassador not to believe that those who had led a life marked by strong moral principles would suffer hellish punishments because of their religion. According to a German pilgrim who went to Jerusalem, his Muslim guide told him that everyone would be saved according to the professed faith. Although at the end of the nineteenth century in Anatolia going to other people's religious buildings was considered only a form of respect, it is relevant that some Orthodox Christians pointed out that a mosque was also 'the House of God.'

The combination of a relaxed atmosphere on these topics and a real convenience is to be attributed to the conduct of some Albanian shepherds in Ottoman times. They were called 'miso-miso (half-half)' because they followed the Christian faith in the mountain pastures during the summer and behaved like Muslims in the winter on the plains. According to the wife of the English ambassador to Istanbul, who passed through Albania in the early eighteenth century, some of the local inhabitants could not decide which was the true religion and so as not to be mistaken they went to the mosque on Friday and to the church on Sunday. During the Ottoman period, this form of double membership also distinguished some Macedonians. When asked what their religion was, they made the sign of the cross and said they were 'Muslims, but through the Blessed Virgin.'

In some remote areas, the lack of a clear differentiation between some of the faithful of the two religions could sometimes lead to not knowing what was the creed of the deceased without relatives. For example, the death of a woman living in a village near the Black Sea, called by some with a Greek name and by others with a Turkish one, caused a dispute between the two communities. This occurred again in the nineteenth century in that type of area. In 1859, a woman buried in a Christian cemetery was exhumed and buried in a Muslim cemetery for that reason. There was, however, no certainty about her religious belief.

Celebrating and partying together

From the previous pages, it is clear that in the House of Islam many Muslims gathered to pray and take vows together with the dhimmis in places and times sacred to all faiths and often explicitly connected to the Christian religion. Several Fatimid rulers showed their favor toward the local Christian population by subsidizing the main religious celebrations and sometimes participating in them, while in Istanbul the Ottoman grand viziers attended Easter ceremonies as a form of respect. In Egypt, on Palm Sunday, Christian clergymen went in procession to the homes of the main Muslim officers singing verses from the New Testament and blessing those faithful of Allah.

For many Muslims, the main Christian festivities became moments of encounter and provided the opportunity to celebrate together with the faithful of Christ and to strengthen friendships and good neighborly relations by exchanging food and gifts, especially at Easter when Christians invited Muslim acquaintances. On that occasion, many believers of Islam loved to be gifted with boiled eggs painted red and blessed during midnight mass. It was a gesture to which they attached great importance, because they believed that the eggs would bring good luck and protect against evil spirits. 'Give us blessed bread and give us red eggs, otherwise we turn into vampires,' said a Turkish proverb. They therefore expected to receive them and were offended if this did not happen. In the Balkans, however, some Muslims imitated their Christian neighbors by dyeing eggs for Easter.

The presence of a large minority of Christians in Egypt and the close connection between their religious holy days and the various phases of the Nile made them extremely popular among Muslims. Those for the baptism of Jesus coincided with the completion of the annual cycle of the Nile; at that time, the river reaches the lowest level from which it then rises. In the evening of that day, Christians made processions toward the Nile carrying candles and torches and singing hymns, after which they immersed themselves in the river. According to a centuries-old belief, in that way, one would acquire protection from disease for the whole of the following year. Although the Christians had been deprived of the right to announce the growth of the Nile, because Egypt would prosper only if it was ruled by those who professed 'the true religion' and police officers circulated through Cairo remembering that Muslims and Christians should not mix, many believers of Islam celebrated that day and performed that ritual together with Christ's faithful. The next morning the Christian religious leaders thanked the authorities for allowing them to celebrate that day publicly by giving a sermon in Arabic and praying to God in favor of the Muslim ruler and his court.

The other important Nile-related festivity was the day when the river level reached a sufficient height to ensure a normal flood, which is essential to ensure a good harvest. Usually this happened between the beginning of August and early September, and on the eleventh of September, the Copts celebrated it during the feast called Nawruz. On the third of May, they also dipped a relic—a martyr's finger—into the river, claiming that the Nile would not have grown without that ritual. Many believers of all faiths attended both celebrations that were followed by great feasts which a large number of Muslims joined. For Nawruz, the Fatimid caliphs and their dignitaries offered banquets and gave gifts, thus turning it into a kind of semi-official state celebration.

Many people took advantage of those events to let off steam and lose the inhibitory brakes, thus transgressing the laws and Islamic precepts. According to a Muslim writer, at Easter many Christians and Muslims went outside of Cairo to a bridge where large tents were set up under which they could eat, drink, listen to music, and dance. The parties, emphasizes the author, degenerated shamefully with the mixing of women and men who drank so much wine that many of them had to be taken away completely intoxicated. Even wilder were the feasts for the martyr's finger immersion ritual. On that occasion, writes another Muslim author, one could see people of all classes, singers of both sexes, prostitutes, transvestites, and evildoers of all kinds. The Christians dared to ride horses and played acrobatic games on them. The amount of wine consumed during the festivities was enormous.

In the fourteenth century, on the occasion of Nawruz, a sort of ceremony was created during which the normal rules were reversed. Elected by the crowd and dressed in red and yellow clothing—the official colors of the Mamluks—the prince of Nawruz was mocked in a ritual similar to those of humiliation practiced by the rulers. Prostitutes, transvestites, and entertainers led the crowd, made up of both Christians and Muslims, in a playful hunt for the rich, who were released after light blows were inflicted on the back of their necks—an obvious parody of the ritual slap sometimes given to the dhimmis during the payment of the jizyah—and after paying a symbolic ransom. It is also noteworthy that that day coincided with the day on which a share of the annual taxes was paid to the state. These celebrations never degenerated into violence and riots, and the reversal of the rules and the public mockery of the powerful took place only during that celebration. The criticism of the rulers was, however, evident.

The Mamluk authorities did not tolerate those feasts for long, and among the obligations and prohibitions concerning the signs of distinction and the use of dhimmis in the public administration, they added some concerning Nawruz. Despite the high sums the state earned in those days through taxes on alcoholic beverages, the martyr's finger feast was banned in 1303. It is important to note that at that time the rumor circulated among the Muslims that the relic belonged to a Christian who had converted to Islam and had then been executed for having publicly repudiated it. That object therefore represented a challenge to the Muslim religion and authorities from various points of view. The re-establishment of the commemoration in 1338, probably caused by the need to replenish the state coffers, was short lived. In 1354, during violent riots against the Christians, an angry crowd razed to the ground the church containing that relic, the finger was symbolically burnt in a public square in front of the sultan, and its ashes were scattered in the Nile so that the Copts could not recover them. The money lost with the lack of income from the taxes on alcohol consumed on that occasion was abundantly recovered through the seizure of all the assets of the Coptic Church that were destined for charitable works.

At the beginning of the fifteenth century, those rituals were no longer celebrated publicly and the Mamluk government thus obtained to dissociate them from the cycle of the Nile and to prevent Muslims from mixing openly with the faithful of Christ. In the following centuries, however, numerous Christian commemorations, attended by many Allah's faithful, were celebrated outside the large urban centers so as not to attract the attention of the Muslim religious and secular authorities. For example, that of the Cross (end of September), coinciding with the ritual for the flooding of the Nile, by order of the patriarch of Cairo was no longer held in the Egyptian capital, but in every Egyptian village. The very popular wrestling competitions and pony races held for the feast of Saint George and organized by the Muslim community did not, on the contrary, cause any controversy in Anatolia.

Although they were not comparable to the celebrations taking place for the main Christian holy days, in the House of Islam, several believers of Christ joined those of Allah on the occasion of the most important Islamic festivities. This phenomenon was quite common after the sunset of the days of Ramadan, when the fasting performed by the Muslims ended, and especially for Bayram, the joyful feast for the end of that period. On those occasions, the main areas of the cities were illuminated, and markets, cafes, and gambling houses were kept open, and music was played everywhere. These entertainments were so popular that when the governor of Damascus ordered during Ramadan in 1819 to arrest a large number of Christians to punish them for a heated dispute between two of their factions, the soldiers did not go to their homes but went to the places just mentioned and took so many believers of Christ that it was necessary to put some in the stables. An Orthodox Christian from Anatolia recalled how, at the beginning of the twentieth century, at the end of Ramadan, his father gave his Muslim 'best friend' a lamb saying 'May your Bayram be blessed,' while a co-religionist from Chios recalled the happiness with which she when a child, had received sweets from her Muslim neighbors on that day. On that occasion, in the nineteenth century, in Istanbul, the dhimmis were sometimes allowed access to the courtyard of some mosques and toward the end of that century to enter the prayer room. An important source for the festivities celebrated together by Muslims and dhimmis is the early nineteenth-century image (reported in this book's cover) portraying a festival held in a large open area in the Ethiopian district of Athens. One can see Muslim women dancing, musicians, vendors offering their wares, and men of all religions, recognizable by their headdresses, socializing with each other. Noteworthy is that the latter are all armed.

In the Christian kingdoms, there was never a phenomenon similar to that taking place for the main Christian festivities in the House of Islam. In Spanish cities, however, some of those ceremonies also had a strong civic dimension and were perceived as a time of celebration and socialization for all inhabitants, including the Muslims. Perhaps because it occurs in late Spring, the one that most took on such aspects was the Corpus Domini. Throughout almost all of the Middle Ages, the faithful of Allah freely participated in the processions held on that day, both as extras and as spectators. They were also allowed to wear traditional clothes and decorate their houses as Christians did. Relations between Christians and Muslims worsened during the fifteenth century and in some parts of Spain, various prohibitions were imposed on the presence of the faithful of Islam at that event. In Valencia, however, the Corpus-Domini processions and celebrations were so popular that even at that time they were able to attend them without any problem and considered it so important to be there that many Muslims came from all over the Valencian region. To prevent ordinary people from participating in Christian festivities, which could lead to conversion, the Mudéjar leaders promoted the commemoration of events not approved by Orthodox Muslims. To the same end, pilgrimages to the tombs of pious Muslims were encouraged. Despite their success, these initiatives did not diminish the number of Allah's faithful attending the celebrations of the Christian holy days.

The faithful of the two religions also found themselves together for collective rituals and prayers not related to entertainment. For example, an Egyptian ruler at the end of the ninth century asked all his subjects, including Christians and Jews, to gather and pray for his recovery. Although the situation of the dhimmis had worsened considerably in Egypt in the fourteenth century, in 1373, during a severe Nile shoal, Jews and Christians participated undisturbed in processions to invoke the rain by holding their sacred texts above them. Similar episodes occurred in various regions of the House of Islam. Even at the beginning of the twentieth century, in case of drought, Anatolian Christians and Muslims went to a certain place to pray according to their own customs and without wearing any distinctive religious signs. In the Lebanese countryside, such processions continued to take place until a few years after the Second World War.

In areas and periods characterized by good relations, the presence of believers of both religions at the funerals of important leaders or of a neighbor of the other faith was quite common. Usually those who did not belong to the religion of the deceased prayed according to their beliefs in a low voice out of respect for the dead and his co-religionists. In 1723, the funeral ceremony of the Dutch consul in Izmir, Hochepied, loved and respected by all, for example, attracted a huge crowd of Muslims, Orthodox Christians, and Jews. The same thing happened for weddings. In 1184, a Muslim traveler passing through Tyre, then under the Christian rule, was fascinated by a wedding procession of two Christians and noticed that faithful of both religions attended it. Numerous testimonies report that this occurred in many villages at baptisms as well.

There were, however, some limitations. At the beginning of the twentieth century, an Anatolian Orthodox Christian, in fact, specified that during those events, Muslims never showed their women. Another Christian of that period added that they too behaved in that way and that the women of the two faiths celebrated together in an area reserved to them. According to another witness, Muslims invited Christians to their wedding feasts, but they did not do the same because the believers of Islam did not drink or dance. The reason for not having them at their celebrations was therefore not religious, but only because they were boring guests.

Residential patterns

In the Middle Eastern Muslim cities, during the Middle Ages and the first two/ three centuries of the Ottoman Empire and in those of the Iberian Peninsula and Sicily, the desire to feel safe and close to their place of worship led to the creation of areas with residents of the same religious background that, however, were not hermetically sealed. The same characteristics distinguished the urban centers of the Christian domains with Muslim subjects. In the kingdom of Jerusalem, in the town of Nablus, in the twelfth century, for example, an inn for Muslims was located opposite a tavern owned by a Christian. Although it was an exception, it is noteworthy that in a rather large town in the kingdom of Aragon like Tarazona at the end of the fourteenth century, there was no Muslim quarter separate from the others. In the main cities of that kingdom, it was not uncommon for Christians to acquire property or settle in the local moreria. In turn, some believers of Islam of Burgos settled in the Christian areas of the city for lack of housing in their neighborhood. In this regard, it should be remembered that in the Iberian Peninsula, the laws on residential segregation did not spread widely until the fifteenth century. Sometimes, it was the Mudéjar communities that requested the construction of walls to separate their neighborhood from the Christian ones in order to avoid contamination and to protect themselves; in some cases, local authorities hindered such requests probably because they did not want to have a fortified enclave. Even in the urban centers where this separation had always existed, the faithful of the two religions lived so closely together that cases such as the one of Lleida were possible. In this Catalan city, Muslim and Christian cemeteries were contiguous, and in some points, they overlapped and graves were not religiously distinguishable to the point that it was discovered that some nonattentive Christians had prayed for the salvation of dead Muslims.

With the passing of the centuries in the House of Islam's great urban centers, there was a progressive move toward a residential model with religiously homogeneous nuclei rather than entire districts with that characteristic. It happened therefore that Christian districts in cities like Cairo were adjacent to areas inhabited by Muslims. As we have seen in the chapter dedicated to justice, in the Egyptian capital in 1485, a Christian bought a house from a believer of Allah and had Muslim neighbors who tried in vain to send her away with the excuse that her dwelling was higher than theirs. Already in 1100, in Cordoba, a Muslim requested the cancellation of a house's purchase when he discovered that he had to share the well with some dhimmis.

In some cases, the mixing was favored by how the Muslims were settled in the cities conquered by the Ottomans. In Thessaloniki, Sultan Murad II (1446–1451), for example, placed them in houses left empty by dead or runaway Christians. In that city, there were some districts still mainly occupied by Christians, but the upper part, the best thanks to the availability of fresh air and water, had mostly Muslim residents. With the passing of time, there was a progressive integration of various areas, and in the nineteenth century, a district of Christ's faithful was within a Muslim area, but still in that period the city resembled a series of villages that communicated with each other. When Thessaloniki was annexed to Greece in 1912, few districts were exclusively inhabited by believers of the same religion. According to the 1913 census, there were 40,000 Orthodox Christians, 45,867 believers of Islam and 61,439 Jews. The upper part was still predominantly Muslim, while in the lower part, strong was the presence of Jews. A high residential integration characterized the other areas; less than a third of the population lived in districts where people of the same faith reached 80% of the residents. About half of the Muslims lived in areas with those characteristics.

Residential integration was instead a little lower in the old part of Jerusalem at the beginning of the twentieth century. Muslims, Christians, and Jews each had a neighborhood in which they represented the majority. The districts with residents almost exclusively of the same religion were a Muslim neighborhood (95%) and a Christian district (93%) and were located near the main entrance to the esplanade of the mosques and the church of the Holy Sepulcher and the Greek Orthodox Patriarchate, respectively. In the other five districts, there were residents belonging to two and sometimes all three religious faiths and their percentage varied between 20% and 40%.

In the first centuries after its conquest, Muslims in Istanbul settled mainly in the old part of the city, located within the walls of the Golden Horn. Half the inhabitants of the capital were dhimmis. Subsequent immigration from the surrounding countryside and other areas of the empire favored a certain degree of mixing in many urban centers, especially in the Balkan area. From the end of the seventeenth century onward, in various Bulgarian cities, associating an area with the Christian population began to exist less and less. In the Balkan and Eastern European cities, different types of residential models were found, ranging from a clear separation to a widespread residential integration. The names of the districts can also be misleading, as in the case of the Kurdish district of Aleppo, where at the beginning of the twentieth century, 93% of the population was Christian.

Although in the eighteenth century, the majority of Aleppo's Christians resided in the northern part of the city, they often had Muslim neighbors. The impossibility for the many Aleppan Christians to live all near the churches forced them to take long walks and to pass through areas inhabited by many believers of Allah to attend mass. The area itself, where their buildings of worship were located and the ecclesiastical hierarchies lived, had Muslim residents who moved there because they were attracted by the prosperity of the area and the economic opportunities it offered. Izmir, the second largest city in the Ottoman Empire, continued to have five districts (the Muslim, Armenian, Greek, Jewish, and 'Frankish' = European), but they never had clear boundaries. In more peripheral areas, like that of Karatash, at the beginning of the twentieth century, the subdivision between Orthodox Christians and Muslims was, on the contrary, more clear-cut. In some cases, the members of the various religious groups preferred to reside according to census as in nineteenth-century Istanbul where most of the wealthy's houses were located around the sultan's palace.

An excellent example of a mixture of different religions' residents and a proof of good neighborliness is provided by an episode that happened in the capital of the Ottoman Empire in the eighteenth century. Five rabbis and more than twenty Greeks, Armenians, and Muslims living in the same district went to an Islamic court and obtained the expulsion of a Jewish prostitute who, working day and night with men of all religions and ethnicities, caused a great uproar in that area. At the same time, in districts with predominantly Muslim residents, the Islamic religious authorities often managed to banish from their neighborhood the dhimmi owners of taverns located in the vicinity of mosques and to have their houses granted to Muslims. This, for example, happened in Istanbul in the summer of 1744 to eight Christians following protests by a delegation of Muslims led by two religious leaders.

In general, the mixing process accelerated in the nineteenth century due to the rapid expansion of several cities in the Ottoman Empire. The property market made a clear division between Christians and Muslims impossible, and many of them lived in areas outside their old neighborhoods. Some even found themselves living in the same building. Many of Christ's faithful also became rich through trade and had the opportunity to buy larger houses, often located in areas inhabited by Muslims. If the house was owned by a religious leader, however, problems could arise, and Christians tried to be cautious and obtain permission to move in. Confirming how this could become a thorny issue and how it was sometimes used to underline the inferiority of Christ's faithful is the case of a Greek agent of the Venetians in Thessaloniki who, wanting to buy a house in the center of the city previously owned by a Muslim religious leader, obtained permission from his successor. Later the new governor of Thessaloniki told him that the Koran did not permit that action.

However, there was not always a gradual move toward greater intermingling among the faithful of the various religions. It happened in fact that, for reasons of security, the opposite direction was followed. The most relevant example is that of Damascus, where in response to tensions during the seventeenth and eighteenth centuries, there was a partial reversal of the trend that occurred in the Middle Ages, when numerous Muslim shopkeepers had settled in Christian districts and mosques had been built there. Although it did not cease completely, residential integration decreased. There were also small and medium-sized urban centers in the Ottoman Empire with a population almost entirely Muslim like Nablus, the capital of a district composed of about three hundred villages, also with the same characteristics as that capital. The surroundings of Tripoli were, on the contrary, marked by various villages whose residents were largely Christians. Many similar cases occurred in Anatolia and especially in the Balkans. This phenomenon sometimes occurred also in the Middle Ages both in the Muslim and in the Christian domains.

In the Ottoman Empire, religious and ethnic mixing was quite common in the hans, commercial buildings that offered accommodation to merchants passing through; later on, employees, soldiers and unmarried men also lived there. Since this happened in the inner courtyards of such structures, this phenomenon was not unusual. In general cohabitation worked, but sometimes it generated disputes and conflicts. For example, in a han in Istanbul in the sixteenth century, Allah's believers protested strongly because they could not stand the prayers of their Christian roommates.

Hangouts/meeting spaces

In addition to religious buildings and shrines, there were also public and private spaces where believers of all religions met and socialized. An almost obligatory meeting point was the public oven, especially in villages and towns where it was not economically viable to build one for one's own family needs and those of the neighbors, and therefore all the inhabitants used them without any restrictions. Also the places used for washing clothes, usually on the banks of a river outside the city walls, were frequented by everyone regardless of their professed faith. Mudéjars and dhimmis had their own markets, but their presence was not unusual in those of others, especially in large urban centers, where the religious background of buyers and sellers was usually of no importance. In the bazaars of Istanbul and the main Ottoman cities, artisans and retailers of all faiths displayed signs in the main languages of the empire so as not to miss any customers. Butchers' shops were an exception, because Muslims required animals to be killed in a particular way. However, various situations could be created. In some areas, the sellers of fabrics and clothes could be of all faiths, while in others, there were only Muslims and in others only Christians. Usually the availability of large areas for the markets favored the presence in the same place of sellers and buyers of all religions.

In Anatolia, during the Ottoman period, in towns and villages with a mixed population, there were usually two squares. The smaller one was located in the Christian area and around it were their main shops and cafes. Food vendors set up stalls there, and weddings and other festivities were held there because the space allowed dancing. The biggest one was in the Muslim district, and it was where the bazaar and the main mosque were located and the believers of Islam held their festivities. Despite these divisions, both places were not precluded to the faithful of the other religion. In the last decades of the nineteenth century in the great cosmopolitan cities of the Ottoman Empire, the old squares were renovated and enlarged and new ones were created where large crowds of subjects of all religions gathered on the occasion of the ascent to the throne of a new sultan, the anniversary of this event, and visits of important foreign officials and dignitaries.

In those years, the European fashion of strolling and carriage rides was adopted in those urban centers at the end of the working day and during the festivities in large open areas of the cities, which were sometimes specially renovated for that purpose. However, it is not clear whether these habits were widespread among the entire population, and probably only the more westernized and wealthy Muslims practiced them assiduously. In Izmir, all ethnic and religious groups frequented the banks of the river Mélés, but the Orthodox Christians and the Europeans preferred strolling along 'La Bella Vista,' a small peninsula located in the north-western part of the city and characterized by the presence of the most luxurious cafes in Izmir. In Beirut, the seaside promenade to the harbor light-house was very popular. The middle classes preferred two gardens in the city. One of them was located in one of the main squares—the entrance fee ensured that only they were present—while the other, English style, was located in a small wood on the outskirts of the city and had been created by an Italian convert to Islam; in the evening, a band played there under a gazebo. Another popular meeting place in Beirut was the hippodrome built in the suburbs in 1893.

In the Mediterranean world, attending public baths was an ancient tradition followed by the members of the three monotheistic religions. It had hygienic-sanitary and ritual implications (for Jews and Muslims) and was a further opportunity to socialize. Despite the prohibitions, in the Middle Ages, both in the House of Islam and in the Christian kingdoms, believers of all religions frequented those places. The prohibitions concerned only males, and it is therefore not clear whether it was taken for granted that they also applied to women. During the Ottoman period, it seems that women of both faiths used the same baths, but in moments of tension, such as in Aleppo in the eighteenth century, on several occasions, the law was passed against this practice. In Istanbul, there were no prohibitions, but it was insisted that the believers of Islam and the dhimmis used different towels. In the kingdom of Jerusalem, the Muslim traveler and ambassador Usama (1095–1188) met Christians on various occasions in the baths and socialized with them. In 1840, a French envoy of his country's Foreign Minister had a different experience during his visit to Sofia shortly after the bloody repression of a revolt of Christian peasants. At that moment of great tension, at the invitation of the governor, he was able to visit the main bath of the city, but when he touched the water of a swimming pool to determine its temperature, a Muslim came out of the pool shouting that the French had contaminated his water.

Places of entertainment and male sociability par excellence, the taverns, to which cafes were added in the early modern period, were locations where men would gather to relax and discuss a wide variety of topics by offering each other drinks, sharing small plates of food, and playing cards. Even though the ubiquitous taverns were intended for the consumption of alcohol, they were, despite the prohibitions, frequented by believers of both religions both in the House of Islam and in the Christian kingdoms. In 1100, an Islamic jurist from Seville, for example, thundered against his co-religionists who crossed the river to go to a

Christian neighborhood for that purpose. In the Middle Ages in the Spanish city of Elche, the excessive consumption of wine in the taverns caused so many fights that the local Mudéjar community asked the king not to allow their members to go to Christian ones. Several Muslims of Izmir enjoyed losing the inhibitory brakes in the taverns in the city's European district, and their excesses were such that in the eighteenth century the European consuls asked, with no success, that they be banned from those places.

To warn the faithful of Christ against the duplicity of the believers of Islam and the danger of frequenting them, especially in those locations, one of the texts about the early-modern neo-martyrs is, not by chance, set in a tavern. A Greek shoemaker, named Nicholas, who had settled in Sofia, was highly esteemed by his co-religionists and the believers of Islam for his work and good character and therefore had friends among the faithful of both religions with whom he often socialized in taverns. One evening, he got drunk with some believers of Islam, and when he woke up, he discovered that his drinking buddies had circumcised him and made him a Muslim.

A judicial source from 1307, on the other hand, allows us to have some details about the clientele of one of those meeting places in an area dominated by Christians with a large number of Muslim subjects. A passing Christian, named Tomas, went to a tavern located in a village near Valencia and joined some patrons intent on drinking wine and playing dice. Among them were Christians, neo-converts to Christianity, and Muslims. Tomas and a believer of Allah lost all their money and even had to pledge their clothes to a Christian. The continuation of the story provides further information on another entertainment that could be obtained in those places. A Christian prostitute gave her contribution to the entertainment of that group by putting herself in the post, but emphasizing that she was available only to her co-religionists. As proof that not all of her colleagues made that difference, in 1311 in the kingdom of Aragon, any contact in the taverns between Christian sex workers and Muslims was forbidden. A mixed clientele characterized the many taverns in Istanbul run by Christians despite various attempts to prohibit the sale of alcohol to Muslims. In them, the believers of Allah could easily obtain dhimmi prostitutes.

The cafes were widespread in the Ottoman Empire—every village had at least one—and most of the time, the believers of Allah and Christ had their own. Muslims frequented those of the Christians looking for entertainment such as alcohol and music, usually absent from their premises, and their number increased considerably at the end of Ramadan. The most common reasons for going to each other's cafes were those related to work; traders and landowners usually met there for business with partners and customers. In the second half of the nineteenth century, some cafes in the great cities of the Ottoman Empire had a cosmopolitan clientele of all religions and became similar to those in Europe. People went there to read the newspapers, to play billiards, and to buy cigars; some offered beer as well.

Inspired by the reforms of the Tanzimat period and the massive presence of Europeans and wealthy traders of various religions, in 1873, the elite of

Thessaloniki founded 'The Thessaloniki Circle,' a club that, imitating the European ones, offered a luxurious meeting place and sociality to the wealthy classes of the city without any distinction of faith and nationality. It was set out in writing in the club's bylaws that nothing should ever endanger its climate of solidarity and harmony. In 1887, it had 159 members among whom were the richest merchants, landowners, bankers, the city's chief of police, and the most famous doctor and lawyer in Thessaloniki.

In those years, the young free thinkers of the middle class and the elite gathered in Masonic lodges that became so widespread that by the end of the nineteenth century every city in the empire had at least one. Here too the religious background was very mixed. In 1869, fifty-three of the one hundred and forty-three members of the 'L'Union d'Orient' lodge in Thessaloniki were Muslims, while at the beginning of the twentieth century of the one hundred and fifty-seven Freemasons in Palestine, 45% were Muslims, 33% were Christians, and 22% were Jews. In addition to being a point of encounter and exchange of ideas between people with different religious backgrounds, the Masonic circles had the function of strengthening solidarity and cohesion among the emerging classes and provided their members with the opportunity to expand their business.

The same considerations expressed about the fashions imported from Europe into the Ottoman Empire at the end of the nineteenth century apply to those who frequented places of entertainment. Izmir, the most cosmopolitan city of the Ottoman Empire and with the highest percentage of Christians, was indeed multicultural, and there were various forms of entertainment—bands, theater groups, and opera house—but, except for the boy scouts, everything always remained rather segregated. In the large Ottoman urban centers, some trade associations were made up of members of both faiths who periodically organized picnics outside the city. In the eighteenth century in Istanbul, this was the case for silk manufacturers. At a certain point, however, Christians refused to participate because of the bad treatment they received.

Although a state school system was created in the Ottoman Empire on the French model from 1869, the students of the public schools were mostly Muslims, and those places therefore did not become a meeting point for children and young people of various religions. On the contrary, this opportunity was provided to the children of elites and professionals, often sent to study in foreign institutes created between the end of the nineteenth and the beginning of the twentieth century in the main cities of the empire. Some of their parents were able to be educated in a religiously mixed environment by attending Christian schools usually considered better than the Muslim ones. For example, despite the strong tensions between the faithful of the two religions in Lebanon, the wealthy Beirut's Muslim merchant Salim Salam studied at the local patriarchal college and sent his sons to the American school in Beirut, while for the girls he first hired Christian instructors and then enrolled the eldest daughter 'Anbara in a nuns' school and then in a girls' school created by an Islamic association, presided by him, and entrusted to a Christian teacher. The marriage between the latter and a friend of Salim Salam was one of the first among the faithful of the two religions of Beirut to take place by free choice. Growing up in such an open and varied environment, as an adult 'Anbara was the first Muslim woman in Lebanon to present herself without a veil in public. Among the first Muslims in Izmir to study in a Christian school was one of the first Turkish novelists, Halid Ziya, son of a rich carpet merchant, strongly criticized by conservative Muslims because of his works.

The domestic space was not exclusively reserved for co-religionists either. Several Europeans who visited Anatolia in the nineteenth century were struck by the absence of animosity between Christians and Muslims and the fact that they were more at ease with each other than the Orthodox Greeks with the Armenians and the Anatolian Turks with co-religionists belonging to other ethnic groups. Telling of his journeys on horseback through Anatolia in the 1860s, an Englishman observed that there was great harmony between 'Turks and Christians' in those areas and that every time he dined with an Armenian, he always found 'Mohammedans' there, while when he went to a Turk's home, there was usually an Armenian. Many of the Orthodox Christians forced to leave Anatolia after the First World War remembered how extremely common it was to exchange visits with neighbors and Muslim friends, underlining the great climate of cordiality. Some landowners said that this often happened with the faithful of Islam of their social class, and in the summer, they spent two weeks in their country estates receiving magnificent hospitality and eating excellent food. Everyone was treated with the utmost respect and the men went hunting together. According to an American missionary, the same thing happened in Palestine in the nineteenth century. Probably, this phenomenon also distinguished other areas and periods for which we do not have such sources.

5

Attacking the other

Hostile attitudes and verbal attacks

The most common forms of hostility toward subjects not professing the rulers' religion were fairly modest in nature and did not go beyond ironic comments and insults. In all likelihood, stereotypes and jokes about the other did not circulate only among coreligionists but were also used to offend those of the other religion and reinforce their inferiority. Verbal hostility toward Christians was quite common in areas characterized by their strong presence. In the Middle Ages, they were often called 'polytheists' to underline that, because they believed in the Trinity, Christ's faithful did not have only one God. Furthermore, the Muslims called 'worshippers of the Cross' the Christians to portray them as idolaters.

According to a popular saying in Egypt, God divided astuteness into ten parts; nine were given to the Egyptian Christians and one to the rest of humankind. During the Ottoman period, it was maintained that a Coptic Christian without slyness was like a tree without fruit. They, however, were the shrewdest of all people in little things and the most ignorant in great ones. Referring to the easy conquest of the Nile's land, it was underlined that the Christians of that region became slaves of whoever subdued them. Attributing to them a scarce adherence to religious practices, it was also claimed that 'the cold lasts as long as a Christian fasts,' that is, not long. According to a story that aimed to denigrate Christians and present them as superstitious savages, they used to drown a virgin in the Nile every year in order to have a normal cycle of flooding. The first Arab governor of Egypt prohibited this ritual, replacing it with the throwing of a piece of paper containing a prayer to Allah, thus demonstrating how a civilized people, following the true religion, behaves. Moreover, the faithful of Islam often called the Christians 'dogs,' one of the worst insults for the Muslims since they believed that dogs were impure and carriers of bad luck and disease.

In some cases, offensive comments about Christianity were intended to provoke a strong reaction in their targets in order to justify inflicting an exemplary lesson on them. As already noted, unable to bear the crude humor about Jesus of his fellow Muslim soldiers, in the fifteenth century, a Bulgarian Christian was sentenced to death for retorting with insulting comments about Muhammad. Christians were sometimes asked their opinions about Islam and its prophet with the same objective. Since they were immediately recognizable and were the most prominent defenders of Christianity, the ecclesiastics were often the victims of such attacks. In the mid-ninth century, for example, in a market in Cordoba, a group of Muslims pestered a monk several times with pressing questions about his views on the Islamic faith. After a few vague answers, the churchman fell into the trap, calling Muhammad a false prophet, and consequently paying for his words with his life. Most of the time, however, such verbal aggressions did not have these consequences. They were either answered with humor or not answered at all.

This type of trap was not used on Muslim subjects in Christian lands, yet the habit of spreading stereotypes and insults about the other was quite common there as well. Islam was labeled a false religion and a concoction of superstitions taken from several heresies, while Muhammad was considered a charlatan who had succeeded in convincing the Arabs that he was a prophet with his tricks and magic. It was said that he had raised a bull from birth and had trained it to come to him and kneel when he heard his master's voice. When he wrote a book on the new religion, he tied it between the animal's horns and hid it in a cave. He then gathered many people, and he started to pray and the bull came to him and did as it had been trained to do. Everyone present interpreted the event as a miracle and converted to Islam.

Other stories that were obvious distortions of Islamic traditions and influenced by beliefs about the Antichrist also circulated about the prophet. According to a medieval author, Muhammad claimed to have received many revelations from the archangel Gabriel, but in reality a vulture had appeared to him. Feeling death approaching, Muhammad prophesied that the angels would resurrect him three days after his demise, but his soul ended up in hell and his body began to rot. Since the miracle did not happen, his followers thought that their presence was preventing the arrival of the angels and so they left the corpse unguarded. Instead it happened that drawn by the stink, some dogs came and ate his hip. According to other stories, pigs devoured the corpse of the 'Arab's pseudo-prophet,' which explained why Muslims did not eat that type of animal.

The faithful of Islam were reputed to be guilty of uncontrollable lust that led them to have homosexual relations, above all with little boys. In this, they were said to resemble their prophet, who was reputed to have wanted to deflower even the mother of Christ. Islam's faithful were, furthermore, teased for not respecting the period of fasting during Ramadan and for their passion for alcohol, the consumption of which is forbidden by Islam (this accusation, however, was not completely without foundation).

The Muslims who were against familiarity between the faithful of the two religions and benevolent treatment of Christians by Islamic rulers underlined the dangers inherent in such attitudes. Since the eighth century, there were writers who, obsessed by the fear of being contaminated by the dhimmis, warned their coreligionists to stay away from them as much as possible. They advised against shaking hands with them; if it occurred by accident, one should wash them immediately. Believing that they were dealing with inferior beings, it was even advised not to reply to greetings and to avoid friendly formulas like 'The same to you' and 'God be with you.' If one erroneously said this, it was recommended to find the person and ask him to take back his greeting. It was also strongly suggested not to keep Christian or Jewish friends as one might risk becoming like them.

Their favorite targets were Christian priests. During the Almoravid rule, which was marked by a strongly anti-Christian sentiment, a writer from Seville advised Muslim women to avoid churches, emphasizing that the priests were libidinous and sodomites. They insisted on their licentiousness, claiming that Christian women went to church to drink wine and have sex with churchmen, who kept two or three concubines. According to a popular fourteenth-century work, a Christian, on the point of death, was given the choice to die like 'a true believer.' He had two visions. In the first, he was told that he could go to heaven if he converted to Islam. In the second, a devil appeared to him in the guise of a Christian priest, who told him that only the faithful of Christ would obtain eternal salvation. He refused the offer of the angel, and he went to hell, where he was subjected to the most terrible pains.

Rumors, often contradictory or without foundation that blamed destructive acts on Christians, constitute further evidence for the existence of hostility toward them. For example, despite the fact that the fire that destroyed the Egyptian city of Fustat in 1168 was ordered by Muslim authorities to counter the attack of the Christians from the Kingdom of Jerusalem, harming Coptic Christians as well as Muslims, it was rumored to have been started by Egyptian Christians as revenge for Caliph Al-Ḥākim's destruction of the Holy Sepulcher one hundred and fifty years before.

Harassments and vexations

Though modest, the phenomena just described indicate the existence of acrimony between Muslims and Christians that authorities tried to keep in check in order to prevent violent outbursts. In addition to underlining the ban on mixing with Christians during the rituals for Christ's baptism, in the Middle Ages, Cairo's authorities also reminded the Muslims of that city that it was prohibited to harass them even if they celebrated that event openly. In the eleventh century, in Alexandria, the public rituals for Palm Sunday were suspended for fifteen years because of some Muslims' aggressive behavior against the faithful of Christ. When they were reinstated, it was with the protection of soldiers, who arrested anyone who insulted a Christian and put a seal on the door of anyone who threw stones at them. Similar measures were also introduced during the parades for the election of the patriarch of Cairo.

Public officials, however, who took advantage of their position to humiliate the Christians, were not lacking. On occasion of the payment of the jizyah, some officers forced the Christians to wear a seal on the nape of their neck that could be removed only after they had fulfilled that obligation. They also slapped them saying: 'Pay the debt to Allah, oh enemy of Allah, oh infidel.' The Ottoman governor of Sidon utilized this humiliating ritual targeting the rich Christians of his city as punishment for the Greek revolt of 1821. When a high-ranking official crossed a public space and greeted the people present, the Christians had to remain immobile, so as not to receive or respond to his greetings. In Islamic courts of justice, several judges followed the recommendations to keep Christians standing and to force them to appear in court on Sunday.

To avoid being beaten, Christians, but probably also Mudéjars, stepped aside when they crossed paths with someone from the faith of the ruling side, particularly when that person was a public official or a religious leader. When Thessaloniki and the surrounding region were annexed by Greece in 1912, the Christian policemen of a village created a rule according to which, if a Muslim on horseback met an officer, he had to dismount and greet him deferentially, otherwise he would be clubbed. The faithful of Islam in Thessaloniki were forced to join the Greek Navy League and to wear a small cross in their buttonhole to prove that they had fulfilled this obligation.

Some Muslim officials extorted money from Christians by requesting donations and imposing unjust fines. For example, seeing some camels urinate on the street in a Syrian city in the ninth century, a governor accused their Christian owner of allowing it on purpose so that Muslims would slip and fall. He confiscated the camels and imprisoned their unfortunate owner until he gave him a donation. On another occasion, that ruler had the donkey of a Christian that had bucked his master to the ground killed on the excuse that it was a dangerous animal. The sentence was revoked after the unfortunate man paid a fine. Christ's faithful were often allowed to harvest grapes only after they had disbursed a certain sum of money to Muslim officials. The same thing occurred for several other agricultural activities. Numerous public officials also expected the Christians to pay undue tolls for using roads and entering cities. In Egypt, a local governor even removed some relics of Saint George from a religious building in order to receive a ransom. During times of great tension with the Christians, there were also governors who imposed heavy fines on them in return for protection and for not inciting violence against them.

Similar behaviors occurred in Christian territories. For example, in 1282, an official in Zaragoza, who was unable to obtain a heavy fine from the local Muslims, of which he himself would have received a high percentage, impounded their cattle. A decade or so later, an official of the same region ordered the faithful of Islam to hand him the fines they usually paid to Muslim magistrates.

He commanded anyone opposing this measure to host traveling nobles and soldiers. Some episodes in the kingdom of Aragon at the end of the thirteenth century, however, show that some officials did the same to Christians under their jurisdiction. In both Muslim and Christian territories, traveling soldiers and those who had not received their salary in months often harassed civilians, becoming particularly aggressive toward the religious minorities.

In general, relations with neighbors of the dominators' religion were fairly friendly. Matters could be quite different, however, if the person of a different faith was also a foreigner. At the beginning of the twentieth century, a Christian from an Anatolian village recalled that, after his grandfather had just arrived there, some local Muslims had thrown him into a ditch and called him 'infidel.' In that region, itinerant Christian peasants suffered similar treatment when they crossed areas where they were not known. Having to go to Damascus, in the second half of the fourteenth century, a young Christian pretended to be a Muslim in order to avoid abuse; the journey went well, but on his return, he was discovered and executed. As has already been noted, in cities, common people often harassed the dhimmis who did not wear the signs of distinction. On festive and celebratory occasions, the atmosphere could sometimes become heated, and even acquaintances and colleagues of different religions could come to blows with each other. At the end of the eighteenth century, the Christian silk workers of Istanbul refused to participate in the traditional picnic of their guild because the Muslim co-workers had previously ill-treated them.

To avoid conflicts, dhimmis preferred not to display wealth, particularly when they crossed areas frequented by Muslims. In 1750, a group of wealthy Copts forgot that rule and paid the consequences. Wishing to go on pilgrimage to Jerusalem, they gave some money to a local Muslim leader to obtain the permit to do so and hired some Bedouins for their protection, but that was not enough to reach their objective. Having left with great pomp and musical fanfare they in fact had to cancel their trip because they were immediately attacked with sticks and stones by Muslims who had been instigated by another Islamic leader hostile to Christian displays.

Violence sometimes degenerated and could end in fatalities, particularly when the faithful of Allah wanted to punish a Christian for having transgressed a relevant prohibition. In the early modern period, in Thessaloniki, some janissaries beat a Christian gunsmith to death, shouting at him that he was an infidel and that with his work he caused a lot of suffering. In 1521, in Egypt, three Christians got drunk publically and then argued with a Muslim magistrate and humiliated him and Islam, and they were, consequently, arrested and put on trial. They were judged guilty, but not punishable by death, because their behavior was caused by drunkenness. Furious because the judges did not order their execution, some soldiers killed two of them and burned their bodies in front of the courthouse. To avoid the same treatment, the third Christian converted and was not punished. Although they are less documented, the Mudéjars also received similar treatment in the Christian kingdoms. Even if they were not the only victims of abuses and of the violence with which disputes were often settled, the Muslim subjects were more exposed to them. In their case, crossing a territory controlled by enemies of their lord could be extremely dangerous. In the fourteenth century, a Muslim wheat merchant was even killed for doing so. Falsely accused of having had sexual relations with a Christian woman, he was immediately burned at the stake.

Muslim rulers against Christian subjects

At the dawn of the eighth century, motivated by the desire to avoid close mixing between Muslims and Christians and probably concerned by the formation of Muslim sects composed by new converts who tolerated the cult of images, Caliph Yazid ordered their destruction in churches and in Christian houses. At the beginning of the eleventh century, the Caliph of Cairo, Al-Ḥākim, on the other hand, issued oppressive laws against his Christian subjects. In so doing, he created such a tense atmosphere that riots against Christians broke out, often promoted by the caliph himself. It was in that period that the church of the Holy Sepulcher in Jerusalem was destroyed. Yet, Al-Ḥākim was characterized by a radical Shiite Islamism with messianic strains and did not specifically target the Christians; among the victims of his persecutions were, in fact, also Jews and Sunni Muslims. Yazid's and Al-Ḥākim's behaviors were an exception, and generally Muslim rulers and public officers never overtly attacked Christian subjects.

Christian communities and their leaders were nevertheless considered responsible for the misdeeds of their coreligionists and for episodes that happened outside the 'House of Islam.' In the second half of the thirteenth century, the governor of Damascus accused the Christians of having sympathy for the Mongolian invaders and of having assaulted some Muslims with their protection. Consequently, he inflicted a very high fine on all the Christians of that region. Accused of setting the main mosque of Damascus on fire (the confessions were obtained through torture), in the thirteenth century, some high ranking Christ's believers were sentenced to death and their community had to pay a hefty sum.

In other cases, the criminal behavior of a Christian public functionary was enough to hold his entire community responsible. After having discovered the abuses of a Christian tax collector, in the 1120s, the caliph of Cairo not only had him executed but imposed heavy restrictions on the use of Christians in the public administration, renewed the obligation to wear signs that identified them, and toughened the rules for paying the jizyah. After the Cypriot Christians raided Alexandria in 1365, the sultan ordered all the Egyptian Christians to give one-fourth of their wealth to repair what their coreligionists had destroyed, to free prisoners, and to finance the construction of a fleet. Noteworthy is the fact that a Muslim religious leader opposed such a punishment, affirming it was against the Islamic precept, according to which, one cannot be responsible for damage caused by others. As retaliation for the campaigns against the faithful of Islam by the Christian rulers of northern Spain around 1100, the Almoravids, on the other hand, ordered the destruction of several churches in Andalusia. In the Ottoman

Empire, the transformation of churches into mosques occurred during the expulsion of the Moriscos from the Iberian Peninsula around 1609 and the war against the Holy League (1593–1606). In turn, Cardinal Cisneros commanded that all Granada's mosques be turned into churches to punish the local Muslim uprising in 1499.

In 1055, a sermon held in the mosque of Constantinople in honor of the caliph of Baghdad, a rival of Cairo's ruler, was sufficient to unleash a vendetta of the latter against his Christian subjects; all the churches in the region were closed for several weeks, the Holy Sepulcher's estates were confiscated, the jizyah was raised for Christians, and monks were forced to pay it. At the beginning of the tenth century, when it was reported that Muslim prisoners had been mistreated in Constantinople, the patriarchs of Jerusalem and Antioch were enjoined to contact the Byzantine authorities to make sure that they put a stop to that behavior and were reminded that they would be held responsible should such a situation arise again. On another occasion, at the news that Muslims were being mistreated in Ethiopia, in the fifteenth century, the sultan of Egypt called on the patriarch of Cairo, rebuked him harshly for what had happened in that Christian territory, had him beaten and threatened with death. In addition, he ordered that the prohibitions for dhimmis be applied to the letter, and he forbade them the assignment of any public offices.

At the beginning of the Greek war of independence in 1821, the sultan reacted very harshly at the news of attacks against the Ottoman army and Muslim civilians in Greece. Even though the Orthodox Christian patriarch of Constantinople threatened to excommunicate anyone who rebelled, the ruler had him hanged at the doors of his palace and had his body dragged through the streets of the city and thrown into the sea, along with those of several other churchmen. The sultan also ordered the execution of a few bishops of his empire, and he inflicted various humiliations upon Christian subjects, as well as confiscating the properties of the wealthiest Christians and raising the jizyah. Moreover, with the cooperation of the authorities, bloody attacks were also carried out against the Greek Orthodox communities of Istanbul, Thessaloniki, and Izmir. In Thessaloniki, as well as inciting his men to kill any Christian they met on the street, the governor had most of the hostages who had been taken before the insurrection killed and many Christians sold as slaves. It took the Christian community several decades to recover from the events of these years. In 1826, Greek revolutionaries conducted a naval raid against Beirut to encourage their coreligionists there to revolt. Although the mission failed, Lebanese Muslims wanted to avenge that attack, by assaulting the local Christians, but the governor of Damascus and the local authorities convinced them to give up their plan. Ottoman authorities, however, satisfied their thirst for revenge by sending five hundred Albanians to Beirut with the order to teach the Christians a harsh lesson.

To eliminate the infidel who is above the faithful

As already seen, in theory, a Christian could not hold an office that would place him above a Muslim. In practice, this happened in several parts of the 'House of Islam,' and their presence created significant frustration and rancor, particularly among the most intransigent faithful of Islam and those belonging to the low social classes. These feelings sometimes resulted in attacks against specific persons. In Baghdad, there was a wave of protests toward the mid-ninth century because Christians occupied important positions in the public administration, while in Palermo at the end of the tenth century, the lynching of a Christian was motivated by envy and the desire to humiliate and eliminate a person who had obtained a prestigious position. After asking for, and receiving from him, a donation that was twice the normal rate, a Muslim insisted that the Court doctor, John, convert. When the physician refused, he was dragged before the ruler of Palermo and accused of blasphemy against Muhammad. After the governor refused to condemn John, the officer easily instigated a crowd of Muslims to lynch him.

In some cases, violence grew from specific situations that depended on both internal and external situations and were used to eliminate an adversary or to oppose rulers too favorable to Christ's faithful. In the 1150s, the caliph of Cairo found himself in a weak position, and his choice of making donations to the Christian kingdoms in order to avoid conflict aroused much criticism. The climate became more heated with the arrival in Egypt of Muslims from the regions attacked by the king of Jerusalem. One of the refugees, a Sunni, vented his anger by criticizing the fact that Christians held important positions in public administration within the House of Islam and by accusing one of them, the court treasurer, Ibn Dukhan, of numerous crimes. In so doing, he also wished to humiliate the Shiite Egyptian ruling class. Ibn Dukhan's refusal to give the refugee a salary certainly increased the latter's hate for that 'infidel.' One of the accusations, that he forced a Muslim to convert, is highly unlikely. It is, on the other hand, relevant that the Sunni Muslim wanted to demonstrate that Ibn Dukhan was guilty just because he was Christian. The charge of having subtracted public money is extremely significant. According to the accuser, a Christian could not be a reliable accountant because he believed that God was one and three. He would therefore take three times as much as the amount that he openly declared from the public treasury. The rumor that Ibn Dukhan had often received emissaries from the kingdom of Jerusalem and had treated certain Muslims with arrogance was enough to make a crowd gather and demand his resignation. The treasurer was arrested at his house and interrogated. Some letters in which he invited the king of Jerusalem to invade Egypt were found, and he was thus punished for being a traitor and a spy. The evidence was likely forged.

A clash over the office of Egypt's vizier in the 1130s caused much tension between Christians and Muslims in that country. The fact that one of the contenders for that position was a Christian and that in that period Western Christians established themselves in the nearby kingdom of Jerusalem, led to an escalation of the conflict that assumed religious undertones. The name of the Christian was Bahram, an Armenian, born in the principality of Edessa, who had moved to Egypt with some of his countrymen to serve in the army. He had been the governor of an Egyptian province and was recognized as the leader of the Armenian Christians in Cairo. The caliph named him vizier to limit the intrusive influence of his Muslim councilors and to facilitate relations with the Norman kingdom of Sicily, and, though Bahram was not a faithful of Allah, conferred on him titles with an Islamic tone, such as 'Sword of Islam' and 'Assistant to the Iman.' The choice of the Egyptian ruler did not stir up any public protest or revolt. Bahram reinforced his power by giving relevant public offices to his family members and to other Armenians, greatly favoring the Armenian Church in Egypt, the head of which was his brother. The bestowal of key positions in the public administration and in the army to newly arrived people and the nepotistic politics of Bahram caused rancor among both Muslims and Copts who represented the majority of Christians in that area. The main opposition to the vizier came from a Sunni Muslim official, Ridwan, who instigated several religious figures to preach against that infidel. The caliph did not intervene, hoping that the two contenders would nullify each other or that at least neither of the two would gain too much power. Ridwan eventually gathered an army and declared that fighting against Bahram was equal to participating in a jihad against infidels; he emphasized this by telling his men to put pages of the Quran on the tips of their lances. The rhetoric worked. The Muslim warriors of the vizier's army in fact deserted *en masse*. Bahram and his Armenians took refuge in southern Egypt where one of his brothers was governor, but his enemies arrived before him and sowed death and destruction among the Armenians of that region. When Bahram saw the mutilated body of one of his brothers chained to the carcass of a dog and thrown on a dump and the desecration of another brother's tomb, he ordered his men to kill any Muslim they met. The conflicts in southern Egypt only lasted a short time because Bahram decided to become a monk and retired to a monastery. In the meantime, in Cairo, an enraged crowd of Muslims destroyed Bahram's house, raping the women of his family and in his service; then they attacked the Armenians, pillaged their churches, and killed their religious leader. The fact that they did not assail any other Christians shows that the fight was seen as conflict with a very specific ethnic-religious group. Ridwan became the new vizier and started to replace Shiite officials and administrators with Sunni personnel. No longer tolerating his behavior, the caliph deposed him and successfully reestablished peace, making sure that the Armenians regained all they had lost, and repairing the churches destroyed in the tumults. Even at the cost of many human lives and by provoking strong inter-religious tension, the ruler succeeded in his attempt to get rid of overly invasive and power-hungry viziers.

Riots against Christians in the Middle Ages

There were always radical Muslims, especially among the religious leaders, who incited their coreligionists to punish the Christians who transgressed the restrictions imposed upon them. Bloody tumults against Christ's faithful, however, did not occur often in the House of Islam. They only took place in coincidence with vacuums of power, famines, epidemics, and economic crisis, moments in which it was possible to gather a consistent number of people in the cities who were ready to find a scapegoat upon which to vent their frustration. Given that those episodes challenged the authority of the rulers and created internal disorder, in the majority of cases, they were immediately repressed. For example, in the tenth century, when the first Fatimid caliph heard that groups of Muslim youths were sowing terror among the Christians of a small Egyptian town, he immediately intervened against the aggressors. As his successor permitted the restauration of some churches in Cairo, many troublemakers turned up in front of these build-ings on the first day of works, but the prompt arrival of troops convinced them to leave. In the same period, again in Cairo, the quick intervention of the army prevented a frenzied crowd from sacking the church of Saint Michael in revenge for the Byzantine conquest of Crete.

Toward the end of the tenth century, a period in which the fear of attacks from Constantinople was widespread, some Muslims from Cairo accused the community of the Amalfitan merchants living there of having set fire to some Muslim ships. They served as triple scapegoats, because, aside from being Chris-tians and rich, they were also foreigners. In fact, one hundred and sixty Italians were killed in the streets, and their houses were pillaged. A representative of the caliph intervened, he had the massacre and the destruction stopped, had any stolen goods given back, and punished the perpetrators severely, thus acknowl-edging the important role of those merchants in Egypt. When Damascus was taken from the Mongols in 1260, some Muslims of that city accused their fellow Christian citizens of having been too friendly toward the invaders and so they assailed them. Yet, this behavior was not tolerated, and the guilty were punished.

On other occasions, the authorities either could not or did not want to in-tervene, especially when the tension was too high and during moments of low government popularity and vacuums of power. In such cases, it was considered more convenient to let the populace quickly vent its rage and to try as much as possible, to make sure that the violence did not spread too much and last for too many days. In the second half of the tenth century, the Byzantines took back some territories previously lost in the eastern Mediterranean and thus created a lot of bad feelings toward Christians on the part of the Muslims of the region. At the news that the troops of Constantinople were approaching Aleppo, the Chris-tians of Antioch were attacked, and some Muslim notables of that city accused the local patriarch of plotting with the enemy, stirring up the population against him. As the religious leader went to the house of one of them who had been a good friend of his until then, the churchman denied having any contact with the Byzantines, but he was not believed and was murdered. Although Christians were not the only victims of the clashes between military factions that occurred in the 1070s in Egypt, many Christian villages and monasteries were ravaged in that period. The patriarch of Cairo's home suffered the same fate, and the reli-gious leader himself was captured, beaten, and freed only after the payment of a heavy ransom. Similar events occurred at the end of Fatimid rule in Egypt; when their adversaries' warriors arrived in the region, a part of the population joined them in devastating and robbing the churches.

During the Mamluk period, the riots against Christians were numerous and particularly bloody. This was not due to a special hatred these rulers nourished for Christ's faithful, but to the intersection of a number of factors that rendered the ground very fertile for such episodes. A long economic crisis and the heavy fiscal policies, levied by the Mamluks to maintain their army and their lavish court life, caused a drastic drop in living standards for many Muslims and produced a vast number of destitute, particularly in the main cities. This, sometimes combined with political crisis, epidemics, and famines, increased the opportunities for having large crowds of malcontents unleashed against the Christians and made the maintenance of internal peace extremely difficult. Some episodes that occurred between the end of the thirteenth and the second half of the following century illustrate the situation of this period very well.

In 1292, at the sight of a Christian functionary passing in front of a mosque pulling a Muslim debtor by a rope tied around his neck, a group of Muslims attempted to free their coreligionist. Because some guards had intervened to defend the Christian, an angry crowd gathered and went to protest in front of the sultan's palace. Intimidated by the great number of people, the ruler ordered the expulsion of all Christians from the public administration and the execution of a few of them. Not satisfied with these measures, the most severe extremists lynched several Christian functionaries and sacked their houses, one of the most important churches in Cairo, and the patriarch's residence.

Since churches were such a powerful visual symbol of the Christian presence in Egypt, they became the favorite target of the most intransigent Muslims. Induced by the insistent requests from the population that churches be destroyed (some had already met this fate in Alexandria and in a city one hundred miles from the capital), in 1301, religious leaders and experts of law met in Cairo and decided that only churches built after the Arab conquest of Egypt in the seventh century should be demolished. The government did not follow this advice and partially satisfied the zealots by closing all Christian religious buildings for an indeterminate period. All the same, it was obvious that resentment against the Christian population was becoming increasingly widespread at all levels of the Muslim population.

In 1303, the sultan did not intervene when a large group of Islam's faithful, angered by a relaxation of the law on Christian identification signs, punished the transgressors by beating them and destroying their houses. The rulers, however, were not always available to satisfy the desires of the radicals and the masses. In 1307, some people who had torn down churches in a southern Egyptian town were arrested, beaten, and subjected to a public humiliation, while a religious leader, accused of having inspired those aggressions, was exiled to a place close to Cairo. In 1314, shouting that he wanted to make Islam triumph and kill Christians and Jews, a Muslim crossed the capital on horseback, injuring three persons. He was arrested and decapitated.

In 1317, the permission to repair one of Cairo's churches provoked many protests, and the sultan therefore decided to halt the restoration work. When he removed the prohibition following the Copts' complaints, a large crowd of Muslims razed the building to the ground. That event prepared the terrain for a much more serious explosion of violence four years later. In 1321, excavation work was stopped in a certain area of the capital because a church was located there. One Friday, after prayers, many faithful of Islam met at that place and destroyed it. This gesture served as a signal, and in a short time, eleven other churches were demolished, and the clergy were either beaten or killed. Similar events took place in all of Egypt's major cities, a circumstance indicating that the actions had been coordinated and that religious leaders had played a major role in this. Nearly sixty churches and monasteries were razed to the ground throughout Egypt. The Christians, however, did not behave as passive victims. In Cairo, some monks set fire to some mosques and the flames consumed some of the neighboring houses. This reaction antagonized the Muslims and led to street fighting between the two religious groups. Some Christians went as far as disguising themselves as Jews to avoid being beaten or killed. When peace was restored, the sultan commanded that all responsible for the brawls, Christians or Muslims, be executed. When some Islamic leaders deemed that the punishments for Christ's faithful had not been sufficient and led an assault on a Christian dignitary, the ruler had them crucified along one of Cairo's streets. In 1324, Mamluk troops were the target of public rage in a town near Cairo. Sent to calm the local inhabitants angered because the Christians had been permitted to repair five churches damaged during the previous riots, the soldiers were stoned. To prevent the situation from degenerating into further violence, it was decided to demolish those religious buildings.

The plague epidemic of 1347–1349 and the worsening of the economic situation that followed it provided the ground for a new, more serious crisis. A Muslim author attributes the outbreak of rage to a Christian who passed in front of a mosque wearing luxurious clothes. After they beat the man, guilty of having dared to exhibit his elevated status in that particular place, during a period that was so difficult for the majority of the population, many Muslims complained about the Christians' behavior to the sultan. He tried to quell the discontent by allowing the demolition of the churches that had been repaired illegally. As already noted, the finger of the martyr used to ensure the regular flooding of the Nile was burned during these riots, and many properties of the Coptic Church were confiscated. The suppression of the disorder was delayed and quite moderate because, due to the sultan's young age and conflicts among his advisors, central power was quite weak, and the remarkable consistency of the crowd suggested prudence. The authorities adopted the same approach with the attacks against Christians that happened in 1365 after the Cypriot Christians sacked Alexandria. A plague epidemic in that year further exacerbated people's feelings. The sultan, too, proved to be influenced by the great tension of those years, having a Christian accused of killing his wife with a magic spell crucified.

Nineteenth-century recrudescences: attacks against Christians in the late Ottoman period

Over the course of most of the Ottoman era, this type of aggression was absent because the above-mentioned conditions that had produced them in the previous centuries did not occur. This does not mean that there were never tumults against Christians, but they did not degenerate into widespread violence. Indeed, in the main Syrian cities, the immediate intervention of public authorities and of Muslim prominent citizens dispersed groups of coreligionists wishing to work off their rancor against the Christians. In that period, the victims were mainly specific individuals. Sometimes they were prestigious religious leaders such as the patriarch of Constantinople, who was sentenced to death in the seventeenth century, during a particularly tense moment between the Ottomans and Russia, with the accusation of having invited the Cossacks to invade Turkish territories. It seems that the charge was due to the misinterpretation of some of his letters in which he asked for financial help from a fellow Christian who lived with the Cossacks.

At the end of the eighteenth century, however, two episodes reveal that the atmosphere was changing. At the beginning of July 1770, at the news that the Russians had defeated the Ottoman fleet, about ninety kilometers from Izmir, a large mob of Muslims from that city assailed the Orthodox Christians, killing hundreds of them. On the 12th of January 1797, again in Izmir, two Greek subjects of the Venetian Republic murdered a janissary and then escaped with the complicity of the Venetian and Russian consuls. Three days later, the fellow soldiers of the victim paraded through the city carrying the bloodied shirt of their companion and threatening death to all Christians, after which they entered the European neighborhood of the city, set fire to some buildings, started to kill all passersby, and chased away anyone who tried to extinguish the fire, thus letting the fire spread to other Christian neighborhoods. The surviving Europeans and the Christians in their service hid themselves in the foreign ships in the harbor; some Venetian and Russian sailors contributed to the disorder by pillaging the port's warehouses. On that day around one thousand five hundred people, mostly Orthodox Christians, died without the city authorities moving a finger to stop the violence.

In the nineteenth century, the progressive decline of the Ottoman Empire's military and economic power, the independence movements in Greece, the Balkans, and eastern Europe, the worsening of many Muslims' living standard and reforms to eliminate all differences among subjects of different religions created the conditions for violent outbursts. In that situation, extremists and proponents of radical Islamism, and in general, all those opposing the changes taking place in the Ottoman empire at that time, had an easy job arguing that their world was collapsing, and that Christians were responsible for those drastic changes. Furthermore, they believed that it was unacceptable that infidels should have the same rights as Muslims. These ideas found fertile ground among the lower classes and those who had been harshly affected by the economic crisis. Among them, there was great fear of seeing their own social and economic status diminish due to the loss of privileges they had enjoyed until this point. At the same time, they considered it intolerable that people who had always been considered inferior could improve their own conditions at the expense of Muslims.

As proof of the Ottoman world's great diversity, violence against Christians did not occur everywhere. In Syria, the presence of fairly small Christian communities and the widespread perception (mostly false) that Christ's faithful were making economic gains and at the same time seriously hurting Muslims thanks to the new economic opportunities offered by the opening of that area to European businessmen created an explosive mix, especially in those cities where populations had recently risen at dizzying rates.

In Aleppo, the tension started to mount in January 1848, following a directive from the sultan that the restoration of churches and the construction of new religious buildings no longer required approval from the authorities. For the ruler, this was only a liberal interpretation of the restrictions present in the Pact of Umar. Yet, Aleppo's Christians took it literally, while their fellow Muslim citizens believed that they would now be allowed to do as they wished. A group of Islam's faithful occupied the place planned for the construction of a church and consecrated it in order to build a mosque, strongly opposing at the same time the plan to erect the Christian Melkites' cathedral. The following year celebrations for the official recognition of the Melkite community caused a huge scandal. Muslims were particularly outraged by the Melkite's public procession with a great unfolding of enormous crosses and men firing into the air, actions that had been forbidden to Christians until a few years before. News of the construction of big churches to underline the new status of the Melkites created the same indignation.

In 1850, news spread among Muslims that there would be a draft of all subjects, Christians included. The idea of seeing them legally armed led to assaults against them. According to a Muslim source, during the riots, twenty Christians were killed and six churches, thirty-six shops, and six hundred eighty-eight houses were destroyed. The perpetrators of the violence wrote to the sultan, claiming not to have rebelled against his authority, but to have actively opposed mandatory conscription. Maintaining that poll taxes should only be paid by Jews and Christians, they also protested this type of imposition. They also reported the arrogant and disrespectful behavior of Christians, who did not have to ring bells, build new churches or keep African slaves because they could be Muslims or pagans intending to convert to Islam. The government in Istanbul could not accept this kind of protest and, under strong pressure from the European powers, sent the army to suppress the uprising. Clashes were particularly bloody because the rebels resisted fiercely. One part of Aleppo was bombed, and in some neighborhoods, it was necessary to fight from house to house.

The 1850s passed without incidents of this type. The outbreak of violence against Christians in various areas of the Near and Middle East—the most serious was in the port city of Jeddah (Arabia) in 1858—shows that fire was smoldering under the ashes. In 1860, in Lebanon, the tensions that in the 1830s and 1840s had led to conflicts between Muslims and Christians reemerged. Feeling displaced by Christ's faithful, the Druze leaders started to incite their coreligionists against them. The first assaults were in villages and in a couple of small towns where hundreds of Christians were killed and their possessions were pillaged. Terrified by the intensity of the violence, some of them responded to the attacks with arms, but the majority fled to Damascus. The great flow of Christian refugees caused significant bad feelings among the local Muslims who were already poorly disposed toward them because of the reforms and economic changes that had occurred in the region. Rumors about the arrival of Druzes and Bedouins threw gasoline on the fire.

During the Islamic festival of the Sacrifice, Muslim boys went to the neighborhoods, prevalently inhabited by Christians, and painted crosses on their houses. A few of them were arrested and forced to remove those signs while kept under an armed guard, but soon a protesting crowd gathered and demanded their release. There was a fight and instigations to attack Christians spread throughout the city. In the meantime, Druzes and Muslims from the countryside arrived, and the killing of Christians and the looting of their goods started and lasted for a week. Without doubt, the massacre was worse than the one in Aleppo ten years earlier; depending on the sources, the number of casualties varies from a few hundreds to around ten thousand. The Ottoman authorities blamed Muslim preachers for inspiring those acts, but there is no evidence. Actually, one of them tried to put an end to the violence.

In this case, too, the majority of rioters were from the lower classes who felt insulted by the reforms and believed that by losing their privileged status everything would be worse for them. At the beginning, the targets were only the richest Christians and those who were protected by the European consuls, and then the situation degenerated. That both Damascus' and Aleppo's massacres resulted from new conditions that inverted the traditional hierarchies and that caused widespread and underestimated anger is proven by the fact that the governors and Muslim elites of those cities, who in the past had made any effort to prevent attacks against the Christian neighborhoods, on these occasions chose not to intervene but to remain inside their houses. Conscious of the disasters caused by those riots, in 1860, Aleppo's governor and prominent Muslim citizens had the streets patrolled so that what had happened in Damascus would not occur in their city. Moreover, the governor walked through the streets predominantly inhabited by Christians and ordered a proclamation to be read. It was stated that no aggression against non-Muslims would be tolerated. In Beirut, the same measures, the reinforcement of the local garrison, and the presence of European warships assured that the lynching of a passing Christian after the discovery of a Muslim corpse did not degenerate further. The storm calmed down all over the Syria-Palestine region thanks to the preventative work carried out by the authorities. Despite the serious economic crisis of the 1870s, episodes on that scale never took place again.

The violence exploded, instead, in Egypt in 1882, where the resentment of the Muslims against the local Christian population and European businessmen, provoked by sudden economic changes and the new status of the dhimmis, added to the intrusive interference by France and above all Great Britain in the internal politics of the country. Widespread corruption, an ineffectual government, a severe economic crisis, and the Egyptian state's heavy debt to European banks further aggravated the situation. The attempt of an Egyptian official, named 'Urabi, to take power and end the serious national crisis prepared the ground for the unrest. France and Great Britain strongly opposed his reforms, thus further embittering the Muslims. On the eleventh of June 1882, in Alexandria, the Egyptian city most affected by the economic and social changes, a Maltese responded to a blow by a Muslim by stabbing him. The brawl then worsened, involving an increasing number of people, and eventually a crowd of enraged Islam's faithful, mostly composed by the lower classes and some soldiers, assaulted the local Christians and Europeans, pillaging their goods and killing around fifty of them (several Muslims also fell in the fighting). A couple of weeks later, in another Egyptian city, another riot caused the death of ten Christians and three Jews. The British then decided to intervene militarily. They had Alexandria bombarded by their fleet, and, after defeating 'Urabi, they assumed control of Egypt.

At the beginning of this section, it was noted that indiscriminate attacks against Christians did not take place everywhere in the Ottoman Empire. As an exemplary case of the lack of violent outbursts despite strong tensions, which emphasizes the special features of the areas just analyzed, we will consider Thessaloniki. Economic boom, great demographic growth, and the presence of a large number of persons belonging to the lower classes characterized this city in the nineteenth century as well, but these phenomena began to emerge from the end of the eighteenth century and resulted from the quick evolution of processes that had been present in earlier centuries. They did not, therefore, have the jarring effect that they had produced in many other regions of the Near and Middle East. Also, in contrast to the cities in those regions, the percentage of Muslims in Thessaloniki's population was not much higher than that of Christians (the presence of many Jews must also be remembered). Finally, it must be remembered that, although the governors of Thessaloniki were unable to face criminality effectively, they were always ready to repress any disturbance immediately. They also tasked themselves with punishing, sometimes indiscriminately, and very violently, Thessaloniki's Christians for terrorist acts as well as the revolts of Christians in other parts of the empire. Therefore, it was the governor's men, not an angry crowd, who assailed Christians in 1821 for punishing them for their coreligionists' insurrection in other parts of Greece. When some Thessalonians of Bulgarian origin carried out some revolutionary acts on the 28th of April 1903 with the aim of provoking Muslim ire against Christians that would justify the intervention of Bulgaria, it was the police as well as the Ottoman soldiers who combed the Bulgarian neighborhoods all night, arresting and often executing hundreds of suspects on the spot. To restore calm, the next day, the governor

himself toured Thessaloniki assuring the protection of all and successfully ad-
monishing the faithful of Islam not to perform any violence against Christians.

The police and the army did not display the same care in 1876 when tempers
rose due to the conversion of a Christian girl who intended to marry a Muslim.
As soon as the young woman arrived in the city from the countryside, in order
to formalize her conversion to Islam, her mother tried to stop her, asking loudly
for the help of the Christians present there who removed her veil and took her
to a secret place, in a carriage belonging to the American vice-consul, who was
a member of a Greek Thessalonian family. As news reached the main bazaar, a
large crowd of Muslims gathered next to a neighboring mosque and refused to
disperse. In the meantime, some protesters captured the French and German
consuls, who were passing by, in order to recover the girl by means of an exchange. The situation, however, degenerated, and the diplomats were lynched.
The crowd did not disperse until they heard that the young woman had been
released. Although no violent acts ensued, tension remained quite high.

News of the bloody event circulated all over the world, the European warships present in the port aimed their cannons at the Muslim part of the city, and
the sultan ordered the immediate arrest of those responsible for the killing of the
two consuls. The governor, with a lot of hesitation, because he knew that most
of the local soldiers were in favor of what had happened, had some thirty people
arrested. Six of those reputed guilty of causing the disorder were hung soon after.
Calm returned little by little, thanks to an active effort to pacify the situation on
the part of prominent citizens of both religions, and, when a few weeks later, a
new sultan took power, a huge crowd of Thessalonians of all religions gathered in
the main streets and squares to celebrate the event with great joy, thus smoothing
over that bloody episode.

Prelude to a genocide: aggressions against the Armenians

In Anatolia, most of the nineteenth century passed without any major action
against the Christians, but the situation became increasingly tense toward the
end of the century. The rise of an antireform sultan who was a proponent of an
aggressive Islamism to power in 1876, the disastrous war with Russia in 1878,
which caused the loss of two-fifths of the Ottoman Empire and the arrival of a
great number of Muslim refugees in various parts of Anatolia, created an explosive mix in that region. Resentment was particularly strong toward Armenians who, in contrast to other Christian subjects, had always maintained a very
strong sense of identity, and in parts of what is today northeastern Turkey, they
had shown little desire to interact and mix with Muslims. Their 'otherness' was
therefore ethnic as well as religious. In this case, too, envy caused by the perception that these ungrateful subjects were growing rich off the backs of Muslims played a significant role. The presence of an educated and entrepreneurial
group as well as of hard-working craftsmen among the Armenians nurtured the
idea that all these infidels had a very high standard of living. At the end of the

nineteenth century, the rumor, not entirely unfounded, that they wanted in-dependence, like the Balkan Christians, or that they wanted to be part of the neighboring and threatening Russian empire, became increasingly widespread. The idea that they were on the brink of organizing an insurrection was held by the majority of Muslims, central and local authorities alike. For this reason, they were convinced that any sign of rebellion had to be harshly suppressed. The Ottoman Empire absolutely could not lose the lands inhabited by the Armenians near the Black Sea and those bordering Russia.

The first massacre took place in the summer of 1894 in the district of Sassoon. The available sources are not unbiased and diverge in their explanation of what led to the attack on the Armenians of this area. Probably their refusal to pay dou-ble the tribute that they owed and their armed resistance to the Kurds' raids pro-voked the intervention of the army and, particularly, of 'irregular' militias that indiscriminately punished the Armenians, resulting in a few thousand casualties. A year later, signs appeared on the doors of some mosques in northeastern Turkey, warning the faithful to be extremely vigilant of Christians, to protect women from their snares, calling all Muslims to act against 'the enemies of the Faith,' and to protect the honor of Islam; the 'wrath of Allah' was threatened against anyone removing the signs. On the day of prayer, many religious leaders gave inflammatory sermons against the Armenians, inciting their congregations to attack the infidel traitors. Similar invitations were graphitized in places Muslims often frequented and appeared the month before the first attacks took place, a de-tail suggesting that there was a coordinated plan. The assaults on the Armenians started at the end of summer 1895 and continued into the autumn of that year. The usual violence of this type of assault took place. Rioting mobs chased the 'other,' mostly killed men, raped women, and sacked and destroyed their prop-erty. That the victims responded with arms in hand led to even bloodier attacks. The difference in numbers between the attackers and those defending themselves is clear in the figures of the casualties recorded in the Ottoman Empire's official sources: in Trebizond, September 1895, one hundred and eighty Armenians and eleven Muslims; at Erzurum, in October, fifty Armenians and five Muslims. The ratio of dead to injured among the former was much higher than among the latter. This clearly indicates the aggressors' intention to kill the infidels. The fact that the victims were adult men and that the other Christians including Catho-lic Armenians were not assailed suggests that, in most cases, there was no blind explosion of violence, but a targeted strategy to eliminate Armenian men. The European press and the Armenians accused the sultan of devising a plan to teach his rebellious subjects a lesson. According to more objective historians, the ruler believed that an insurrection was imminent, and he ordered the local authorities to suppress any sign of rebellion with the maximum force. As has been seen, however, there is no doubt that in some areas the aggression was premeditated.

In a few cases, the fuse leading to the explosion of violence was lighted by episodes attributed to Armenians, like the attempted murder of a pasha in Tre-bizond at the beginning of October. Yet, that event occurred more than a month after the first attacks in the region. Bloody clashes also took place in Istanbul. On September 30, 1895, a few thousand Armenians headed toward the seat of government to present a petition in favor of reforms for the status of non-Muslims. Many of them were armed with knives and pistols. When the police stopped them, there were a few scuffles that, after a few gun shots, turned into a bloody fight; about one hundred protesters and fifteen officers fell in the clashes. Several groups of Muslims immediately gathered and assailed the Armenians all over the city, causing another hundred deaths. The false news on the 17th of October that the sultan had conceded to pressure from the European powers and had given the Armenians independence reignited the fires of aggression, which continued until the following year. The worst massacre occurred in Bitlis, considered one of the most radical centers of Islamism. Again, on Friday, during prayers at the main mosque, a shot was heard. Blaming it on an 'infidel,' the faithful of Islam streamed into the streets killing all the Armenians they met. According to some estimates, the death toll that day was between five and eight hundred.

The police and the army rarely intervened in the riots, either from indifference or from a sense of impotence in the face of such major violence; the police and soldiers sometimes joined the rioters. In that year, in a small town, where a dog's carcass tied to a cross-shaped sign, containing insults in Turkish, had been thrown into an Armenian church, the troops put themselves between a hundred irate Armenians and the local Muslim population, thus preventing bloodshed. In general, it was hoped that the Kurdish attacks, which were most prevalent in the countryside and the mountains, would end in the winter. Nevertheless, with the return of good weather in 1896, other sporadic massacres took place.

In Istanbul, on the afternoon of the 26th of August 1896, a few members of the Armenian revolutionary party performed a sensational act in the hope of drawing international attention to their cause. They occupied the Imperial Ottoman Bank and threatened to blow it up if their request to change Armenians' status was not accepted. Their intention had already leaked both to their coreligionists (many of whom abandoned Istanbul that morning) and to the Ottoman authorities, who did not prevent the action in order to blame the whole community and to have an opportunity to teach all Istanbul's Armenians a harsh lesson. Bands of armed men had already been organized for several days, tasked with striking the 'infidels' immediately after the news of that unacceptable provocation. They had a free hand until the evening of the following day. The casualties on this occasion were around five thousand, mostly males, and from the lower classes, who, evidently, had not been informed of what was going to happen or had not been able to leave the city. The Istanbul incident was significantly magnified, and there were several other assaults against Armenians in the areas that had been hit the previous year. Terrorized by those massacres, those who were able to chose to move to communities of their fellow Armenians in the Russian empire.

In the following years, there were no massacres comparable to those of this period. Nevertheless, the tension remained high and the revolutionary activities of the Armenians continued to throw gasoline on the fire. The intervention of the Ottoman troops against the Armenians in Sassoon had the features of an insurrection's suppression because the Armenian revolutionaries had distributed weapons to the civilians. The extermination of a Kurdish tribe, guilty of many killings, by a group of Armenians from Persia and the failed bomb attack against the sultan, which resulted in twenty-six deaths, caused great clamor but no immediate retaliations.

A very serious massacre instead took place in the Adana region (southeastern Turkey), which had not suffered any violence up until that point. On the 24th of July 1908, the Young Turks performed a coup d'état, intending to give a new institutional form to the empire. As a result, the sultan was forced to renew the Constitution. In the wake of the initiative of some reactionaries who had succeeded in restoring full power to the sultan in April 1909, aggressive actions were taken against the Armenians in Adana, who, since July of the previous year, had supposedly behaved unacceptably to Muslims. A few hours after the coup, various Muslim leaders incited their coreligionists to attack those insolent infidels, and the troops who were sent to calm the unrest participated in the assaults. The European warships' arrival in the city port and news that the Young Turks had returned to power unleashed more attacks, which also took place in the surrounding villages. The riots were contained in that area, but the number of casualties was high. The new government made real efforts to collect funds to repay survivors for the damage they had suffered and instituted a court martial to punish those responsible for the riots. Fifty people were executed for committing homicides and instigating violence; among them were five Armenians. It was one of the first ever cases of Muslims being hung for killing Christians in the Ottoman Empire and for causing riots against them.

Attacks against Muslims in Christian lands

In Sicily, the constant increase in the number of Christians during the course of the twelfth century, the growing envy toward well off Muslim craftsmen and farmers, the widespread discontent at the use of non-aristocrats and of eunuch converts to Christianity (who were suspected of continuing to practice Islam) in the royal administration, as well as the weakening authority of King William in the 1150s, created a situation favorable for the explosion of violence against Islam's faithful on the island. The murder of the king's main councilor in November 1160, in Palermo, was followed in March by an attack on the royal palace by a crowd of Christians led by some nobles. The sovereign was imprisoned, the royal archive was destroyed, and a manhunt was unleashed against the palace eunuchs, which soon spread to the streets and houses of Palermo against any Muslims. The faithful of Islam retreated to a neighborhood on the city's periphery, where, taking advantage of the narrow streets, they managed to defend themselves against the Christians effectively. Attacks against Muslims then occurred throughout Sicily, both in the countryside and in the urban centers. Many faithful of Islam took refuge in the Southwest of the island, a safe area for them because there were many royal properties. Other Muslims, however, abandoned the island all together. The unrest ended a few months later, thanks to a group of aristocrats, loyal to the king, who liberated him and punished the rebels. Numerous Muslims returned to the cities, including Palermo, but the clashes had poisoned relations between the two religions' faithful. They degenerated again when King William II died suddenly in November 1189. The lack of a direct heir created a power vacuum, which encouraged a new series of brutalities against Palermitan Muslims. This time, however, Allah's faithful preferred to abandon the city and take refuge in fortified centers in the mountainous area, south of Palermo. In addition, the election as king of one of the aristocrats who had orchestrated the rebellion of 1161–1162 was interpreted as the inevitable worsening of the situation, further encouraging the majority of Sicilian Muslims to move to that zone and to rebel.

In the rich, densely populated region of Valencia, attacks against Muslims started immediately after Christians conquered the city in 1238. Evidently convinced that the war against the Moors was not finished and that it was still possible to loot their properties, a nobleman gathered irregular troops and conducted raids against the local Muslims, causing such serious devastations and so many deaths that the king had to suspend a military expedition in southern France and come back swiftly in order to restore peace. In the following years, on several occasions, Christians refused to obey the order of the sovereign to respect his Muslim subjects' rights and illegally took possession of their lands, kidnapped them to sell them as slaves, and sometimes killed them. Many Muslim communities asked that walls be built around their neighborhoods to protect them from harassment and assaults by the Christians, who, though still inferior in number to the Muslims, were becoming more and more numerous. The sudden defeat of the Castilians in 1275 against the Moors from southern Spain and the Maghreb and the fear of the Valencian Muslims' insurrection, believed to have too many rights and to be too numerous, created a climate that was ripe for riots against them. In Valencia, however, these were directed mostly against royal officials and symbols of royal power. The faithful of Islam were not particularly targeted. There were, in fact, Moors among both the victims and the perpetrators. In contrast, in other cities of the region, the Muslims were the target of attacks in which royal officials sometimes took part; however, there were some cases in which nobles were injured while defending their Mudéjar employees. In the meantime, a knight gathered a militia and led his men against the Muslim communities in the countryside. Homicides, rapes, destruction of property, looting, and the enslavement of Moors ensued in many places in the Valencian region. The king did not tolerate this disorder and sent his troops to fight the marauders, killing those who fell into their hands and bringing peace back to that area. The sovereign also imposed heavy penalties on the Christian citizens guilty of those crimes. Only those who could prove that they had been unable to help their fellow Muslim citizens were not punished.

In the two following centuries, attacks against the Muslim communities in the Valencian region continued but were sporadic and not comparable to those just described. As has already been noted for Egypt under the Mamluks, usually tension increased during serious economic crises, rising prices of staple goods, epidemics, and droughts. Even in Christian territories, those were the moments when it was possible to gather a consistent number of people wishing to vent their frustration and anger against 'others' who thus functioned as scapegoats. In the second half of the fourteenth century and throughout the 1400s, such conditions occurred quite often. For example, the Muslim neighborhood of a city near Valencia was pillaged in 1386 after an earthquake, while this happened in Valencia itself in 1391 and 1399. In those years, the Mudéjar communities in the south of Valencia were attacked on several occasions. It was only due to the immediate intervention of the city and royal authorities that the situation did not degenerate.

In general, there were not many casualties and attacks were mostly directed at property. The Muslims' ability to predict assaults and to abandon their homes quickly helped greatly to limit the number of homicides. This strategy was particularly effective in Valencia in 1455. In May of that year, bands of young people celebrated the election of a Spanish bishop as pope by touring the Moorish neighborhood and harassing its residents. When the (false) rumor spread that the new pope promised indulgences to anyone killing Muslims, the number of Christians wishing to eliminate them began to grow, and the city's officials did nothing to calm them. The majority of Islam's faithful, then, abandoned their homes. The prediction was correct. At the beginning of June, some Christ's faithful pillaged the Moorish quarter, causing great damage to the houses and killing some of the few Muslims who had not left. In some cases, the violence was specifically provoked by extremist churchmen. For example, in 1457, a Dominican friar was relieved of his duties because he had instigated the persecution of the Mudéjars. Toward the end of that century, the virulence with which the bishop of Zaragoza incited his flock during mass to attack the Muslims provoked the intervention of the king who asked him to put an end to his incendiary attitude.

Another factor that exacerbated the relationships with the local Muslims was created when troops gathered for campaigns against the Moors of the Andalusian potentates. In these cases, heated sermons were given to galvanize the Christian population and soldiers against the 'infidels,' and on several occasions, the royal officials and the nobility intervened, often with success, to block fanatics wishing to start fights with the native Muslims. Rumors about the imminent offensive of Granada's Moors provoked a similar reaction and sometimes were exploited to justify aggressions that had already occurred and to spread panic.

An episode from 1491, during the Corpus Domini parade in Valencia, well illustrates both how tense the situation was and how quickly inaccurate news circulated. A Mudéjar took advantage of the great crowd to kill a Muslim adversary, but a rumor spread that the victim was a Christian and Christ's faithful took up arms to assail the Moors. The swift reaction of the local authorities, who calmed the crowd by telling them what had really happened, prevented a blood bath. On another occasion, the widespread talk about an offensive by Granada's Muslims after Ramadan induced Valencian authorities to contact King Ferdinand, saying that the Mudéjars were 'public enemies with ears raised and lances sharpened.' The sovereign, however, maintained a steady nerve and simply had surveillance increased. The rumors proved to be false. Ferdinand had the same reaction in 1487 when he was told that the Moors of Valencia had invited the Turks to invade Spain and that the Mudéjars were all ready to rebel. He made no special provisions. He conducted an accurate inquiry and discovered nothing. During the organization of the crusade against the Maghreb in 1496–1497, the king ordered that no Maghreb merchants be attacked in his kingdom.

A panic crisis, originating in France, was also treated the royal officials and the sovereign with calm and efficiency. In 1321, word spread that, on the instigation of the Jews, the lepers wanted to eliminate the Christians by poisoning the wells. This news reached Catalonia and Aragon where the Jews were attacked. The Muslims were also accused of contaminating the water at the suggestion of the lepers. As proof of the quite good relationships between Christians and Mudéjars and the economic value of the latter in that region, however, there were not indiscriminate assaults against them. In August of that year, the king wrote to the authorities of Zaragoza not to believe those accusations but, as some Muslims had confessed (confessions obtained through torture), he ordered those people executed and all the others liberated. In Catalonia, the royal officials entered the lands of some aristocrats to arrest those Moors charged with that crime and, failing, instead accused a few nobles of harboring criminals. The sovereign decided not to prosecute them. The case of a Muslim believed to be a leper and accused of poisoning wells is also significant. While waiting for a thorough inquiry, the suspect's family members were told to keep him quarantined, and they were threatened with a heavy fine if they failed to do so.

6

Eliminating the other

Deportations and eliminations of Muslim subjects during the Middle Ages

In the Middle Ages, clashes with the faithful of the Crescent gave Christians opportunities to deport entire Muslim communities. The first to do this were the Byzantines during their campaign to reconquer a part of Syria in mid-tenth century. In order to secure that border area, Muslims who refused to convert to Christianity were enslaved and taken to the heart of the empire. Constantinople's authorities tended to adopt such drastic measures during their military operations against recently subjugated 'infidels.' Even Sicilian Muslims suffered this same fate in the thirteenth century, but in their case, it was in an area that had been under Christian rule for about one hundred and fifty years. The complete deterioration of the relations between the faithful of the two religions made the forced transfer of the Sicilian Muslims appear to be the only way to restore internal order. Throughout the chaotic power struggles in Sicily at the turn of the 1200s, the Christians there had repeatedly attacked the Muslims, who then reacted by fleeing the urban centers and counter-attacking. Adhering to the ancient proverb, 'the enemy of my enemy is my friend,' Islam's faithful allied with Markwald von Anweiler, a pretender to the German crown, and besieged Palermo for about twenty days. Strongly opposed to that German nobleman, the pope harshly condemned the impious alliance by demonizing Markwald and the Muslims siding with him. According to the pontiff, that 'new Saladin' attracted them to his side, giving them to drink Christian blood and venting their lust on Christian women. The pope then offered his co-religionists absolution of their sins to fight against the infidels. The struggle against Islam's faithful, therefore, intensified and took on religious significance.

The end of the infighting among Christians and the ascent to the throne of Frederick II, the legitimate heir to the throne, did not however bring peace to the island. Exasperated by many years of violence and abuse, many Muslims refused to lay down their arms. Moreover, taking advantage of the absence of the sovereign, who was engaged on other fronts, they led raids in various parts of Sicily and even attempted to create an Islamic state in Sicily. The most charismatic of the rebels assumed the significant title of 'Prince of the Believers,' used by caliphs and leading Islamic figures, and minted his own coinage. Soon after his coronation in 1220, Emperor Frederick II was able to focus upon Sicily and decided to quell the rebel Muslims by force. He gave them no quarter and his armies attacked all urban centers that rejected his authority. During this time, many Muslims hid in the mountains of the island, and Frederick II was often engaged on other fronts. Subsequently, this allowed Allah's followers to lead guerrilla campaigns that lasted many years. Resorting to 'scorched earth'-style tactics to eliminate the most difficult rebels while attempting to control all nonhostile Muslims was often counterproductive, very expensive, and sometimes impossible to implement. As a result, the emperor ordered that all the Sicilian Muslims be moved to another area of his kingdom far enough from Sicily, the sea, and the mountains, while remaining easily controllable.

The Apulian city of Lucera matched this outline. The first deportations took place around 1230 and continued for over ten years. Some fled and returned to Sicily, but were hunted down and brought back to Apulia. These actions provoked some uprisings that were promptly and bloodily stifled. By 1247, the last of the operations to deport Sicilian Muslims could be considered completed. About forty thousand Allah's faithful were taken to Lucera. Christians paid a high price to obtain their vision of a Muslim-free Sicily. The Muslims had provided much of the skilled labor, and their removal left many Sicilian trade centers and farms in disrepair and led to other negative consequences for the island. However, Lucera did not become a prison camp. Frederick II granted Muslim farmers numerous oxen to work their lands hoping to circumvent future revolts and transform the land into an asset. In addition, the emperor provided artisans with tools to produce weapons and other implements for the army. Sicilian rulers used some of Islam's faithful in the military campaigns against their Christian enemies. The emperor also granted Lucera's Muslims freedom of worship. These concessions raised many suspicions regarding Frederick II, to the point that his enemies called him 'the Sultan of Lucera.'

After the emperor's death in 1250, feelings toward Lucera among Christians gradually changed. The faithful of Allah were dislodged from the villages surrounding Lucera and forced to move into the city which became crowded, and the Muslim population found itself with scant resources. While no open revolts took place, many Muslims resorted to thievery and banditry out of necessity. On many occasions their Christian neighbors led punitive expeditions against the Muslims, sometimes resulting in indiscriminate killings. Accordingly, Muslims found more and more barriers to trade in Christian markets. The beatings at the market of the neighboring town of San Severo signified an end to such relations for the Muslim community. Still, no one in the Christian camp listened to complaints by Muslims. In 1269, Lucera's Muslims sided with Christian enemies of the king of southern Italy, and even though the sovereign punished the Christian rebels more harshly than the Muslims, because the latter were considered a valuable asset, this episode contributed to the intensification of hostilities between the believers of the two religions. Consequently, the existence of that 'Muslim island' began to be perceived as a thorny problem. External factors also fostered problems between Christians and Muslims. For example, Catholic preachers called for forcing all non-Christian subjects in European kingdoms to convert. Moreover, the failure of the king of France, uncle of Charles II of Anjou, king of southern Italy, to reclaim the Holy Land whose last Christian stronghold fell in 1291, contributed to worsen the feelings toward the Muslims of Lucera. The urgent need of Charles II of Anjou to obtain resources to finance the war against his enemies in Sicily and his personality should also be taken into consideration. Since he was unable to go to the Near East to fight the Muslims, perhaps Charles II of Anjou decided to eliminate those who lived on his lands.

In the end, drastic measures were taken to deal with the problem of Lucera. Because Muslims were considered 'servants of the king,' the Crown decided to take the city by force. In August 1300, Christian troops entered the city and took possession of it in a few days killing on the spot all those who resisted (including those who surrendered after taking up arms), and immediately deported the community leaders to the capital of the kingdom. Thanks to the collaboration of a Muslim knight and the members of his family, who earned the restitution of a portion of their properties and authorization to settle in a nearby city where they embraced Christianity, Christian authorities were able to develop an accurate census of Lucera's Muslims and find hidden foodstuffs, things necessary for organizing their orderly transfer. Muslims were divided into several groups, set on forced marches to the main cities of the kingdom, and within just over a month sold as slaves. The majority of those who converted were also subjected to the same treatment. Only those who had connections with members of the royal court and practiced professions for which there was a high demand, such as physician, managed to avoid that fate. Despite the severe prohibitions of the king who was eager to preserve those precious economic resources, Christian raiders killed and robbed numerous Muslims during their transfer and plundered their properties in Lucera. Some Muslims were able to run away, and in 1301, the sovereign issued several edicts promising rewards for the capture of the fugitives. As proof of some good will between Christians and Muslims, and of the fact that not everybody approved the king's decision, some Allah's faithful found protection among Christians. It is worth noting, for instance, the case of the monastery of St. Sofia of Benevento, one of the most famous in Campania, which offered hospitality and protection to a Muslim knight until it was explicitly ordered to turn him in to the authorities. It seems that some Christians purchased a few neo-converts of Lucera with the intention of freeing them.

In order to pursue the total elimination from the city of the 'infidels,' Christians destroyed the main mosque and built a cathedral as well as other religious buildings. Moreover, to rid themselves of the memory of the Muslim city known as Lucera, they christened their reborn city as 'City of Saint Mary.' The name Lucera continued to be used, but to stress the change, it was specified that it was 'Lucera of the Christians.' Although the king's order to track any remaining Muslims in his kingdom to make them pay taxes implies the presence of a certain number of free Muslim residents in southern Italy, Lucera's episode constitutes the first radical solution in a Christian kingdom to eliminate its Muslim subjects.

Spanish solutions: converting all the infidels and expelling all false Christians

The substantial number of Muslims in the Iberian Peninsula, their economic relevance, and probably the lack of sovereigns with the mentality of Charles II of Anjou, prevented the implementation of similarly harsh measures in Iberia during the Middle Ages. At the end of the fifteenth century, thanks to the marriage between Isabelle, Queen of Castile, and King Ferdinand of Aragon, as well as the subsequent fall of the Muslim kingdom in Granada, all of Spain came under Christian rule. The first step toward creating an identity suitable to the new situation was to eliminate non-Christian population. The Muslim and Jewish subjects were, therefore, given the option of either converting to Christianity or leaving the land their ancestors had inhabited for many centuries. Most Muslims decided to stay and embrace Christianity. Despite this, old Christians derogatorily called them Moriscos in order to emphasize their Moorish and Muslim origin. Following the precepts of Muslim jurists and religious leaders, which allowed for the dissimulation of the Islamic faith in case of danger, the majority of converts continued to see themselves as Muslims and to practice their faith in secret. Most Moriscos maintained separate communities, and the 'Old Christians' always regarded the 'New Christians' with suspicion.

All the same, their treatment, varied in accordance with the area in which they lived, their social standing, and the economic contributions they provided to the Crown. Considering the highly efficient manufacturing and commercial system of the Kingdom of Granada and the large amount of money generated in taxes by that region after the Christian conquest, Spanish rulers preferred to maintain the structure of Muslim society before conversion and avoided intervening in the cultural and religious affairs of Moriscos. Rulers also pushed Spanish churchmen to behave accordingly. As a result, these 'New Christians' kept most of their traditions; most of their elites became strong supporters of the new regime, and some of them cooperated with the royal court. In the rest of Spain, there were areas exclusively inhabited by Moriscos and others by 'Old Christians.' When the groups were co-mingled, the 'New Christians' were constantly reminded that they were second-class subjects. Although the sovereigns tried to propitiate marriages between the two groups, the vast majority of their subjects ignored this suggestion. With the exception of the conversion to Christianity, there was therefore a strong continuity between the Mudéjar and Morisco communities, and the latter continued to play a relevant role in the Spanish economy. The need to keep their farmers and artisans satisfied and therefore productive led the Christian lords to ignore their Morisco dependents' religious practices. This was so widespread as to induce the Inquisition to conduct careful inquiries about what was happening in the countryside. In a few cases the inquisitors accused some nobles of having allowed their Morisco tenants to practice Islam publicly.

The situation was different in the cities. In many cases, the accusations alleging the secret practice of the Islamic faith became a strategy for eliminating economic rivals or those enjoying a status superior to many 'Old Christians.' For instance, over the course of the sixteenth century almost all the wealthy Morisco families of Huesca were eliminated in this way. In Zaragoza, the local highly skilled masons, who descended from 'New Christians,' were denounced to the Inquisition, and many of them were burned at the stake for disavowing Christianity. Even if nothing could be uncovered about their behavior, Moriscos were always perceived as false Christians, and their actions deemed offensive. Authorities constantly forbade Morisco women from covering their heads and faces in public. Both legally and informally, the Moriscos were subjected to open discrimination which created an unsurmountable barrier to the integration between the 'New' and the 'Old' Christians. The former were not allowed to attend public baths with the latter and to bury their dead in churches. For changing residence or going to the coastal regions, Moriscos needed a permit that was not easily obtainable.

At the suggestion of the royal court's churchmen, in 1526, the sovereign issued a series of prohibitions aimed at suppressing the Morisco culture. Laws forbade the use of the Arabic language, Middle Eastern-style clothing, the veil for women, and numerous popular traditions of Muslim origin, including songs and dances. Moriscos were also ordered to adopt Christian names, and numerous restrictions concerning the practice of medicine were imposed on them. Additionally, the Church had to be in charge of their children's education. The New Christians, however, managed to obtain the suspension of the new laws for forty years through the payment of a very high sum to the king. To emphasize the fact that the atmosphere was changing, in 1526, the Inquisition was allowed to operate in Granada. Although the inquisitors acted cautiously, they implemented procedures that came to be adopted throughout the rest of Spain. For example, in order to garner help in discovering 'false Christians,' a share of their confiscated assets went to their accusers. Inquisitors also promised protection to the members of Morisco families who denounced their relatives. Moreover, the inquisitors often used anonymous denunciations as evidence and applied torture during interrogations. The discovery of large networks of Moriscos practicing Islam further encouraged the use of these methods. Rumors about the escape of many Moriscos with the help of Maghrebi Muslims, and the existence of small groups of Granada's Moriscos, who, having refused to convert, fought against Spanish soldiers and led raids against Christians, intensified the resentment toward Moriscos.

The situation in other parts of the world further exacerbated matters in Spain. In the 1500s, the Turks exerted great pressure on both Europe (in 1529 they besieged Vienna and shortly after they invaded almost all of Hungary) and the western Mediterranean. Moreover, they made Algeria part of the Ottoman Empire and, from there, launched numerous raids against the Spanish coasts. At the same time, the alliance between the king of France and the Turks against the Spanish spread the idea that the false Christians in Europe were ready to side with the Muslims to defeat the true Christians. Simultaneously, the emergence of the Reformation in Germany contributed to the feelings that Catholics were under siege. In the meantime, the King of Spain, Charles, received the imperial crown, and European Catholics came to see him as the defender of a Christendom that had to be protected from internal and external enemies. A clear sign of the tension between the 'Old Christians' and the Moriscos occurred in 1521 during the uprisings of the Valencian brotherhoods that were composed mainly of artisans. At first, the rebels attacked aristocrats, then they also assaulted the Moriscos as a way to harm both the nobles and the king. The fact that many 'New Christians' were among the militias of the great landowners provided a further reason for 'Old Christians' to assault the Moriscos indiscriminately, especially the wealthiest among them as they were considered economic rivals. At that time, it was unacceptable for 'false' Christians to be richer and have a better standard of living than true Christians. On that occasion, the troops charged with suppressing the uprising certainly did not behave as saviors of the Moriscos because they had no scruples against plundering the properties of the 'New Christians,' who, therefore, often found themselves between two fires. There were also other assaults in 1526. In this case, the hostilities were preceded by the appearance of a wandering Franciscan friar carrying a large crucifix while inciting the Old Christians to assault the 'New Christians,' shouting, 'Long live the Christian faith and war against the Moriscos.'

These episodes and the tightening measures against the 'New Christians,' however, had the effect of strengthening Morisco communities many of which continued to practice the Islamic faith, sometimes adopting forms of syncretism. The bravest among the wealthy also made the traditional pilgrimage to Mecca that every Muslim should undertake at least once in his life. Unlike most men who did not wear Morisco clothing in order to avoid confrontations with the old Christians, many women challenged the bans, continued to cover their heads, and even hid the Koran under their skirts during inspections. This atmosphere embittered the hearts of those among the 'New Christians' who actually had fully acculturated themselves and probably did genuinely accept the Christian faith.

In 1566, the extension of the anti-Morisco legislation enacted forty years earlier expired, and despite all attempts to prolong it, measures against the 'New Christians' were put into place. The cultural and socio-economic effects on the Moriscos were devastating and riots broke out immediately, the most serious of which took place in Granada. Declaring themselves faithful to Allah, the rebels elected a ruler following the ritual used in the former Muslim kingdom of

Granada, and, along with the help of Maghrebi volunteers, assaulted Christians. The king sent an army, and the fighting lasted over a year. After the defeat of the rebels, the sovereign removed by force Granada's 'New Christians' and sent them to every corner of Spain. There had been tension between generations of older and younger Moriscos, but this measure led to the strengthening of their cultural identity and communities throughout all of Spain. Morisco banditry became widespread in the kingdom and was no longer limited to the area surrounding Granada. The insurgency provoked a considerable escalation of propaganda against the 'New Christians,' who were explicitly compared to a foreign object that the Christian body had to expel. The fear that other revolts and plots might happen was very widespread among all social classes. Starting in 1580, a series of famines and epidemics created an ideal climate to commit and justify any violence against the false Christians and provide the true Christians an outlet for their frustrations at the same time. The most serious incident occurred in Aragon, where Christian shepherds killed Morisco peasants with impunity while local authorities turned a blind eye; on one occasion public officials even took part in the indiscriminate killing of 'New Christians.'

Meanwhile, the search for a decisive solution to the Morisco problem became more and more pressing. On several occasions, the king was presented with 'final solution' proposals including drowning all of them at sea or castrating the men and sterilizing the women. Unique in its inventiveness (the cruelty part is obvious) was the idea to send those who might survive the mutilation to Canada, where they might become extinct. Among the more 'charitable' plans was to enslave all of the Moriscos. The desire to avoid appearing as a bloodthirsty tyrant, as well as the fear of reprisal from the Ottoman Empire, convinced the sovereign to lean toward the option of expelling the Moriscos. Some members of the court and clergy opposed this plan, but calls for moderation went unheeded. To contrast the protests of churchmen, troubled by the idea of expelling a high number of Christians who once in Muslim lands would certainly renounce their Christian faith, the royal court presented the project as a way to put an end to an indomitable revolt, rather than solving a religious problem. For many years, both the Spanish Church and the court had portrayed the Moriscos as apostates and incorrigible rebels. According to a report given to the king, the disappearance of the Moriscos would have seriously damaged only the noble landowners in the Aragon and Valencia regions. As they had refused to pay new taxes to the Crown in the previous years, the sovereign perceived that measure as a beneficial side effect of expulsion. The king was also told that the confiscation of Morisco property would represent a great economic advantage to the monarchy.

Eventually, in September 1609, the king decreed that all the Moriscos in Valencia region had three days to present themselves to their local authorities in order to be transported to designated ports and then be expelled from Spain. In the countryside, six out of one hundred Moriscos had to remain on their estates in order to instruct the 'Old Christians,' to whom those properties had been allocated, about the functioning of mills and irrigation systems. Opposition to the edict was to be met with death but, at the same time, it was forbidden to attack and harass the Moriscos during their transfer. The vast majority of the Moriscos obeyed the orders (very few fled into the hills), after which they were taken to the Spanish enclave in Algeria, and were free to go where they wished. By the end of November of the same year, the expulsion from the Valencian region was completed. Even though the measure was no longer a surprise, the expulsion of the 'New Christians' of Aragon and Catalonia began in the spring of the following year. The bishop of Tortosa prevented the deportation of two thousand Moriscos residing in his diocese, stating that they were all 'good Christians.' The king of France offered the Moriscos the opportunity to settle in the northern reaches of his kingdom provided they were 'good Catholics.' On the contrary, the Ottoman sultan's request to the king of England to grant them asylum was completely dismissed. Almost all of the Moriscos from Aragon and Catalonia were transported to the coast of Maghreb.

In other parts of Spain, the Moriscos were given more time to leave, particularly to those living in territories far from the main ports, and were asked to leave voluntarily. They were allowed to sell their properties, and a 50% tax was imposed on the money they were taking away with them. With the exception of the aforementioned Moriscos of Tortosa, the only 'New Christians' to remain were the Maghrebi renegades, who had recently converted to Christianity, as well as the slaves of Christian masters, and the Moriscos of the Canary Islands who were exempted from the expulsion decree thanks to their particular origin and identity. Members of a community about nine miles from Murcia, who claimed they were Christians, disobeyed the edict, but were all forcibly deported any way. The local authorities were ordered to comb the entire kingdom to search for fugitives and 'New Christians' who had returned from Africa, but by February 1614, Spain declared itself free of Moriscos. Estimates suggest that around three hundred and twenty thousand Moriscos were expelled. Despite the promises made to the king, that measure caused serious damage to the Spanish economy. The loss of revenue resulting from such a large reduction in a tax base was actually one of the minor results of the expulsion. A larger problem was that the 'old Christians' could not replace the skillful Morisco artisans and farmers in the medium and long term. Moreover, many areas, characterized by elaborate irrigation techniques capable of creating varied and bountiful crops, disappeared almost completely and were replaced by less productive farming and animal herding activities. The Morisco expulsion was one of the factors that contributed to the decline of Spain in the second part of the early modern age.

Deporting and eliminating Christian subjects

Throughout the pre-modern age in the House of Islam, there were very few Christian insurrections against Muslim authorities, and therefore very rare were the cases in which it was considered necessary to deport or eliminate an entire community of Christian subjects. The most striking case occurred in southern Egypt, around 830, when a group of Christians rebelled justifying their actions with the very high taxes imposed on them by the region's governor, indiscriminate imprisonments, numerous homicides, and violence against their women. After several clashes with Muslim troops, that population surrendered and agreed to be transferred to Syria and Iraq, but almost all of them, narrates a Syrian Christian author, either died along the journey because of cruel treatment, or were sold as slaves. It was probably higher the number of Christian subjects from the main Andalusian cities who were exiled in 1126 to Morocco under suspicion of collaboration with the Christian king of Castile, who had attacked southern Spain that year. The fact that the Muslims wanted to prevent the Castilian sovereign from taking the Andalusian Christians into his dominion suggests that entire communities of Christ's faithful were subjected to this measure. The strict enforcement of bans on the dhimmis in Maghreb and the hostility shown by the locals toward the Christians convinced some of them to convert to Islam and generally prevented the growth of that community. In the case of the Christian subjects of Cyprus, who had rebelled in the eighth century, however, the opinion of those opposing deportation prevailed, as they pointed out that it was contrary to the agreements granted to Christian subjects in the seventh century. In the early modern period also rare were the episodes of expulsion of all Christian subjects of a region or a city for fear that they could collaborate with Christian enemies. The most famous instance occurred in 1099 when the Muslims drove away the Christians of Jerusalem when they learned of the approach of crusaders.

During the early Ottoman period, forced relocation of Christians to little-populated districts in need of economic revitalization took place. Nevertheless, those measures were not enacted as a form of punishment but, rather, as attempts to prevent the Christians from residing only in some areas. Moreover, in those years, population relocation was a provision adopted especially for Muslims, often forced to settle in Christian territories that the Ottomans had conquered. Sultan Muhammad II paid particular attention to this problem and, after the conquest of Constantinople, repopulated the city with Christians from the Black Sea and Turks from Central Anatolia. His successors adopted similar strategies, for the same reasons, in various parts of Greece and in the Aegean islands. For instance, in 1572 Christians from Cappadocia were brought to the recently conquered Cyprus. On the other hand, the transfer of a Bulgarian village's inhabitants to Anatolia was a punishment. After the Tanzimat edict they had revealed to be Christians. Half of them apparently died of hardship and illness during the journey.

It was not until 1915 that an entire Christian population was deported and nearly eliminated in a Muslim ruled state. As previously emphasized, in the case of the Armenians, beside the fact that they were Christians, their strong tendency to maintain their cultural identity played a significant role.

The efforts of the Young Turks government to establish a harmonious existence with the Armenians after the massacres of the late nineteenth and early twentieth centuries were jeopardized, then progressively nullified, due to external factors. The disastrous wars with Bulgaria, the Balkan countries, and Italy created, also among the Young Turks, an atmosphere that made them feel besieged by Christian powers, and that sometimes turned into paranoia. Several factors contributed to the creation of that atmosphere. First, the arrival in Anatolia of half a million Muslim refugees from the areas the Ottoman Empire lost in those wars (those refugees joined those who had fled for similar reasons in previous decades); the insistent rumors about the Europeans' desire to take possession of all the Ottoman Empire implying that 'infidels' would rule over Muslims; and finally, the persistence of Armenian guerilla fighters' activities.

The events precipitated with the outbreak of World War I. The Kurds, long-standing adversaries of the Armenians, had always perceived them as a kind of prey, and therefore feared punishment for violence that they had previously inflicted on the Armenians, particularly in the scenario of a Russian victory. Completely unprepared for modern warfare, the Ottoman Empire suffered numerous defeats. The landing of the Allies in Gallipoli, near Istanbul, on April 24, 1915, Ottomans' disastrous losses in the Caucasus regions at the hands of the Russian army, which included Russian Armenian troops, and the successful rebellion of the Armenians of Van, which led to the Russian occupation of that city on May 17 of the same year, induced the Ottoman government to seek a scapegoat that could justify those failures and give the Muslims of the region an outlet for their frustration. The Young Turks also felt a strong desire for revenge because, before the war, the Armenian revolutionaries had promised the Young Turks that they would not help the Tsarist Empire in exchange for the creation of an autonomous Armenian state in the event of an Ottoman victory. At the same time, the Young Turks threatened to take drastic measures if the Ottoman Armenians helped their enemies. When it became clear that Armenian volunteers were part of the Russian army and that Armenian guerilla fighters continued to operate in the Ottoman territories, the Ottoman authorities, believing that the Armenian civilians would lend their enemies logistical aid, reacted with brutality. On April 24, 1915, while the Allied troops were landing in Gallipoli, the Ottoman government ordered the suppression of every Armenian political organization, as well as the arrest and transfer to locations far from the front of all their members. They enforced those measures immediately in Istanbul and detained nearly two-thousand people, of whom nothing was heard of again; the same provisions were taken across all of Anatolia. Because of the intensification of Armenian revolutionary activities near Van, it was decided to extend that measure to all Armenians. At the end of May, the authorities issued the order of deportation to Iraq for all Armenians from central and eastern Anatolia, Cilicia, and Syria (they excluded the capital cities of the latter two zones). Additionally, they approved 'a temporary law concerning the measures to be taken by military authorities against those who obstruct state operations in the war.' Thanks to it, the Ottoman army could relocate the populations of villages and towns 'in response to any indications of rebellion and betrayal.'

As several studies based on nonpartisan sources emphasize, the Ottoman Government did not want the total physical elimination of the Armenians. Although some Young Turks' leaders held radical ideas about that people, there is no clear evidence to indicate that the decree was just a way to cover their true intentions. Moreover, the authorities did not possess the means to transport several hundred-thousand people. Suffice it to say that the inability of the Ottoman government and its army to provide medical assistance to the wounded and manage adequate provisions to its soldiers resulted in the deaths of hundreds of thousands of Ottoman soldiers during World War I. In addition, the railway designated for the transport of the Armenian sick, women, and children did not actually exist, and many had already died by the time the mass of deportees arrived at the railway heading to Baghdad. Moreover, it was inconceivable that, while the Ottoman forces were engaged on multiple fronts, a peaceful conduct of operations could take place in areas characterized by hatred and clashes for so many years. The rumors about the atrocities committed by the Armenians against the Muslims in Van strongly reactivated those hostile feelings. No central command was even formed to coordinate the logistics of the transfers. Local authorities carried the burden of implementing these efforts; even those officials who were willing to obey the orders properly could do almost nothing. Moreover, the Armenians had little time to prepare for the transfer and often found themselves at gathering points without any food. In some areas, local authorities conducted thorough searches among the Armenians and publicly displayed any discovery of weapons, thus, creating an atmosphere of strong suspicion toward them and justifying the arrest of men who were executed in isolated locations. Harput province suffered particularly bloody massacres. In their attempts to save their families, some girls agreed to marry Muslims or join their harems. Some Armenians converted to Islam, while some paid large sums to hide themselves or be included in the lists of highly specialized artisans who were exempt from deportation. These tactics did not always work. In the hopes of saving their children, some women sold them to Muslims. In the camps, it was not unusual to see officers accompanied by doctors looking for beautiful and healthy girls. Under pressure from European and American diplomats, the Sublime Porte exempted Protestant and Catholic Armenians from deportation in August, but many of them had already been forced to leave their homes.

The only significant clash between the Ottoman forces and the Armenians was in the city of Urfa, in the Aleppo district. This location had been spared from the deportation decree, but a series of indiscriminate arrests, killings, attacks, and counterattacks in the summer of that year further stirred up the tension between the local Armenians and the Muslims. The sight of long columns of desperate, stranded deportees throughout Urfa contributed to worsen the situation. It reached the point of no return when an Armenian deserter killed two police officers, leading to the massacre of several hundred Armenians at the hands of a Muslim crowd. The Armenian revolutionaries of Urfa persuaded their community to rebel if such a bloodbath were to take place again. In late September, the Armenians, by force of arms, forced the retreat of a police patrol investigating gunshots in their neighborhood. The rebels also fought off other policemen, who came to put down the uprising, and consequently the army intervened. Follow-ing an organized plan, the bells tolled to prompt the Armenians to defend their homes, and barricades were erected in the streets. Ottoman authorities needed to deploy no fewer than six thousand soldiers with heavy artillery to stamp out the Armenian resistance. Many Armenians committed suicide rather than be captured, and the soldiers executed anyone who surrendered. They only spared the men who could prove they did not participate in any rebellious activities.

Ottoman gendarmes were in charge of rounding up and escorting the Arme-nians to the gathering centers. Traditionally recruited from the lower strata of the Muslim population, these men were notorious for their poor training, use of violent methods, and rampant corruption (the government paid them poorly and infrequently during the war). The great need for soldiers caused a serious short-age of gendarmes, which the government then attempted to remedy by recruit-ing convicts. Among the policemen, there was also a high number of Circassians, who having moved to Anatolia, following the Ottoman defeats by the Russians in the second half of the nineteenth century, had always displayed a particular hatred toward the Armenians. These were clearly not the appropriate forces to perform peaceful deportations. The scantiness of the escorts assigned to the long lines of the displaced gave free hand to those who sought revenge or to pillage the refugees, especially in Kurdish territories. Those same escorts sometimes assaulted those whom they were supposed to protect, and bribing the escorts did not always guarantee safe passage. In order to share the spoils of the Armenians with the attackers or not risk their lives to defend them, some gendarmes fled upon the arrival of bandits. The latter after killing all the men and robbing them of their possessions, including clothing, dragged away young women and left the survivors completely naked with no food or water. On other occasions, the guards sold the Armenians to the Kurds as slaves.

The march to Iraq resulted in a very high number of deaths from hunger, hardship, disease, and violence; obviously, the longer the journey, the higher the casualties. The plight of the deportees did not end at their destination. Diseases, caused by appalling hygienic conditions, lack of food and water, and aggres-sions further decimated those who had survived the deportations. Even then, only those who still had money managed to secure protection and food, and sometimes, they even succeeded in being transferred to a safe location. In those conditions, the guards had no difficulties in finding women willing to prostitute themselves for a piece of bread. The Armenian labor battalions of the Ottoman army suffered a similar fate. At the start of the war, they were disarmed and used for heavy labor. Poor hygienic conditions and reduced rations caused a very high number of deaths. Despite their utility, many of these units were deported and many men were summarily executed.

Not all Muslims showed implacable hatred toward the Armenians. Harshly affected by the war and influenced by their government propaganda, most of the Ottoman Muslims were indifferent to the Armenians' sufferings. However, in spite of the harsh punishments for helping the Armenians, some Muslims fed and hid some of them (usually in exchange for some compensation). The Kurdish tribe of Dersim, who was traditionally friendly toward Christians, assisted those who could not pay. Some Ottoman army officers tried to protect the Armenians and punished those who attacked them. The most important of them was Gemāl, commander of the fourth army in Syria–Palestine, an area characterized more by the passing of large swaths of deportees than by transfers. He forbade violence against the Armenians in his district and did not hesitate to execute those who disobeyed his orders. Moreover, he succeeded in stopping the transfer of 150,000 Armenians to Iraq and kept them in Syria and Lebanon where he improved their living conditions. According to Gemāl, the deportation of the Armenians was necessary for the security of the Ottoman Empire, but defending their lives and property was a matter of moral integrity. Beyond his scruples, his benevolent attitude was likely influenced by his desire to offer a separate peace to the Allies as he envisioned an Asian Turkey in which he would rule, as well as an autonomous Armenian province. However, his membership in the Young Turks was not forgiven, and two Armenians assassinated him in 1922 during a vast operation to eliminate the leaders of that group.

At the end of August, the Ottoman government ordered the end of all deportations, yet the decree was largely ignored. Following protests and pressure from the international community, as well as from their Austrian and German allies, the Ottoman authorities repeated those orders on several occasions. The decree to end deportations excluded people deemed to be dangerous to the state and offered many officials the excuse to continue the transfers that took place until the beginning of 1917.

We will never know the exact number of the victims of those deportations, but its outcome for the Armenians of northeast Anatolia was close to a complete genocide. Although some areas of the Ottoman Empire were unaffected by the decree, the chaotic post-war situation in Turkey, the fear of being attacked, and the terrible economic and sanitary conditions convinced the majority of Ottoman Armenians to emigrate. The failed attempt by the Greeks to occupy large areas of Anatolia, culminating in the near-total destruction of Izmir in 1922 (the local Armenian district was the first to be set on fire when Turkish troops arrived in the city) greatly accelerated that process. It is estimated that in 1914 the Armenian population of the empire amounted to about two million and that currently about ninety thousand Armenians live in Turkey.

Twentieth-century epilogue: Muslims with Muslims and Christians with Christians

In the nineteenth century, the independence movements of the Ottoman Empire's Balkan provinces, often aided by foreign powers, ultimately resulted in the loss of those territories by the Sublime Porte. On those occasions, both Christian rebels and the Ottoman army often carried out attacks against civilians as well. The revolutionaries' aggressions against the Muslims aimed to provoke brash reactions from the Ottoman troops, thus hoping to gain more support from the Christian civilian population. Resentments and tensions, that had been under control for centuries, exploded provoking a spiral of retaliations. The use of undisciplined irregular militias by both sides, formed by ethnic groups that held a particular grudge against the other, made matters worse. The Ottomans, for instance, hired Albanians in the War of Independence of the Greeks and Circassians in the Bulgarian uprising in 1876 and in the war with Russia that supported the Bulgarian revolutionaries (1877—1878). In turn, the Russians employed Cossacks in that conflict. On that occasion, the number of civilian casualties resulting from violent clashes, illness, and hardship was high, and for the first time in the modern period, this phenomenon also affected Muslims extensively. The Turkish press and various observers indicated how the Russians and the Bulgarians were implementing a well-conceived policy to eliminate the Muslims, but this was an exaggeration. According to the 1887-Bulgarian census, about 50% of the pre-war Muslim population still lived in that nation. Approximately two-thirds of the missing Muslims migrated to Ottoman territories. Bulgaria's independence caused a notable change in the composition of its inhabitants, of whom Muslims had constituted 38%. Following the war, the country became more Christian. Still, despite the postwar climate remaining tense for many Bulgarian Muslims, there were no official attempts to expel them. Although with less violence, these phenomena also distinguished the other Balkan countries, which became independent or were annexed by a European state.

The humiliating defeats suffered by the Ottoman Empire in 1913 at the hands of Greece, Montenegro, Serbia, and Bulgaria signaled the end of a process marking the near-total loss of the Sublime Porte's European territories. The losses stretched from the Adriatic to the Black sea including parts of southern modern Albania, Serbia, and Bulgaria, along with northern areas of Greece, comprising the regions the Ottomans had conquered in the fifteenth century and Thessaloniki, one of the largest cities in the empire. Prior to the Balkan conflicts, the Muslims in those areas made up about 51% of the population. Even with a reduced number of casualties, what happened during and after the war with the Bulgarians and Russians in 1878 took place on that occasion as well. In the countryside and in the cities, the Muslims were subjected to abuse and violence from gendarmes and irregular troops, as well as Christian refugees coming from the few European territories still under Ottoman rule. Even in the safest neighborhoods in Thessaloniki, Muslims were harassed. Christian refugee groups settled in their homes and looted their shops. The Muslim population decreased between one half and two thirds, depending on the geographic area, and a substantial majority of Christians inhabited those lands again. Even in this scenario, governments did not implement Muslims' expulsions.

In the Ottoman Empire, the suspicion that Christian recruits had boycotted war operations and their co-religionists in Anatolia had provided economic aid to the Sublime Porte's enemies was very widespread. From that moment onward, most Ottoman Muslims believed that the European powers aimed to divide the Empire with the support of Christian subjects. This therefore furthered the idea that it was necessary to create a Turkish state inhabited only by Allah's faithful. The fact that the conflict with the Balkan countries displaced nearly 177,000 Muslims from Serbia and, particularly, Bulgaria to Istanbul and Anatolia reinforced these belligerent attitudes. Moreover, Muslim emigration fostered the belief that those nations only wanted Christian citizens. In 1913, the Sublime Porte and Bulgaria reached an agreement for the exchange of members of the religious minorities residing near their border, and similar negotiations were held with Greece on the following year. All this indicates that the Ottoman and Balkan governments planned to create nations inhabited exclusively by people of the same creed and to expel the religious minorities. That idea began to proliferate even among western European politicians and diplomats. In 1914, the British ambassador in Istanbul pointed out with regret that this was the only way to resolve a tragic situation that had lasted for over a century.

The defeats suffered by the Ottomans in World War I made the situation much worse. Though not comparable to the violence and deportations inflicted upon the Armenians, Orthodox Christian communities were affected as well. Those in close proximity to war zones—Thrace, the coasts of the Mediterranean and the Black Sea—and railways were taken to areas believed not to be prone to war operations. Even then, the number of people who died from hardship, disease, and bandit attacks during forced marches was very high. The Ottoman army conscripted almost all adult males into their labor battalions where the mortality rate was very high as well. However, the situation completely deteriorated at the end of the war. The Ottoman Empire was among the losers, and the behavior of the victors confirmed the worst suspicions of the Sublime Porte's Muslim subjects. The French and British occupied Istanbul and some Near-East regions of the Ottoman Empire. Furthermore, after obtaining the region surrounding Izmir, the Greeks tried to take possession of a large amount of territory in central Anatolia. The conflict ended in 1922 with the Turks emerging victorious. Both the Greeks and the Turks inflicted numerous atrocities upon the civilian population; a European eyewitness stated that after that conflict, the Greeks could not consider the Turks as champions of barbarism and violence any longer. Armed clashes, massacres of civilians, illness, and emigration caused a significant drop in the entire population of Anatolia during and after the war; in 1923, the population had decreased by about 20% compared to ten years earlier. What changed above all, however, was the proportion of its inhabitants. In those years, the percentage of Muslims in Anatolia rose from 80% to 98%. This statistic along with the hatred and feelings of retaliation aroused by the conflict to drive out the Greek invaders—significantly called the War of Independence by the Turks—had therefore created the conditions for a state formed exclusively of Muslim citizens.

Peace negotiations between Greece and Turkey took place in Lausanne in 1922 and 1923. The Turks initially proposed to exchange all Christians living in their state for the Muslims who still resided in areas once belonging to the Ottoman

Empire. The absence of an Armenian delegation and, more importantly, the fear of renegotiating with the Soviet Union, convinced the Turks to exclude the Armenians and to limit their request to the Orthodox Christians. The exchange was to take place exclusively with Greece. Because both governments were facing the problem of the previous years' refugees, they hoped to solve the issue of resettlement by using the properties of the 'exchangeables,' and therefore pressed for the exchange to be mandatory. Only after lengthy discussions and intense pressure from the Allies, did the Turkish government agree that the 'Greeks' of Istanbul (about 110,000) were exempt from the exchange as long as they did not require any privileges. Two-thirds of them, who had been subjects of the Ottoman Empire, received Turkish citizenship. The other third, having settled in that city before March 1918, received permission to stay. According to a clause in the agreement, the Orthodox Christians, who had resided in Istanbul before World War I and then left it, were permitted to return to their houses. Yet, seeking to harm that community, the Turkish government decided that this allowance was reserved only for those who had a Turkish Republic passport and, therefore, only those who had left after October 29, 1923 could return. As a result, the authorities excluded almost thirty thousand Orthodox Christians who lived in Greece and had Ottoman passports. Instead, they expelled those who lived in the Asian area of the city. The others suffered many intimidations after Allied troops left Istanbul, and many seizures of Christians' properties occurred. The Greeks committed similar violations of the agreements against the Muslim populations of northeast Greece, that had been excluded from these exchanges.

Both the Greeks and the Turks decided to implement the exchange, adopting a criterion based on the exchangeables' religion and their ideas regarding Greek and Turkish identities; usually, ethnicity and cultural background did not affect this. For instance, in Turkey, the Karamanlides, who spoke Turkish and only shared a common Christian faith with the Greeks, were, in spite of their firm opposition, listed among the exchangeables. In Greece, that list included Greek-speaking Cretan and Albanian Muslims and descendants of Thessalonian Jews, converted to Islam in the seventeenth century, still speaking the language of their ancestors, i.e., the Jews expelled from Spain at the end of the fifteenth century, who had then settled in the Ottoman Empire. Another paradoxical occurrence happened to the Gagauz Turcomans, a Turkish tribe established in northeastern Greece before the Ottomans. Even though they were Christians, they were considered 'exchangeables.' To prevent Muslims from acquiring Albanian passports and avoiding expulsion, the Greek authorities established that only those whose fathers were born in Albania, were residing in Greece, and had no 'Turkish awareness' were considered Albanians.

The exchange operations officially began in December 1923 (often times, it was just making official an in-progress process) and finished at the end of the following year. These measures affected approximately 350,000 Muslims and 290,000 Christians. Most of the 'Greeks' of Anatolia (about a million) had already begun to emigrate to Greece when the tide of war between Greeks and

Turks began to favor the latter. Except for the aforementioned Karamanlides, who hoped to be spared from the expulsion, the Orthodox Christians continued to emigrate even during the Lausanne negotiations. The majority of eligible Muslims in Greece instead waited for the ratification of the agreements. Both the Turkish and Greek authorities expropriated the assets of the dispossessed minorities for sums much lower than their actual value; the Turks included properties sold to foreigners and those that the 'Greeks' of Istanbul owned in Anatolia.

The agreement signed in Lausanne raised considerable protests from both sides. In Greece, many Muslims asked the government for exemptions by declaring that they were completely satisfied with how they were treated and that they did not want to leave their homeland nor the graves of their ancestors. They even went further, saying that they did not wish to go to a foreign land and return under 'the bad Turkish administration.' In Thessaloniki, they attempted to appeal to the consciences of the politicians by arguing that the decision was 'a scandalous barter of bodies that offends modern civilization.' Nearly all eight thousand Muslim inhabitants of that city did not want to leave. Among the few who were allowed to stay was a former Ottoman colonel and court photographer who had opposed the formation of a secular Turkish nation to the point that he fought alongside the Greeks during their invasion of Anatolia. Impoverished and abused, the majority of Islamic farmers were, on the contrary, very eager to move to Turkey.

In Turkey, many also sought exemption from the exchange, but the vast majority of requests failed. The few successful exceptions concerned those who succeeded in demonstrating that they had helped the Turkish troops during the war against the Greek invasion. For example, a doctor was allowed to stay for having saved the lives of many Muslims in that conflict. In response to the wave of Christian conversions to Islam during the Lausanne negotiations, the Turkish authorities suspended further conversions. Afterward, the newly converted were added to the number of those to be expelled, and marriages between Christians and Muslims after the ratification of the agreement were invalidated.

Many protests concerned the manner in which these exchanges were conducted. In most cases, the Christians only had two weeks to leave their homes, bringing with them only a few personal effects. In addition, they had to pay for maritime passage to Istanbul. Even if the Greek authorities declared that they could not provide such a great number of refugees with accommodation, food, and transportation to Greece in so little time, the Turks kept sending thousands of Christians to Istanbul. This time, the massacres and appalling conditions in which the Armenian deportations took place in 1915 did not occur, but Turkish bandits often robbed Christians during the transfers. The great crowding and the deplorable hygienic conditions in the Turkish deportation centers also favored outbreaks of typhus and cholera causing many casualties. In the eleven-day voyage by ship from Istanbul to Thessaloniki, a ten-year-old boy whose father had died in Turkey described how he and his fellow travelers starved, and five refugees died of hardships. These problems also characterized the transfer of the Muslims from Greece to Turkey, but to a much lesser extent. Complications at the port of Thessaloniki arose with the arrival of thousands of Yugoslavian Muslims hoping to settle in the now-abandoned properties of the Anatolian Christians. They were so numerous that the Turkish government had to temporarily stop any further boarding. The Cretan Muslims experienced far more efficient operations. For a bitter coincidence, both the Turkish and Greek government leaders of that period, Mustafa Kemal 'Atatürk' and Eleftherios Kyriakou Venizelos, were born and raised in areas heavily affected by the expulsion of the Muslims; the first was from Thessaloniki, while the second was from Crete. Fortunately, clashes between those arriving and those leaving were rare. In Thessaloniki, hungry Christian refugees sacked a few Muslim shops. Due to scarce housing and the general misery of the camps, others lived in the homes of the Muslims, sometimes with the owners still residing there. Most of the time, this cohabitation worked out, and a Muslim remembered how some of the intruders were kind people who knew Islamic customs and spoke Turkish. On the other hand, after publicly boasting about selling some cows at high prices to refugees, a Muslim man and his wife were murdered.

In addition to the trauma caused by the displacement of the people directly involved and the controversy surrounding how the exchanges took place, the relocation of hundreds of thousands of people caused serious social and economic damage. Although both governments touted the process as a great success, the chaos and occupation of abandoned properties by local populations in both countries obstructed the process. Furthermore, the attempts at resettling the new arrivals with the goal of accommodating the skillsets that they brought from their home countries failed. Even though a Turkish parliamentarian would claim that 'the arrival of every single individual is a source of wealth for us; and the departure of every single individual is a blessing for us,' this could not be further from the truth for both countries. Including the prelude to the exchanges, the entire process had significant consequences for many areas in Anatolia. A large ruralization of those regions took place, and the disappearance of the Orthodox Christians — most of whom were artisans — had serious effects on Turkish economy, that for a generation was essentially based on farming. This also slowed the formation of a middle class capable of expanding and prospering autonomously with little reliance on the state.

In Greece, the final number of refugees had a much stronger demographic impact as they formed about one fifth of the indigenous population. In this period, the inhabitants of Athens and Thessaloniki doubled. and 'new towns,' that were actually refugee camps, arose around the main urban centers. In Thessaloniki, the old Muslim cemetery outside the walls became the first refugee camp because it was considered an 'exchangeable asset.' Many newcomers remained there for several years and often for all their lives in very precarious conditions, and most only managed to obtain temporary and low-paying jobs. This prevented their integration into Greek society and caused strong tensions with the local population that sometimes resulted in violent clashes. The cultural differences between the groups fed the resentments, and the socioeconomic gap between them furthered the divide, as many refugees had actually come from more educated and prosperous backgrounds. Many did not even consider themselves as Greeks, but rather as Eastern Christians or Anatolian Christians. To the great surprise of the Greeks, these co-religionists spoke strange dialects and often knew the Turkish language better than Greek, sometimes only knowing the former (some Muslims from Crete shared similar experiences in Turkey because they only spoke the Cretan dialect). In Greece, prejudices and stereotypes toward the 'other' were widespread in both communities. The refugees were referred to as 'Turks' and 'baptized with yoghurt.' In turn, they considered most Greek peasants primitive. The frustration of having lost their socioeconomic status, a sense of alienation, and the nostalgia for their homelands were strongly felt among the new-comers. Their living conditions in rural areas were not any better. Native Greeks immediately acquired the best lands that the Muslims were forced to abandon, both legally or illegally, making life for the refugees problematic. Many of them had to go into debt with local elites and were forced to live as sharecroppers or laborers. The newcomers also triggered significant effects on the political scenario that gradually became more fragmented and increasingly radical, shifting from being monarchists versus liberals to Right versus Left. Relying on the support from the slums created with the arrival of refugees, the following two decades saw the Greek Communist party assume a relevant role in Greek politics. The problems created by the arrival of the Anatolian Greeks undoubtedly contributed to the reasons that led to the creation of military dictatorships and the civil war (1949—1951).

The exchange of populations did not mark the normalization of relations between Greece and Turkey, nor did it signal the improvement of relations with the respective religious minorities in those countries. Despite the strong campaign to secularize Turkish society, the notion that Muslims were the only true Turkish citizens did not disappear. The constant tension between Turkey and Greece kept religious discrimination and general disdain for the other alive. For instance, in the period between 1942 and 1944, the exorbitant taxes on assets applied almost exclusively to the Turkish citizens of Christian and Jewish faiths. Since Greece was under German occupation at the time, the Turkish government was certain that this measure would not stir strong opposition among its targets. The dour climate between the Turkish and Greek states surrounding the question of Cyprus induced most of the Orthodox Christians of Istanbul with Turkish citizenship to leave Turkey in the 1950s and in the 1960s; particularly violent were the aggressions the Turkish government promoted in early September 1955. By the end of the 1990s, the Orthodox Christian population of Istanbul fluctuated between 2,500 during winter and 5,000 in the summer time.

Another example of this tension occurred in the small islands of Imbros and Tenedos in the Aegean Sea, mostly inhabited by Christians. At Lausanne negotiations the Turkish government succeeded in getting them back even though they had been under Greek rule since 1912. In the late 1960s and early 1970s, a series of restrictions concerning the education of the Christian population and a massive expropriation program of their assets led to the emigration of almost all the island's inhabitants who were then replaced with Anatolian Turks. The names of the islands and towns were changed, and the first mosque created in the islands in 1965 was built on a confiscated property and symbolically called the 'Mosque of the Conqueror,' that is, the very same name of the mosque the Ottomans constructed over the Basilica of the Twelve Apostles a few years after the conquest of Constantinople in 1453.

The Greek government granted citizenship to about one hundred thousand Muslims who had always lived in northeastern Greece and had been excluded from the exchange in 1923. They could practice their religion freely, have their own schools, newspapers, radio, and television in Turkish. Until the worsening of the Cyprus crisis, the Greeks tended to ignore their presence. Tensions rose as the crisis deepened, particularly during the rule of the military junta (1967—1974), which implemented a series of restrictive measures against them. However, those restrictions were not comparable to what the Orthodox Christians suffered in Istanbul and the Aegean islands. Greece's entry into the European Community led it to pay more attention to the civil rights of the Muslim minority.

The impossible task of reaching a peaceful agreement between Muslims and Christians in an area once part of the Ottoman Empire, distinguished by a substantial presence of religious minorities, resurfaced in Cyprus, a British colony until 1959. The strong disagreements among the Christians, who wanted to join Greece, and the Cypriot Muslims, who preferred to be a substantial minority in a British colony (most of whom feared expulsion), degenerated into bloody clashes after Cyprus's independence. The presence of extremists on both sides, of supporters of the union to Greece among the Christians, and of advocates of the division of the island into two parts among the Muslims prevented the Cypriot parliament from functioning and the formation of a mixed public administration, police, and army. All these problems further fueled the conflicts that led to the disappearance of numerous towns inhabited by believers of both religions. Only the UN deployment of an interposing force avoided civil war. To the coup d'état of the Cypriot national guard that in 1974 put in power a strong supporter of the union with Greece, Turkey replied by occupying about a third of the island and half of the capital; the Turkish government justified the military intervention with the role of guarantor of Cyprus' independence the treaties of 1959—1960 assigned to Turkey. This action caused Cypriot Christians to flee from that area and the flow to that zone of the Muslims still residing in the other section of the island. Both areas founded a republic consisting exclusively of co-religionists and, in so doing, dispelled the illusion of being able to create a democracy in which there was a strong religious minority.

Conclusions

Both Muslim and Christian rulers allowed their subjects who were of a faith different from their own to continue practicing their religion, provided they accept their acknowledged state of inferiority. The rulers nonetheless created different systems based on varying forms of legitimacy. The system created by the faithful of Allah was established by the Koran and therefore had a religious foundation, while in the system developed in the Christian kingdoms, Muslim subjects were classed in the category of 'servants of the king.' They were thus placed under the direct protection of the monarchs against all and any abuses, but that status underscored their complete dependency on the will of the rulers, with whom they often had to negotiate rights and duties, making them legally subject to the occasionally drastic decisions of the sovereigns.

All those who followed the religion of the dominators and those professing the faith of the dominated generally led separate but intertwining lives. For the most part, relations among them were peaceful and even though there were still significant differences in treatment and a certain degree of contemptuous superiority among the former toward the latter, the prohibitions and discriminations toward second-class subjects still did not tend to exert a powerful impact on the policies of the rulers and on the realities of daily life. Attributing to a religion, period, or population a special and intrinsic predisposition to peaceful coexistence and tolerance with regard to religiously diverse subjects, whose inferiority is determined legally, is not a correct approach because, in point of fact, those conditions were the product of very particular economic, social, demographic, and political circumstances. At the same time, explaining the existence of tolerance and peaceful coexistence as a product of mere convenience is too reductive, because it attributes to human beings an all-too-mechanical behavior, linking actions and results in an extremely articulated field, where the relationship among those factors is not always obvious and immediate. While not attempting to provide a general interpretation of such complex themes, we can reasonably state that once the second-class subjects had accepted their condition of inferiority, respected the less discriminatory measures, refrained from flaunting whatever wealth they might have accumulated, and cultivated good relations with the authorities, the members of the faith of the dominators then by and large proceeded to ignore them or else carried on nonconflictual relations with them and in some cases even collaborated with them, sharing beliefs and locations and even feasting with them, thereby acknowledging more or less implicitly that communities prosper when there are no tensions and conflicts. What instead tended to be inspired by convenience were the policies and behaviors adopted by rulers and rich land-owners for whom those types of subjects worked, as long as they continued to adhere to the roles they were supposed to embody, that is, productive, obedient, and silent. On both micro and macro levels in these relationships and in their de-velopment, it was always the numerical bulk of these subjects and their economic and social roles that were particularly fundamental.

While it is necessary to avoid demonizing those relations, and taking into account the numerous nuances, it is also incumbent upon us to avoid idealizing them, which might thereby mean presenting an imaginary world of peaceful co-existence and fecund multiculturality. In fact, societies were not created in which those special subjects were different from the others merely because they paid an extra tax and were required to respect certain prohibitions. They were often denied access to public employment and military service, and their opportunities for social and economic improvement were decisively inferior, factors that, com-bined with the discriminations of the legal system and, in some cases, economic difficulties, in various situations proved so intolerable a difference that it pushed them to simply adopt the religion of the dominators.

Likewise impossible to maintain is the position of those who attribute to a religion, people, or period a particular tendency to intolerance and persecution. Christianity and Islam are monotheistic religions, and are therefore not inclusive ones. Their faithful believe that they worship the only true God. There have al-ways been Muslim and Christian extremists, especially among the religious lead-ers, who did not limit themselves to underscoring that notion, but instead made a strong point of calling out the falseness of the others' religion and emphasizing how much of a threat they were to their own faithful, because they contam-inated the rituals and the sacred space of the true faith, menacing and infect-ing the true believers. Those radicals often demanded ironbound application of laws concerning those subjects and their segregation, if not, in certain cases, their outright elimination. In periods of prosperity and in the absence of catastrophic emergencies, there were relatively few persons who shared that type of ideas and attitudes, and as a result, they did not constitute a problem. For the most part, the extremists obtained only the partial result of reminding their coreligionists of those concepts, instilling in them an extra bit of contempt and a sense of superi-ority, rather than any outright hostility toward those people. Grave economic cri-ses, along with epidemics, natural catastrophes, and heavy defeats at the hands of outside enemies nonetheless tended to exacerbate the need for a scapegoat, as well as envy toward the second-class subjects who had achieved success. At those times, the affinities and peaceful relations were soon forgotten, and clearly distinct identities emerged. In particular, there was a sharp increase in the number of people willing to lend an ear to the extremists and ready to attack the other. The graver those crises became, the more numerous the radicals and the greater the likelihood of an explosion of violence and its resulting intensity. It was the combination of long-term factors and specific contexts that produced the conflicts. In those circumstances, slaughters and plundering practiced against those subjects ensued, both in the House of Islam and in the kingdoms of Christendom. That violence could be unleashed when the central authorities were weak and therefore incapable of securing the preservation of domestic order. In the Ottoman Empire, the explosions of violence occurred only in the modern age because powerful tensions, caused by some of the factors previously mentioned as well as the reform meant to eliminate all differences among subjects, arose exclusively in the nineteenth century and at the beginning of the twentieth century. Those episodes and the great difficulties encountered in carrying out that change clearly make it obvious that a stroke of the pen would never be sufficient to eradicate a centuries-old system designed and created to emphasize the superiority of Muslims.

The ways in which the Christian and Muslim rulers managed to eliminate those religious minorities were different, but even this difference was due to very specific contexts rather than approaches dictated by religion. In the cases of the Sicilian and Iberian faithful of Islam, their elimination was no doubt facilitated by their status, which technically made them property of the Crown. In both cases, these were not immediate processes. The more rapid of the two processes had to do with the Sicilian Muslims, who were first subjected to the grueling experience of a forced transfer to Lucera, triggered by their indomitable revolt. In their case, the presence of a monarch who had been raised in a setting devoid of Muslim subjects and assailed by economic problems, and their relatively limited number, made it possible to reduce them all to a state of slavery and subsequently sell them off. Considerably more complex was the situation of the far more numerous Iberian believers in Islam whose almost forced conversion did nothing more than to delay by a century their expulsion which was influenced by factors both external and internal. In the House of Islam, conditions that induced the rulers to undertake large-scale transfers and eliminations as well as to expel subjects of differing religion, on the other hand, took place only in the first part of the twentieth century. The high number of victims and refugees on those occasions should constitute a sobering warning with respect to what can happen in societies where written and unwritten differences are created on the basis of religious affiliation. The absence of a complete integration between Christians and Muslims, caused by the persistence of preconceptions, and the continual occurrence of bloody attacks against the other in western nations and in Muslim ones, as well as the existence of laws punishing with death sentences any act of blasphemy against Islam in nations such as Pakistan, remind us that the topics treated in this book do not merely concern a distant past.

Glossary

Almohads   Moroccan Muslim dynasty that ruled over northwest Africa and a part of the Iberian Peninsula between the 1140s and the beginning of the twelfth century.

Almoravids   Moroccan Muslim dynasty that ruled over northwest Africa and Islamic Spain from the late eleventh to the mid-twelfth century.

Anatolia   Area corresponding approximately to present-day Turkey.

Andalusia   It is derived from the Arabic word Al-Andalus, which was used for the Iberian Peninsula (Modern Spain and Portugal)

Caliph   It literally means 'successor.' The leader of the Muslims held this title. In the tenth century, the rulers of Andalusia and of Egypt claimed this title. Consequently, there was a caliph in Baghdad, one in Cordoba, and another one in Cairo.

Copts   Indigenous Egyptian Christians who have a liturgy and beliefs different from those of Catholic and Orthodox Christians.

Dhimmis   Free Jewish and Christian subjects living in territories under Muslim rule.

Druzes   Religious group of Muslim origin that was created in the eleventh century and was, and is, still mainly present in Lebanon.

Emir   Regional Muslim ruler.

Fatimids   Shia Muslim dynasty that ruled over a part of North Africa, Egypt, and Syria between the tenth and the twelfth centuries.

Jizyah   As a sign of their subjugation, male dhimmis aged approximately ten and up were required to pay a tax known as the jizyah, the amount of which varied depending on income (three categories were created).

Maghreb   It literally means 'the West.' It indicates the region corresponding approximately to present-day Morocco and western Algeria.

Mamluks   They were former slave soldiers who were able to create an independent state in Egypt and Syria (mid thirteenth century – beginning of the sixteenth century.

Melkites   Orthodox Christians.

Moor   Definition used for the Muslims of the Iberian Peninsula.

Moreria   Muslim neighborhood of the urban centers of the Iberian Christian kingdoms.

Mudejar   Free Muslim subjects of the Christian kingdoms of the Iberian Peninsula.

Ottomans   Turkish population which settled in Anatolia at the end of the thirteenth century. This term later designated all the subjects of the empire they had created.

Ramadan   Holy Muslim period during which Islam's faithful fast and abstain from sex from dawn to sunset.

Shiites   Muslims believing that the descendants of Ali, cousin and son-in-law of the prophet Muhammad, are the legitimate leaders of the Muslims.

Sublime Porte   Definition used for indicating the government of the Ottoman empire.

Sultan   It is derived from an Arabic word that means 'authority/power.' From the late Middle Age, some Muslim rulers, who had full sovereignty (for example, the Mamluk and the Ottoman rulers), used sultan as their title.

Sunnis   'Orthodox' faithful of the Islam community of which they are the majority. They assumed this name to emphasize that, unlike the Shiites, they are following the true tradition (sunna) of the prophet Muhammad.

Tanzimat   On November 3, 1839, the Ottoman sultan issued the edict of *Tanzimat* (reforms) in which he established the principle of equality between dhimmis and Muslims.

Vizier   The highest office in the Muslim courts.

Young Turks   An early-twentieth-century movement that aimed to create a constitutional government in the Ottoman Empire.

Timeline

1187.	Saladin defeats the kingdom of Jerusalem's army at the Battle of Hattin, and then he occupies Jerusalem
1195.	The Almohads defeat King Alfonso III of Castile at the Battle of Alarcos.
1212.	A coalition of Christian Iberian kings beat the Almohads at the Battle of Las Navas de Tolosa.
1236.	King Ferdinand III of Castile conquers Cordoba
1238.	King James I of Aragon takes possession of Valencia
1300.	Elimination of Lucera's Muslims
1385.	The Ottomans conquer Sofia (Bulgaria)
1389.	The Ottomans defeat a coalition of Balkan states at Kossovo-Polje
1430.	Ottoman capture of Thessaloniki
1439.	The Ottomans annex Serbia
1444.	The Ottomans defeat a coalition of west and central European states at Varna (Bulgaria)
1453.	Ottoman conquest of Constantinople
1492.	Fall of Granada, the last Muslim principality of the Iberian Peninsula
1517.	The Ottomans take possession of Egypt
1526.	Hungary becomes a vassal of the Ottoman Empire
1529.	The Ottomans besiege Vienna
1541.	Ottoman annexation of Hungary
1609–1614.	Moriscos' expulsion from Spain
1669.	The Ottomans conquer the capital of Crete, Candia
1683.	The Ottomans besiege Vienna
1798.	Napoleon attacks Egypt
1839.	Edict of Tanzimat
1876.	First Ottoman Constitution
1908.	The Young Turks take the power
1914–1918.	World War I
1915–1916.	The Ottomans deport the Armenians of northeast Anatolia. A very high number of Armenians die during the transfers
1923.	Proclamation of the Republic of Turkey
1974.	The Turks occupy a part of Cyprus

Maps

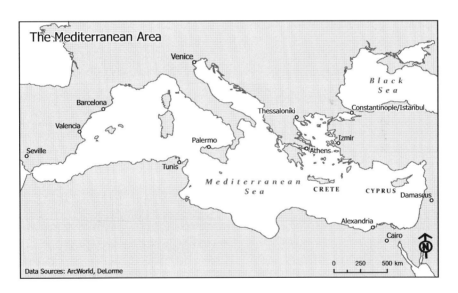

The Mediterranean Area

Venice

Barcelona

Valencia

Seville

Palermo

Tunis

Thessaloniki

Black Sea

Constantinople/Istanbul

Izmir

Athens

Mediterranean Sea

CRETE

CYPRUS

Damascus

Alexandria

Cairo

Data Sources: ArcWorld, DeLorme

0   250   500 km

MAP 1

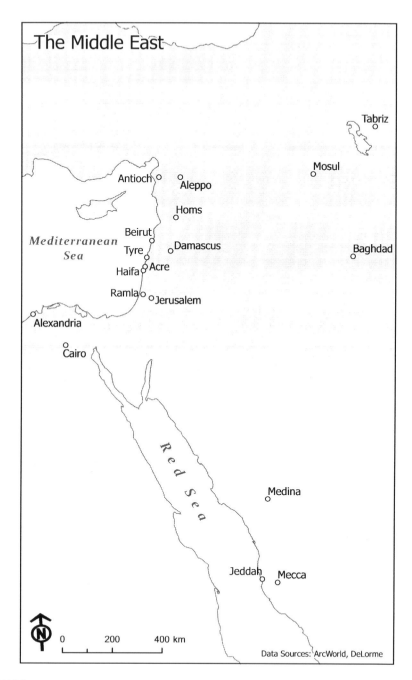

MAP 2

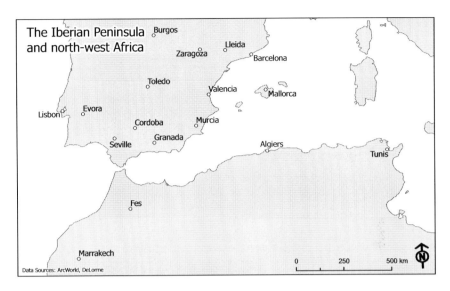

The Iberian Peninsula and north-west Africa

Burgos
Lleida
Zaragoza
Barcelona
Toledo
Valencia
Mallorca
Evora
Lisbon
Cordoba
Murcia
Seville
Granada
Algiers
Tunis
Fes
Marrakech

0   250   500 km

Data Sources: ArcWorld, DeLorme

MAP 3

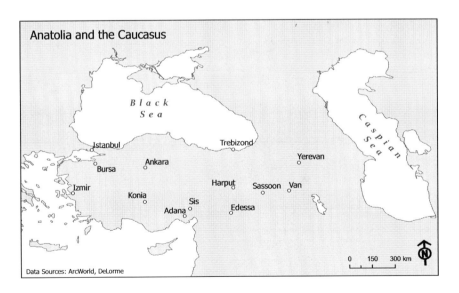

Anatolia and the Caucasus

Black Sea

Caspian Sea

Istanbul
Trebizond
Yerevan
Ankara
Bursa
Izmir
Harput
Sassoon
Van
Konia
Sis
Adana
Edessa

0   150   300 km

Data Sources: ArcWorld, DeLorme

MAP 4

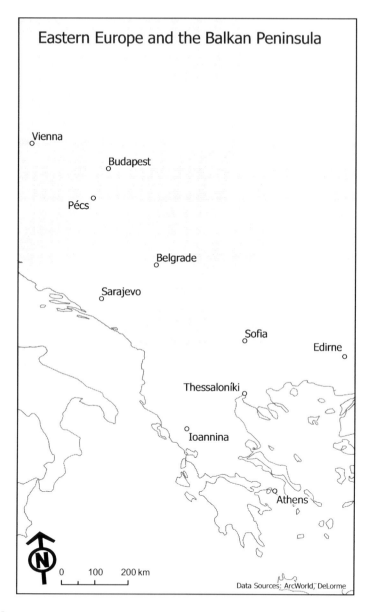

Eastern Europe and the Balkan Peninsula

Vienna

Budapest

Pécs

Belgrade

Sarajevo

Sofia

Edirne

Thessaloníki

Ioannina

Athens

0   100   200 km

Data Sources: ArcWorld, DeLorme

MAP 5

Bibliography

This synthesis is based on a great amount of works written in several different languages and considering the features of this book, it has been necessary to make a selection and, with a few exceptions, to give preference to works written in English. I have only cited below the secondary sources from which I have drawn the information mentioned in this volume (I have not utilized works based on biased sources). I apologize to the scholars who have not been mentioned. Further information about this book's topics, and primary and secondary sources can be found in those works.

The works that have been used in several chapters are:

F. Armanios, *Coptic Christianity in Ottoman Egypt* (Oxford, 2011).

G. Augustinos, *The Greeks of Asia Minor: Confession, Community, and Ethnicity in the Nineteenth Century* (Kent, 1992).

L. A. Berto, *Christians and Muslims in Early Medieval Italy: Perceptions, Encounters, and Clashes* (Abingdon – New York, 2020).

B. A. Catlos, *Muslims of Medieval Latin Christendom, c.1050–1614* (Cambridge, 2014).

N. Doumanis, *Before the Nation: Muslim-Christian Coexistence and Its Destruction in Late-Ottoman Anatolia* (Oxford, 2012).

A. Ducellier, *Chrétiens d'Orient et Islam au Moyen Âge VIIe–XVe siècle* (Paris, 1996).

B. Dutheil, *Les chrétiens du Bilād al-Šām dans la première période mamlūke (1260–1382)*, Mémoire de Master 2, Université Paris I Panthéon-Sorbonne (2015–2016).

T. el-Leithy, *Coptic Culture and Conversion in Medieval Cairo, 1293–1524 A.D.* (Ph.D. diss. Princeton University, 2005).

E. Freas, *Muslim-Christian Relationships in Ottoman Palestine: Where Nationalism and Religion Intersect* (New York, 2016).

Y. Friedmann, *Tolerance and Coercion in Islam: Interfaith Relations in the Muslim Tradition* (Cambridge, 2003).

T. W. Gallant, *Modern Greece: From the War of Independence to the Present* (London, 2016, 2nd edition).

A. García-Sanjuán, 'Jews and Christians in Almoravid Seville as Portrayed by the Islamic Jurist Ibn Abdūn', *Medieval Encounters*, 14, 1 (2007), pp. 78–98.

M. Greene, *A Shared World: Christians and Muslims in the Early Modern Mediterranean* (Princeton, 2000).

M. Greene, *The Edinburgh History of the Greeks, 1453 to 1768: The Ottoman Empire* (Edinburgh, 2015).

R. C. Jennings, *Christians and Muslims in Ottoman Cyprus and the Mediterranean World, 1571–1640* (Oxford, 1992).

S. Kassir, *Beirut* (Oakland, 2010)

M. J. Kister, "Do Not Assimilate Yourselves," *Jerusalem Studies in Arabic and Islam*, 12 (1989), pp. 321–53.

T. Krstić, *Contested Conversions to Islam: Narratives of Religious Change in the Early Modern Ottoman Empire* (Stanford, 2011).

T. Ladjal, 'The Christian Presence in North Africa under Almoravid Rule (1040–1147 CE): Coexistence or Eradication?', *Cogent Arts & Humanities*, 4, 1 (2017), pp. 1–17.

R. M. Levy, *Non-Muslims in the Early Islamic Empire: From Surrender to Coexistence* (Cambridge, 2011).

G. Lewy, *The Armenian Massacres in Ottoman Turkey: A Disputed Genocide* (Salt Lake, 2005).

Ph. Mansel, *Levant: Splendour and Catastrophe on the Mediterranean* (London, 2010).

A. Marcus, *The Middle East on the Eve of Modernity: Aleppo in the Eighteenth Century* (New York, 1989).

M. Mazower, *Salonica: City of Ghosts: Christians, Muslims and Jews 1430–1950* (London, 2005).

A. Metcalfe, *The Muslims of Medieval Italy* (Edinburgh, 2009).

M. D. Meyerson, *The Muslims of Valencia in the Age of Fernando and Isabel: Between Coexistence and Crusade* (Berkeley, 1991).

Muslims under Latin Rule, 1100–1300, ed. J. Powell (Princeton, 1990).

Sh.-A. Naguib, *Government Relations with the Coptic Community in Egypt during the Fatimid Period (358–567 A.H. /969–1171 C.E.)* (Ph.D. diss. University of Chicago, 1995).

D. Nirenberg, *Communities of Violence: Persecution of Minorities in the Middle Ages* (Princeton, 1996).

M. O'Connell and E. Dursteler, *The Mediterranean World: From the Fall of Rome to the Rise of Napoleon* (Baltimore, 2016).

D. Quataert, *The Ottoman Empire, 1700–1922* (Cambridge, 2005, 2nd edition).

J. M. Safran, *Defining Boundaries in AlAndalus: Muslims, Christians, and Jews* (Ithaca, 2013).

H. J. Sharkey, *A History of Muslims, Christians, and Jews in the Middle East* (Cambridge, 2017).

J. V. Tolan, *Saracens: Islam in the Medieval European Imagination* (New York, 2002).

N. M. Vaporis, *Witnesses for Christ: Orthodox Christian Neomartyrs of the Ottoman Period, 1437–1860* (Yonkers, 2000).

Vivre dans l'empire Ottoman: Sociabilités et relations intercommunautaires (XVIIIè–XXè siècles), eds. P. Dumont and F. Georgeon (Paris, 1997).

K. J. Werthmuller, *Coptic Identity and Ayyubid Politics in Egypt, 1218–1250* (Cairo – New York, 2010).

M. Winter, *Egyptian Society under Ottoman Rule, 1517–1798* (London – New York, 1992).

R. J. Zorgati, *Pluralism in the Middle Ages: Hybrid Identities, Conversion, and Mixed Marriages in Medieval Iberia* (London – New York, 2012).

E. J. Zürcher, *Turkey: A Modern History* (London – New York, 2017, 4th edition).

1. Laws and justice

N. Al-Qattan, 'Dhimmis in the Muslim Court: Legal Autonomy and Religious Discrimination', *International Journal of Middle East Studies*, 31, 3 (1999), pp. 429–44.

B. A. Catlos, *The Victors and the Vanquished: Christians and Muslims of Catalonia and Aragon, 1050–1300* (Cambridge, 2007).

A. Fattal, 'How Dhimmis Were Judged in the Islamic World', in *Muslims and Others in Early Islamic Society*, ed. R. Hoyland (Aldershot, 2004), pp. 83–102.

The Legal Status of Dimmī-s in the Islamic West (Second/Eighth-Ninth/Fifteenth Centuries), eds. M. Fierro and J. Tolan (Leuven, 2013).

A. Ozil, *Orthodox Christians in the late Ottoman Empire: A Study of Commnunal Relations in Anatolia* (London – New York, 2013).

D. Quataert, 'Clothing Laws, State, and Society in the Ottoman Empire, 1720–1829', *International Journal of Middle East Studies*, 29, 3 (1997), pp. 403–25.

2. Conversions

M. D. Baer, *Honored by the Glory of Islam: Conversion and Conquest in Ottoman Europe* (Oxford, 2009).

M. Balivet, *Byzantins et Ottomans: Relations, Interaction, Succession* (Istanbul, 1999).

B Bennassar and L. Bennassar, *Les Chretiens d'Allah: L'histoire extraordinaire des renegats, XVIe et XVIIe Siècles* (Paris, 1989).

A. Bryer, *Peoples and Settlement in Anatolia and the Caucasus, 800–1900* (London, 1988).

S. Deringil, *Conversion and Apostasy in the Late Ottoman Empire* (Cambridge, 2012).

Ch. C. Sahner, *Christian Martyrs under Islam: Religious Violence and the Making of the Muslim World* (Princeton, 2018).

3. Working

J. Beinin, *Workers and Peasants in the Modern Middle East* (Cambridge, 2001).

Y. H. Erdem, *Slavery in the Ottoman Empire and its Demise: 1800–1909* (London – New York, 1996).

S. Faroqhi, *Artisans of Empire: Crafts and Craftsmen under the Ottomans* (London – New York, 2009).

S. Faroqhi, *Travel and Artisans in the Ottoman Empire: Employment and Mobility in the Early Modern Era* (London – New York, 2014).

Ch. Lowney, *A Vanished World: Medieval Spain's Golden Age of Enlightenment* (New York, 2005).

D. Quataert, 'Ottoman Workers and the State, 1826–1914', in *Workers and Working Classes in the Middle East: Struggles, Histories, Historiographies* (Albany, 1994), pp. 21–40.

A. Wharton, *The Architects of Ottoman Constantinople: The Balyan Family and the History of Ottoman Architecture* (London – New York, 2015).

4. Sharing beliefs and spaces

N. Al-Qattan, 'Litigants and Neighbors: The Communal Topography of Ottoman Damascus', *Comparative Studies in Society and History*, 44, 3 (2002), pp. 511–33.

Armenian Smyrna/Izmir: The Aegean Communities, ed. R. G. Hovannisian (Costa Mesa, 2012).

M. U. Campos, *Ottoman Brothers: Muslims, Christians, and Jews in Early Twentieth-Century Palestine* (Stanford, 2011).

B. B. Doumani, *Family Life in the Ottoman Mediterranean: A Social History* (Cambridge, 2017).

R. Gradeva, *Rumeli under the Ottomans, 15th–18th Centuries: Institutions and Communities* (Istanbul, 2004).

J. Grehan, *Twilight of the Saints: Everyday Religion in Ottoman Syria and Palestine* (Oxford, 2014).

Muslims and Others in Sacred Space, ed. M. Cormack (New York, 2013).

S. Peychev, 'The Image of the City: Public Baths and Urban Space in Western Travellers' Descriptions of Ottoman Sofia', in *The City in the Muslim World: Depictions by Western Travel Writers*, eds. Mohammad Gharipour and Nilay Özlü (London – New York, 2015), pp. 101–20.

E. Semerdjian, 'Naked Anxiety: Bathhouses, Nudity, and the Dhimm Woman in 18th-Century Aleppo', *International Journal of Middle East Studies*, 45, 4 (2013), pp. 651–76.

The Urban Social History of the Middle East, 1750–1950, ed. P. Sluglett (Syracuse, 2008).

Vivre dans l'empire ottoman: sociabilités et relations intercommunautaires (18.–20. siècles), eds. F. Georgeon and P. Dumont (Paris, 1997).

E. S. Wolper, 'Khidr and the Politics of Translation in Mosul Mar Behnam, St George and Khidr Ilyas', in *Sacred Precincts: The Religious Architecture of Non-Muslim Communities across the Islamic World*, ed. M. Gharipour (Leiden, 2015), pp. 379–92.

F. Zarinebaf, *Crime and Punishment in Istanbul: 1700/1800* (Oakland, 2011).

5. Attacking the other

B. A. Catlos, *Infidel Kings and Unholy Warriors: Faith, Power, and Violence in the Age of Crusade and Jihad* (New York, 2014).

J. R. Cole, *Colonialism and Revolution in the Middle East: Social and Cultural Origins of Egypt's Urabi Movement* (Princeton, 1993).

B. Masters, *Christians and Jews in the Ottoman Arab World: The Roots of Sectarianism* (Cambridge, 2001).

6. Eliminating the other

J. A. Taylor, *Muslims in Medieval Italy: The Colony at Lucera* (Lanham, 2003).

O. Yildirim, *Diplomacy and Displacement: Reconsidering the Turco-Greek Exchange of Populations, 1922–1934* (New York, 2006).

Further readings

N. Antov, *The Ottoman 'Wild West': The Balkan Frontier in the Fifteenth and Sixteenth Centuries* (Cambridge, 2017).

S. Barton, *Conquerors, Brides, and Concubines: Interfaith Relations and Social Power in Medieval Iberia* (Philadelphia, 2015).

Christians and Jews in the Ottoman Empire: The Abridged Edition, ed. B. Braude (Boulder, 2014).

S. H. Griffith, *The Church in the Shadow of the Mosque: Christians and Muslims in the World of Islam* (Princeton, 2007).

Islam and Christianity in Medieval Anatolia, eds. A.C.S. Peacock, B. De Nicola, S. N. Yildiz (London – New York, 2020).

M. S. A. Mikhail, *From Byzantine to Islamic Egypt: Religion, Identity and Politics after the Arab Conquest* (London – New York, 2014).

A. Minkov, *Conversion to Islam in the Balkans: Kisve Bahası Petitions and Ottoman Social Life, 1670–1730* (Leiden, 2004).

The Routledge Handbook of Muslim Iberia, ed. M. I. Fierro (Abingdon – New York, 2020).

L. E. Weitz, *Between Christ and Caliph: Law, Marriage, and Christian Community in Early Islam* (Philadelphia, 2018).

Index